Environmental Crisis in Young Adult Fiction

Critical Approaches to Children's Literature

Series Editors: **Kerry Mallan** and **Clare Bradford**

Critical Approaches to Children's Literature is an innovative series concerned with the best contemporary scholarship and criticism on children's and young adult literature, film, and media texts. The series addresses new and developing areas of children's literature research as well as bringing contemporary perspectives to historical texts. The series has a distinctive take on scholarship, delivering quality works of criticism written in an accessible style for a range of readers, both academic and professional. The series is invaluable for undergraduate students in children's literature as well as advanced students and established scholars.

Published titles include:

Cherie Allan
PLAYING WITH PICTUREBOOKS
Postmodernism and the Postmodernesque

Clare Bradford, Kerry Mallan, John Stephens & Robyn McCallum
NEW WORLD ORDERS IN CONTEMPORARY CHILDREN'S LITERATURE
Utopian Transformations

Alice Curry
ENVIRONMENTAL CRISIS IN YOUNG ADULT FICTION
A Poetics of Earth

Margaret Mackey
NARRATIVE PLEASURES IN YOUNG ADULT NOVELS, FILMS AND VIDEO GAMES
Critical Approaches to Children's Literature

Andrew O'Malley
CHILDREN'S LITERATURE, POPULAR CULTURE, AND *ROBINSON CRUSOE*

Christopher Parkes
CHILDREN'S LITERATURE AND CAPITALISM
Fictions of Social Mobility in Britain, 1850–1914

Michelle Smith
EMPIRE IN BRITISH GIRLS' LITERATURE AND CULTURE
Imperial Girls, 1880–1915

Forthcoming titles:

Elizabeth Bullen
CLASS IN CONTEMPORARY CHILDREN'S LITERATURE

Pamela Knights
READING BALLET AND PERFORMANCE NARRATIVES FOR CHILDREN

Kate McInally
DESIRING GIRLS IN YOUNG ADULT FICTION

Susan Napier
MIYAZAKI HAYO AND THE USES OF ENCHANTMENT

Critical Approaches to Children's Literature
Series Standing Order ISBN 978–0–230–22786–6 (hardback)
978–0–230–22787–3 (paperback)
(*outside North America only*)

You can receive future titles in this series as they are published by placing a standing order. Please contact your bookseller or, in case of difficulty, write to us at the address below with your name and address, the title of the series and the ISBN quoted above.

Customer Services Department, Macmillan Distribution Ltd, Houndmills, Basingstoke, Hampshire RG21 6XS, England

Environmental Crisis in Young Adult Fiction

A Poetics of Earth

Alice Curry

First published 2013 by
PALGRAVE MACMILLAN

Palgrave Macmillan in the UK is an imprint of Macmillan Publishers Limited, registered in England, company number 785998, of Houndmills, Basingstoke, Hampshire RG21 6XS.

Palgrave Macmillan in the US is a division of St Martin's Press LLC, 175 Fifth Avenue, New York, NY 10010.

Palgrave Macmillan is the global academic imprint of the above companies and has companies and representatives throughout the world.

Palgrave® and Macmillan® are registered trademarks in the United States, the United Kingdom, Europe and other countries.

ISBN 978–1–137–27010–8

This book is printed on paper suitable for recycling and made from fully managed and sustained forest sources. Logging, pulping and manufacturing processes are expected to conform to the environmental regulations of the country of origin.

A catalogue record for this book is available from the British Library.

A catalog record for this book is available from the Library of Congress.

10   9   8   7   6   5   4   3   2   1
22   21   20   19   18   17   16   15   14   13

Printed and bound in Great Britain by
CPI Antony Rowe, Chippenham and Eastbourne

We may wonder which is more realistic – recycling or abandoning our appliances altogether and growing our own food; which is more visionary – taking care of the earth we have or turning our backs on its problems and seeking a pristine wilderness? It is sometimes hard to distinguish the positive, activist stance from the negative, reactionist one and to determine which addresses root causes and which only superficial effects. Ecology 'experts' do not agree on the solutions to our environmental problems; should children's literature?

Betty Greenway (1994: 146)

Contents

Series Preface   ix

Acknowledgements   x

Introduction: Ecofeminism and Environmental Crisis   1

1 A 'Poetics of Planet': Apocalypse and Our
  Post-Natural Future   18

2 Ideologies of Advancement: Writing on the Body   43

3 Regimes of Gender Difference: An Ecofeminist
  Ethic of Care   74

4 Situated Knowledges: Competing Epistemological
  Frameworks   101

5 A Poetics of Earth: Ecofeminist Spiritualities   129

6 Deep Ecology or Ecofeminism: The Embodied,
  Embedded Hybrid   160

Conclusion: Apocalypse as Ecopoiesis   192

Notes   199

Bibliography   203

Works Cited   204

Index   215

Series Preface

The *Critical Approaches to Children's Literature* series was initiated in 2008 by Kerry Mallan and Clare Bradford. The aim of the series is to identify and publish the best contemporary scholarship and criticism on children's and young adult literature, film and media texts. The series is open to theoretically informed scholarship covering a wide range of critical perspectives on historical and contemporary texts from diverse national and cultural settings. *Critical Approaches* aims to make a significant contribution to the expanding field of children's literature research by publishing quality books that promote informed discussion and debate about the production and reception of children's literature and its criticism.

Kerry Mallan and Clare Bradford

Acknowledgements

My sincere thanks go to John Stephens, Professor Emeritus at Macquarie University, whose tirelessness, thoroughness, insightfulness and humour made the writing of this book an unexpected pleasure. My thanks also go to Macquarie University's Arts Faculty for the generous affiliation it has afforded me as Honorary Associate. I am enormously grateful to the Commonwealth Education Trust for its wholehearted support for my research endeavours, and in particular to Judith Hanratty CVO OBE, for offering me the invaluable opportunity to broaden my knowledge as Children's Literature Advisor to the Trust.

I extend further thanks to Clare Bradford and Kerry Mallan, whose encouragement and advice in the writing of this book were enormously appreciated, and to my editors at Palgrave Macmillan for their constant friendly professionalism. I am also grateful to Beverly Lyon Clark, Kate Rigby and Naomi Wood for their insightful and constructive feedback on my manuscript in its earlier stages.

I am indebted to Lydia Kokkola for her advice and hospitality during my three-month research period in Finland and to the staff at the Internationale Jugendbibliothek München whose exhaustive collection of international children's fiction was an invaluable resource during my three-month research fellowship in Germany. My more general thanks go to those scholars who have offered helpful and informed feedback at conferences and seminars over the course of my writing.

I am also grateful to The Johns Hopkins University Press for its kind permission to reprint an extract from *Children's Literature Association Quarterly* as an epigraph to this book.

Last, but not least, I am enormously grateful to my friends and family, and in particular my father, mother, sister and partner, for their unlimited love and support throughout the writing of this book.

Introduction: Ecofeminism and Environmental Crisis

Ecofeminism is rooted in the critical insight that environmental crisis is a feminist issue. Ecofeminist discourses draw from feminism and critical ecology to identify comparable mechanisms of exploitation that affect women and the environment and to challenge both the theoretical underpinnings and actual manifestations of these mechanisms. Ecofeminism is informed by several different strands – some of which are complementary, some competing – yet all ecofeminisms address, at base, this connection between women and nature. In this work I extend this connection to encompass children and young adults alongside women and nature, in a tripartite analysis informed by the critical history, philosophy and ethics of ecofeminism. In bringing ecofeminist theory to bear on a study of contemporary literature for young adults I identify some of the common constructivist discourses imposed on women, children (or 'the child') and nature that invest certain members of these categories with comparable discursive attributes. An ecofeminist reading of fiction for young adults can offer to children's literature an examination of the processes and productions of gender difference that 'feminise' categories lying outside the parameters of the adult white male subject. It further enables an exploration of the ways in which young adult novels attempt to develop a sustainable ethic of care that can encompass such 'feminised' peoples and spatialities, including nonhumans and the environment. It is especially apt for engaging with the construction of young adult subjectivity in novels in which radically ruptured post-apocalyptic societies struggle to create new – more caring – world orders based on the dismantling of social and biosocial inequalities.

  Commonly thought to have begun with the coining of the term 'l'eco-féminisme' by Françoise d'Eaubonne in 1974, ecofeminism as a movement had its first major proponents in the US in the 1980s, and has since flourished both geographically and critically, expanding its interdisciplinary theorising outwards into the social and political fields. Since its foundation, ecofeminism has been a practical movement for social change as well as a theoretical academic discipline, with an emphasis on social and political activism that crosses scales and spaces, from localised grassroots movements to global advocacy for change. The parameters of the movement have extended beyond gender to include what Karen Warren (1997: 30) terms 'any "ism" which presupposes or advances a logic of domination' such as racism, sexism, ageism, classism and speciesism, and what Erika Cudworth (2005: 2) neatly summarises as 'multiplicities of domination'. Thus understood, ecofeminism constitutes a 'strategic response' to the global corporate practices that inhere in interlocking discourses of self-advancement, economic progress and 'development' and that can result in the pejorative treatment of women, the natural environment and other marginalised categories (Carlassare 2000: 100). As Cecilia Herles (2000: 109) puts it, the underlying association between women and the natural world 'can operate as a source of both subjugation and resistance, exploitation, and inspiration'. Ecofeminists frequently adopt a mode of resistant positioning in a hopeful bid to revalue, rather than deny, the woman–nature connection as a caring and transformative response to environmental crisis.

Underpinning the counter-hegemonic potential of much ecofeminist critique is resistance towards the segregation of the natural world from human conceptions of identity and selfhood. The understanding of today's neoliberal societies as hierarchies structured upon socio-political notions of difference is a premise common to most, if not all, ecofeminisms. The drive to identify what are widely believed to be the false divides between the categories man/woman, culture/nature and human/nonhuman has been, and continues to be, a major shared preoccupation for ecofeminists. Much ecofeminist scholarship points to the inapplicability of dualistic thinking within the ambiguities and intersectionalities of a rapidly changing global society and the ways in which such historical dualisms are often in fact 'mutually constitutive' (Fincher 2004: 50). A less hierarchical mode of valuing women and the environment arises from attempts to undertake a relational analysis of the global forces that currently impact women and the local landscape. Such an analysis identifies interdependencies and connections rather than privileging autonomous binary categories. As Colleen Mack-Canty (2004: 174) notes, attempts 'to reweave dualism generally and the nature/culture duality specifically' and to dismantle value hierarchical thinking in its many guises and incarnations can further ecofeminist efforts to construct non-oppositional models of biosocial engagement.

Two primary positions in ecofeminism have had a major impact on subsequent theorising and both address the connection between women and nature in different ways. The first, often labelled 'affinity' or 'cultural' ecofeminism with its roots in 'radical' feminism, constitutes the (now rarely instantiated) first wave of ecofeminist theorising that centres on a physiological connection between women and nature arising out of female reproductive processes (the menstrual cycle, birthing, nursing) and a woman's consequent propensity towards care, nourishment and nurturance. These 'female' qualities are perceived to invest women with a spiritual and embodied understanding of nature unshared by men. 'Affinity' feminism has been much critiqued by proponents of second wave ecofeminism, often labelled 'social', 'socialist' or 'materialist' ecofeminists, who note no inherent woman–nature connection but instead argue for a material connection between the treatment of women and nature under current socio-political regimes, namely those systems of gender-defined uneconomic labour (child rearing, housework, food preparation, sanitation and so on) that circumscribe the 'natural' female role under neoliberal capitalism and define the 'natural' environment as a capitalist resource. In the former essentialist position, male-domination is often glossed as a biological phenomenon whilst in the latter, male-domination is seen to arise through the intersection of particular social, historical and material contexts.

Important foundational insights underpin alternative ecofeminist models of ecological engagement, as will be explored throughout this study. One key insight is the 'disproportionate responsibility' borne by women for the biological processes that inescapably tie humans to the natural world, namely their embodiment (Mellor 1996: 160). The subordination of nature, ecofeminists argue, results from a failure to acknowledge human embodiment and ecological embeddedness as preconditions of existence, a failure that Mary Mellor (2000: 111) suggests 'becomes most destructive in the divided societies of capitalist patriarchy'. I here take embodiment to signal an ontological acknowledgement that 'subjectivity and identity emerge not from disembodied consciousness, but from the experience of acting through – and on – the physical, visceral and mortal vehicle of the body' (Bakker and Bridge 2006: 15). It is the overwhelming adherence to embodiment as a vital element of ecofeminist reappraisal that obligates an ecofeminist reading of place, place-situatedness and grounding within the natural world as indicative of the need for alternative embodied epistemologies. Place-situatedness, in the sense of an embodied connection with the earth, gives rise to situated knowledges, rather than the abstract universal theories of normative ethics and philosophy, and underpins the ecofeminist assertion that 'to know' should be subsumed beneath 'to experience'. This emphasis on the experience of human-nonhuman connection, moving beyond feminist standpoint theory to engage plural perspectives, collective viewpoints and localised subject positions, is important to all aspects of contemporary ecofeminist engagement.

It is only fair to note that the ecofeminist movement has not been without its critics.[1] An early focus on spiritual and emotional reconnection with the natural world has been critiqued as being apolitical, atheoretical and essentialist and likely to do little to transform current neoliberal policies that condone gender marginalisation and environmental destruction. In attempting to reclaim the connection between women and nature – whether physiological or material – as a way to empower the female subject, ecofeminists have come under fire in other branches of feminism for their perceived failure to acknowledge the long history of feminist struggle from the suffragette movement to the present day to transcend their association with 'the natural'. In celebrating women's embodied connection with the earth, earlier ecofeminists have been further critiqued – from within the movement itself – for universalising, totalising and essentialising women's relationship with nature, a criticism that follows the more general drive in third wave feminist theory to account for racial, cultural and economic differences amongst women. This debate still continues to open up important new areas of enquiry. For the purposes of this study, I foreground the importance of an ontological-representational distinction in ecofeminist theorising. What is of most relevance is not the validity of a historical connection between women and nature, but the ways in which such a connection has been perceived, abused and exploited under the auspices of gender difference. Phoebe Godfrey (2008: 104) puts it well: in critiquing the women–nature connection, liberal feminists (and others) fail to distinguish 'women's material embeddedness in natural relations *as distinct from* capitalist patriarchal depictions or representations of that material relationship' (my italics). It is this shift from ontological to representational thinking in ecofeminist theorising that I bring to bear on an analysis of young adult subject positioning within the novels under consideration.

The ecofeminist discourses on which I mostly draw in this study in order to construct my own literary ecofeminist position are materialist since I situate my critique of ecological representation in the novels under consideration within a framework of globalised neoliberal values arisen in today's particular, historical context. In reading young adult texts through an ecofeminist lens, I take the young protagonists to be products of their social and familial contexts and thus engage with materialist ecofeminism by suggesting that young people's social and political struggle and maturation is indivisible from the needs of the earth, particularly at this moment of accelerating environmental crisis. The understanding of ecological thinking given by Lorraine Code (2006: 20) as 'a conception of materially constituted and situated subjectivity for which place, embodied locatedness, and discursive interdependence are conditions of the very possibility of knowledge and action' is central to my thinking. I note a tendency, however, within the young adult novels under consideration to adhere to a dualistic conception of human/nonhuman, culture/nature and male/female categories. My study as a whole, in fact, highlights a preoccupation in contemporary young adult post-disaster fiction with the unfolding of individual agency against a backdrop of more or less starkly defined oppositional dualisms.

With this in mind I trace instances of greater and lesser success in these novels in reconceiving or dismantling these purported dualisms, and identify a tendency within the novels to reclaim cultural ecofeminist notions of spirituality and personal transformation, often largely dissociated from their historical, material contexts.[2] This is indicative of a major preoccupation in fiction for children and young adults with the protagonists' potential for subjectivity and agency within largely disempowering social systems and the hopeful association of much young adult fiction with individual empowerment through negotiation of the protagonists' interrelationships with the outside world. My final chapter focuses on what I term a 'hybrid' notion of ecofeminist engagement that promises to revalue and revision, rather than deny, a connection between children, women and nature in a move beyond dualisms that aims to empower the juvenile subject. This last chapter is designed to foreground the 'usefulness' of ecofeminist theory to children's literature 'as a positive and creative philosophy that can teach us about existing and available *alternatives* to oppression' (Cuomo 2002: 10). Whilst I allude at various points to complementary or competing theoretical positions such as deep ecology and feminist political geography, I nevertheless ground my analysis within 'the power and the promise' of ecofeminist thinking in both its critical *and* restorative reifications (Warren 1990).

Ecofeminism and the child

Almost twenty years ago Beverly Lyon Clark (1993: 172) could claim that 'feminist theorising has rarely recognised, let alone addressed, the position of the child'. Twenty years on the situation is somewhat different, yet the 'ambivalences' Clark (1993: 171) suggests characterise feminist engagement with the child are still apparent. Whilst feminist theorists now make forays into children's literature that are useful contributions to the field, one can still note a certain reticence in mainstream feminism to engage more generally with children's literature.[3] Whilst ecofeminism has been criticised for its lack of a homogenous theoretical standpoint, instead evoking what Elizabeth Carlassare (2000: 90) terms 'an open, flexible political and ethical alliance that does not invoke any shared, singular theoretical framework or epistemology', its very openness, I suggest, endows it with the potential to forge useful connections between these two fields. Clark (1993: 174) in fact prefigured – in her own discursive turn of phrase – the potential of ecofeminism to work towards such an aim when she challenged theorists to 'start unearthing' new relationships between feminist theory and children's literature. I here suggest that the flexibility and integrative nature of ecofeminist discourse leave it scope to encompass 'the child' as a third category of analysis alongside women and nature, and foreground the relevance and appropriateness of ecofeminism as a conceptual tool with which to interrogate the positioning of young adults in contemporary literature.

My conflation of 'child' and 'young adult' is here deliberate. I use the word 'child' or 'the child' to mark the essentialist or constructivist values imposed onto children in contemporary discourses on childhood and suggest that the young adult is equally subject to constructivist readings. The young adult, however, is a borderline identity, situated on the threshold between childhood and adulthood. As I shall go on to explore in my first chapter, the borderline positioning of the young adult is key to the construction of young adult subjectivity. I suggest that the imminent entry of young adults into systems of adult responsibility places them in a unique position to critique the discourses of childhood essentialism on which I focus. Today's young western adults are also in the privileged position of growing up in societies in which the long history of feminist struggle and its relative successes is an accepted and acknowledged aspect of life. Whilst practices of gender difference and prejudices based not simply on gender and sexuality but also on class, race, religion and so on still undoubtedly remain, today's youth are more aware than ever before of the legal freedoms and responsibilities they have inherited from their feminist foremothers.[4] As such, my focus on the young adult enables me to examine the interplay of global forces that position young adults on the cusp of social and political responsibility and interpellated by the ethics and epistemologies of the feminist present.

In the burgeoning field of childhood studies, the purported adult/child dualism is a perpetual locus for examination and critique. Whilst the plethora of critical responses to the categories of child and adult suggest a drive to interrogate these dichotomies, Chris Jenks (2005: 3) nevertheless cautions that '[t]he relationship adult-child appears locked within the binary reasoning which, for so long, both contained and constrained critical thought in relation to issues of gender and ethnicity'. Patrick J. Ryan (2008: 553) points to the ways in which the child has been viewed as a 'special' category distinct from its adult purveyors, noting the 'special importance that is granted to childhood in the discourses on being human'. Heinz Hengst's (2005: 21) comparable contention that decentredness in childhood analysis 'transcends the dualism of childhood–adulthood distinctions and abandons any fixation on a presumed experiential space on the part of children that is primarily understood with reference to these distinctions' echoes a similar call voiced by ecofeminists to undertake a relational analysis of the multiplicities of systemic processes that affect women in plural ways. This association of women, children and nature illuminates a historical tendency within the west to allocate both difference and distance to these non-hegemonic categories and points to a potential locus for collaborative revisioning.

An ontological distinction between women's actual and perceived affinity with nature has much in common with the historical positioning (and repositioning) of the 'natural' child in critical discourses on childhood from Romanticism to the present day. Locke's empiricism and Rousseau's 'original innocence' have both been formative in imbricating the child and the natural world under the romantic framework of a shared ontological purity.[5] Both of these thinkers have had a formative influence on the romantic poetics of place, particularly in their contributions to developmental theories of the child in relation to the natural world. In the 'poetics of childhood' delineated by Roni Natov (2003), the child has been further perceived to embody a 'naturalness' that is lacking in adulthood – innocence, imagination, harmony, embodiment – whilst the natural world has been informed by a 'childishness' of representation – immediacy, wildness, uncultivated simplicity. This isomorphic troping centres on the semantic paralleling of the romantic landscape with the romantic child; as Natov (2003: 92) puts it, the 'child may lead us into the garden, but also may become the garden'. When set alongside the romantic poetics of place, this naturalising of childhood characteristics gains additional relevance for designating the child and the natural world comparable sites on which constructivist accounts of 'nature' are discursively enacted.

Ryan (2008: 555–6) outlines the three tenets of a 'paradigm shift' in thinking that has produced a 'new' social study of childhood:[6]

> The first is that the topic should be explored as a political and cultural construction rather than as natural phenomenon. ... The second tenet is that children are active subjects operating within a social field rather than mere products of heredity and environment. ... The third tenet...[challenges] the adult-child distinction...[and] allows us to move beyond modern dualisms.

If we compare these tenets, reflective of how children are perceived as 'different from' adults, to the four ways in which ecofeminist Ariel Salleh (1997: 161) shows women's relations to nature to be 'qualitatively different from men's', we find various levels of overlap within and between the categories:

> The first...involves experiences mediated by female body organs in the hard but sensuous interplay of birthing and suckling labours. The second...are historically assigned caring and maintenance chores which serve to 'bridge' men and nature. A third involves women's manual work in making goods as farmers, weavers, herbalists, potters. A fourth...involves creating symbolic representations of 'feminine' relations to 'nature' – in poetry, painting, philosophy, and everyday talk.

With the exception of Salleh's third labour-based set of female experiences, the other three categories – biological, historical and symbolic – are replicated in Ryan's delineation of the basic tenets of childhood studies which implicate the authentic child (natural, biological), the political child (cultural, historical) and the conditioned child (ideological, symbolic). The general move in childhood studies away from the authentic child of romantic developmentalism towards the agential political child capable of moral and social action – the preferred child for contemporary authors of fiction for children and young adults – is on par with the current conception of childhood as 'a permanent structural form or category' that nevertheless varies significantly in different cultures, periods and historicities (Corsaro 1997: 4). Children, like women, occupy an ambivalent space between their biological, historical and symbolic constructions and thus are also subject to the ontological–representational paradox underpinning ecofeminist theorising mentioned previously. In Alan Prout's (2005: 11) call for childhood studies to 'take a step back from...the dualisms between childhood and adulthood...if they are to become closer to the open-ended interdisciplinary form of enquiry necessary to present-day conditions', we can see a complementary correlative in ecofeminism's preoccupation with the interdependencies of global processes on the experiences of women in the modern day.

If we return briefly, however, to Ryan's tenets of modern childhood studies, we can identify a significant point of departure between ecofeminism and childhood studies in the 'new' incarnation as delineated by Ryan. In pointing to the current trend in thinking that sees childhood explored as anything *but* natural phenomenon, Ryan instead argues – in the second tenet – that 'children are active subjects operating within a social field rather than mere products of heredity and environment'. Whilst 'nature' and environment' are invoked to avoid an essentialist reading of the child as 'product' rather than 'actor', the tenets fail to situate the child within his or her *ecological* setting. An ecofeminist reading of this conception of childhood would foreground a failure to see children as operating within a social *and environmental* field. Thus when Ryan (2008: 572) contends that '[v]iewing children as social actors with a part to play in the construction of their own intellect, abilities, and identities requires immersion in (rather than departure from) the landscape of modern childhood with all of its complications and dualisms', immersion in (rather than departure from) the *ecological* landscape is quite conspicuously missing. As Code (1999: 65) argues, '[e]cological thinking redirects theoretical analysis towards situated knowledges, situated ethico-politics, where situation is *constitutive of*, not just the context for, the backdrop against which, enactments of subjectivity occur'. In Ryan's delineation of modern childhood studies, the natural world that actively constitutes the subjectivity of the child, appears to have become lost somewhere between the poles of the authentic child, the political child and the conditioned child. In foregrounding humanity's position as embodied and embedded beings within the natural world, ecofeminism brings to childhood studies an understanding of children, like women, as contextually-bound and thus potentially capable of rejecting the abstract and universal categorisations that are implicated in dualistic conceptual frameworks and in the degraded natural landscapes of the twenty-first century.

Ecofeminism and literature

Since ecofeminism is a multidisciplinary theoretical position with its foundations in philosophy and ethics and its goals in political and social activism, it might not at first appear obvious how literature, and specifically literature written for young adults, constitutes an appropriate object of analysis. That novels for any age offer insights into the culture in which they are produced is an adage that requires no further explanation. That novels for children offer insights into the adult culture in which they are produced *and also* into adult constructions of child subjectivity, agency and identity as well as conceptions of responsible pedagogy, also now goes without saying. What *is* worth mentioning is that the strong moral and ethical standpoint from which human attitudes towards the environment must necessarily be critiqued invariably becomes lost – or is hard to swallow – when couched in the abstract moral discourse of philosophy and ethics, particularly when addressed to young people. With this in mind, literature can be instrumental in grounding such abstract discourse in concrete settings and making such moral reappraisal accessible. As environmental ethicist R.J.H. King (1999: 27) suggests, 'we need to articulate the meaning of moral concepts by embedding them in wider narrative structures and imaginatively embodying them in images of possible life practices'. By laying forth such 'images of possible life practices' the novels under consideration open up a space for moral and ethical exploration in a way that can promote long-lasting attitudinal change.

Hubert Zapf (2008: 855) notes that 'the opening of traditional ethics to ecological issues seems to go hand in hand with a shift in focus from the paradigm of philosophy to the paradigm of literature in recent discussions of ethics'. He argues that four key elements of debate are present in what he terms 'literary ecology and the ethics of texts' (2008: 853):

1) the ways in which the narrative mode is necessary to provide a medium for the concrete exemplification of ethical issues that cannot adequately be explored on a merely systematic–theoretical level;

2) the ways in which literature, as a form of knowledge that is always mediated through personal perspectives, reflects the

indissoluble connection between ethics and the human subject, a subject, however, not understood as a mere cognitive ego but a concrete, bodily self implicated in multiple interrelationships;

3) the ways in which the imaginative staging of other lives in fictional texts provides a forum for the enactment of the dialogical interdependence between self and other, and beyond that of the irreducible difference and alterity of the other which is central to ethics; and

4) the ways in which literature and art are not merely illustrations of moral ideologies but also symbolic representations of complex dynamic life processes, whose ethical force consists precisely of their resistance to easy interpretation and appropriation.[7]

If we take these elements to be generally representative of the achievements of ecocriticism in general and literary ecofeminism in particular, we can see that they are conducive to furthering the goals of ecofeminism as a critical, strategic discourse of resistance to hegemonic understandings of human relations with nature.

Zapf's first point foregrounds the need for 'concrete exemplification' of systematic–theoretical ethical tenets and thus echoes the ecofeminist call for situated knowledges in the face of abstract and monistic moral theorising and its tendency to accord a privileged status to universalist principles that often overlook the actual lived experiences of marginalised groups. Zapf's second point builds from the first by acknowledging the embodiment and embeddedness of the ethical actant, an acknowledgement that ecofeminists contend should be extended to all those nonhuman actors who play a part in the 'interconnected web of life' of the earth's ecosystem (Orenstein 1993: 172). The mediation of literature through personal perspectives is correlative with the mediation of the natural world 'through linguistic forms' (Stephens 2010: 214). The longstanding constructivist/essentialist debate in ecocritical theorising has seen such textual mediation fiercely debated. Materialist feminists such as Alaimo and Hekman (2008: 3) have suggested that the postmodernist position that defines 'materiality, the body, and nature as products of discourse' has compounded a denial of human embodiment in western society. Zapf's point, however, addresses this concern by arguing that the human subject must 'not [be] understood as a mere cognitive ego'. As Bonnie Foote (2007: 751) suggests, '[n]o storyteller speaks, no author writes, no text is printed, no reader reads outside of some interactive environment'. The embodiment of the authors of the novels here discussed can themselves be seen as determinate of the construction of embodied subject positions within the textual medium.

Zapf's third point signals the capability of the literary text to provide a 'forum' or open up a space for the performance of intersubjective and interdependent relations between self and other. In noting the importance of 'the irreducible difference and alterity of the other' in ethical theory and praxis, Zapf touches on a major strand of ecofeminist theorising that sees the natural other not as an incorporated or assimilated self but as an entity with its own subjective agency and intrinsic value. In according such 'difference' to the natural world, ecofeminists encourage the human subject to extend the traditionally underplayed values of empathy, solidarity and mutuality towards nonhuman others; such values can be enacted persuasively within the imaginative space opened up by literary texts. Ecofeminist Lori Gruen (2009: 32) points to the added relevance of this particular function of literature to the child, as opposed to the adult, reader on account of a child's natural 'storied empathy'. Defining 'storied empathy' as 'the ability that we have as children to empathise with fictional beings', Gruen (2009: 32) argues that our 'capacity to engage with very different others through narrative, literature, art and storytelling...if honed, may help us to empathetically engage with the more than human world'. Literature, under this formulation, actively furthers the aim of ecofeminist theorists to encourage personal and social transformation. In the 'symbolic representations of complex dynamic life processes' of Zapf's final point, such transformation occurs not through prescriptive moral conditioning but through reflexive self-exploration via the literary text.

Like ecofeminist theorising more generally, ecocriticism has productively foregrounded the concept of place-situatedness as a means of counteracting the tendency towards dislocation inherent in processes of globalisation. This notion of place can be taken further to encompass the situatedness of narrative structures within textual discourses. Arguing that literary texts are positioned 'at the boundary line of the culture–nature interaction' Zapf (2008: 853) contends that they are thus ideally poised to become sites 'where ecological concerns and the ethical self-reflection of the human species are brought together' (859–60). Such liminal positioning accords literature the ontological status of 'an important medium and connecting frame for the dialogue' between the discourses of ethics and ecology (Zapf 2008: 855). Ecofeminism, as a strategic response to global corporate practices, can use such a borderline medium productively and fruitfully to explore the interlocking and overlapping power relations that contribute to socio-political inequality. The usefulness of narrative as a 'connecting frame' for ecofeminist – as much as ecological and ethical – discourse, can be perceived 'in terms of interaction,' to appropriate a phrase used by Foote (2007: 739–40):

> To think of narrative in terms of interaction means to acknowledge that every narrative is shaped by and acts within a unique and intricate environment (inter-) and produces a very specific, if not necessarily an intended or a simple, effect on that environment (-action). To think of narrative as interaction pushes into the foreground the power and dynamism of narrative as something that *happens* (-action) *between* things (inter-), that causes change and creates something new.

To view literary texts as interactive mediums *happening between* culture and nature, male and female, adult and child is to view narrative liminality as enabling of transformation: 'caus[ing] change and creat[ing] something new'. From an ecofeminist perspective, the use of narrative texts as connecting frames grounded in their environment and affecting that environment can enable the desired trajectory from personal awareness to social and political transformation by foregrounding that borderline space in which attitudinal renegotiation can occur.

Ecofeminism, the child and literature: apocalyptic imaginings

Ecologically-oriented children's literature has primarily been analysed for its ecopedagogical potential: how it can promote, and engender, responsible pedagogy in and out of the classroom. Criticism has tended to focus on novels for younger readers, and particularly the modern picture book. Dobrin and Kidd's (2004) edited collection of ecocritical analyses of contemporary children's literature, media and other cultural forms usefully foregrounds the scope and potential of this melding of children's texts and ecological concerns. Greta Gaard (2009: 327; 328; 330) raises 'three important questions' about the capacity of children's environmental literature to increase ecological literacy: 'First, how does the text address the ontological question, "who am I?"'; 'Second, how does the narrative define the ecojustice problem?'; 'Third, what kind of agency does the text recognise in nature?'. Whilst my analysis engages with all of the above, my parameters for analysis are different from those outlined by Gaard. First, my focus on young adult fiction means that the processes of identity formation, subject positioning and constitution of agency are worked through within the novels to different ends.

The young adult protagonists are positioned on the brink of entry into, rather than simply subsumed beneath, the systems of domination that Gaard wishes to critique. These characters' potential, and imminent, complicity with these oppressive systems inheres in a more overtly political narrative trajectory. Secondly, the novels of my chosen corpus have been written by western authors; whilst my analysis therefore does not do justice to the growing canon of non-western novels for young people, my choice is in fact deliberate. The tension perceived in my focused novels over the young protagonists' potential complicity with the dominant hegemonies of western neoliberalism is heightened by their cultural alignment with these same systems. My analysis is thus designed to foreground the troubling scenario of growing up within – and as a product of – the oppressive social structures that materially disadvantage certain women, children and ecologies and that leave the readers differentially implicated in the object of ecofeminist struggle.

Thirdly, the novels of my corpus are not avowedly 'environmental'. Whilst some are overt in their ecological agendas, others employ a degraded natural landscape as backdrop to social critique. It is this implicit construction of landscape that best gives us access to current representational frameworks for ecological engagement. And since these novels are set in a post-apocalyptic world, often in some far-distant future, their responses to crisis are not designed to be taken as a literal and practical jumping off point for children's or young adult activism; instead they are ideologically resonant, necessitating an interpretative reading with a view to attitudinal change. As Bradford *et al.* (2008: 80) suggest:

> Children's texts will not typically incorporate the full range of benefits which might flow from positive environmental policies, but rather seek to convey them by metonymy and analogy, while dystopian narratives allude to them as absence or loss.

Whilst my focused novels might be included amongst those Bradford (2003: 116) critiques when she contends that many children's books are 'strong on articulating ecological crises, but weak on promoting political programmes or collective action', I would suggest that such a 'weakness' is less a political failure and more a deliberate narrative strategy to engender reflexive ethical engagement with the text. The lack of an overt framework for action neither precludes nor delimits interrogation of the ways in which 'human rights and social justice issues are linked to ecological issues', as Kamala Platt (2004: 186) notes.

Thus these novels are highly political in scope, if not always in practice, and – as shall be shown – employ discursive techniques such as those noted above by Bradford *et al.* (2008) to engender a restorative and transformative response to environmental crisis.

The analysis to follow centres on a selection of recent post-disaster novels for young adults and the ways in which these novels can be analysed productively and creatively as a response to environmental crisis through use of an ecofeminist theoretical framework. Throughout the work I conflate the terms 'post-apocalyptic' and 'post-disaster' since both terms – in my use of them – capture the sense of a world recovering from a large-scale breach of cultural normativities. The American, British, Australian and South African landscapes in which the novels were written are particularly apt for an examination of the contentious environmental positioning of contemporary young adult readers. The novels written in the US – and particularly those of Scott Westerfeld and Carrie Ryan – are metonymic of America's situatedness in a history of colonialism, marked by the rise of a mythologised national frontier and a literature inscribing the wilderness as a space both of threat and salvation. Justin D'Ath's novel is equally attuned to Australia's colonial history and explores political and ethical dilemmas regarding the respective rights of native peoples and indigenous lands. Jenny Robson's novel reflects the contentious environmental positioning of South Africa's native peoples with regards to a history of stratified landscape management in the maintenance of wildlife sanctuaries and safari parks. The novels written in Britain – particularly those of Meg Rosoff and Nina Bawden – exhibit tension over spatial division within the ecological landscape, with a particular focus on the space of the garden as a contentious site reflective of the eighteenth century 'enclosure' acts that drove peasants off the land to retain the natural beauty of the countryside. This authorial preoccupation with national environmental history lends to the novels an implicit awareness of further complicity and an arguably stronger teleological progression towards restorative narrative closure.

In my first chapter I explore the apocalyptic conditions that spawn the decaying landscapes of crisis fiction. This chapter offers a 'poetics of planet' to foreground human dislocation from the earth within a discourse of apocalypse that posits planetary alienation as a consequence of transgressed social and environmental tipping points.[8] This alienation sees the earth become a 'blind space': a site of cultural production, lacking in self-determination.[9] In my second chapter I contend that environmental crisis has occasioned a crisis of embodiment for young adults who are faced with the prospect of growing up in a post-natural world. This crisis is reflected in the contentious relationships between the young protagonists of the novels and their social and ecological surroundings, relationships that are enacted on the discursive site of their own bodies. In novels that envisage enhanced technology as instantiating an increasingly disembodied world, the body – and particularly the female body and the posthuman body – becomes a locus of control and a site of potential resistance. I read these first two chapters as reflective of the world's current context of global warming, climate change and increasing natural disasters. These first chapters illuminate a masculinist model of understanding in current discourses of climate change which posits science and technology as abstract solutions to planetary disaster.

In my third and fourth chapters I situate my analysis of the post-disaster novels more thoroughly within a theoretical ecofeminist framework in order to provide an alternative ethical model with which to critique the interlocking discourses of crisis and disembodiment portrayed in contemporary young adult fiction. In the first of these two chapters I analyse the ideologies of neoliberal individualism that value self-advancement at the expense of wider community engagement. I argue that the language, theory and praxis of normative ethics are usefully mediated by the 'feminine' values, such as compassion and empathy, traditionally underplayed within individualist ideologies. My reading of the young adult novels calls attention to the ways in which such novels succeed or fail to instantiate an ethic of care in response to planetary disaster. The second of these two chapters extends this analysis to encompass the various epistemological frameworks available under globalised neoliberalism, deemed limited and limiting by ecofeminists, before moving to an exploration of ecofeminist epistemologies and their capacity to reconfigure such frameworks. One important way in which such reconfiguration is accomplished is through a narrative focus on storytelling and mythmaking to express the value systems necessary for a transformation of ecological attitudes.

In my fifth and sixth chapters I read contemporary young adult fiction through the ecofeminist lens established in my previous chapters and note the tendency of such fiction to challenge the processes of globalisation implicated in earth-dislocation by promoting localised interaction between humans and the land. The first of these chapters moves from an analysis of the western secularisation of nature to counter-hegemonic attempts – promoted by ecofeminists – to reclaim an embodied notion of the sacred within the landscape. Such reclamation is informed by conceptions of indigenous holistic sanctity and ecological immanence often via a romantic association of nature and the child. In my final chapter I propose the notion of the hybrid body as a symbol of resistance to human–earth dislocation, following the ecofeminist call for personal transformation as a necessary preliminary to political engagement. The hybrid form, in my conception, is key to a responsible understanding of young adult identity formation within our current ecological context. Hybridity constitutes the melding of human and nonhuman forms, and the imbrication of human and nonhuman exigencies. Such a figure is socially transformative (unlike the incorporated and assimilated other critiqued by some ecofeminists) and paves the way to the attainment of a re-envisaged relationship between humans and the natural world by embedding the human actant firmly within his or her ecological context. I conclude by noting the importance of this type of re-envisaged attitude in novels for young adults positioned on the brink of adulthood and entry into adult systems of power and control, able – theoretically at least – to materially occasion the aforementioned changes. I note the capacity of these texts to re-envisage the 'blind space' of both the post-apocalyptic earth and the female body and to advocate a more embodied and embedded ecological identity for humans at this time of escalating crisis.

1
A 'Poetics of Planet': Apocalypse and Our Post-Natural Future

'Apocalypse', writes Lawrence Buell (1995: 285), 'is the single most powerful master metaphor that the contemporary environmental imagination has at its disposal.' In post-apocalyptic fiction, the ecocatastrophe of tomorrow is graphically invoked to reflect upon the worsening crisis of today. Climate change is envisaged not as a general process of environmental decay and social degeneration but as an immediate and devastating shattering of cultural norms. Such a dramatic erasure of previous knowledges serves to interrogate the current epistemological frameworks held responsible for crisis whilst laying the groundwork for new and different modes of human–earth interaction. The new world orders put forward in the old world's stead are predicated on a variety of ethical standpoints that are rendered more, or less, able to engender sustainable human relationships with the earth. These standpoints pivot around the alienation and dislocation engendered by crisis: of humans from the earth and of planetary exigencies from anthropocentric systems of value. In focusing on environmental apocalypse as a representational determinant of a more integrated and agential attitude towards earthly belonging I work from the ecofeminist premise that crisis calls for interrogating established ethical and epistemological frameworks to bring about a radical change in environmental thinking. Yet, as Betty Greenway (1994: 146) warns, when ecology experts themselves cannot agree on a solution to the world's problems, should children's literature be any more likely to? In their attempts to establish an ecoconscious framework for environmental reappraisal it is unsurprising that the young adult novels discussed are more successful in constructing resistant subject positions that reject or refute existing ontologies, than on creating fully-fledged new ones.

It has been well documented that in the history of western thought human 'culture' has undergone a socio-spatial segregation from wild 'nature'. Scott Hess (2010: 85) delineates the pejorative effects of this systemic distancing of nature from culture as an enforced 'blindness':

> [The] tendency to locate 'nature' apart from ourselves skews our environmental awareness and priorities in ways that blind us to the devastating ecological impact of our own everyday lives and incapacitate us from pursuing realistic alternatives. If we seek nature apart from our lives, how can we restructure those lives – not just individually, but socially, politically, and economically – in order to change the current patterns of environmental destruction?

By advocating the integration of human and natural concerns, Hess adheres to a general trend in environmental thinking: a move from what Michael P. Cohen (2004: 23) terms the 'praise song' school of first wave ecocriticism in which nature writing was lauded for celebrating the beauty of such a segregated nature to a second wave concern with humanity's intimate and integral place *within* nature. Hess's words are designed to instigate change: to restructure environmental perceptions that currently 'blind us' to our ecological impact. The metaphor of blindness in western ecological thought can be instrumental in elucidating current modes of crisis representation in young adult fiction. Novels that envisage the natural world as removed from human dwelling effectively construct the environment as a blind space, contoured by anthropocentric ideologies.

The earth, contends Bonnie Mann (2005: 57), 'seems, more than any other "notion," to always exceed its discursive boundaries'. Like climate change, it exists in its own epistemic blind space, at once too tangible and too amorphous, too material and too immense. Always phenomenologically accessible – we can feel it under our feet, we can crumble it in our hands – the earth is nevertheless invisible as a planet. The transcendent image of a dematerialised planet has been used to overwhelming effect as a slogan or icon to unite peoples of all nationalities and political orientations in service of the earth. The image of the globe as a contained and distant sphere that humans may contemplate, remotely, in its entirety – a perspective labelled by Frank White (1998) as 'the overview effect' – can, however, also engender a sense of dislocation from humanity's material context, or what I term a 'planetary consciousness'. A planetary consciousness is one of disengagement from local community; it denotes an ontological failure to account for the incommensurability of human relationships and a dehistoricised engagement with place on a scale that delimits closer readings of human–earth interaction. From an ecofeminist perspective, the dislocated view of the earth from space seems largely incommensurate with the caring values that underpin responsible place-based engagement with the earth.

Julien Knebusch (2004: 20) interprets our tendency to dematerialise the planet as product of our 'relationship with the idea of the "planetary"'. Such an idea is born out though narrative formulations of environmental crisis that situate climate change and the deterioration of planetary health within a blind space in the contemporary western imagination. Sarah Amsler (2010: 139) notes that 'instead of the threat of conceivable suffering, we encounter...the unfathomable possibility of collective non-existence, wrought by a confluence of human and non-human factors, unfolding somewhere out of our control, and happening in an unspecified future'. Kearns and Keller (2007: 1) similarly point to the intangibility of crisis rhetoric by suggesting that climate change 'seems at once too flat in its realism and too dramatic in its rhetoric, too factual and too speculative, too complex and too immense to bear in mind'. If the globe as a material entity defies human comprehension then we might question how climate change, as a phenomenon occurring at the planetary level, can be drawn out of the blind space to engender activism and enable socio-political change. By interrogating the scaling of planetary symbolisation in contemporary climate rhetoric, ecofeminists contemplate the potential for a sense-based relationship between humans and an earth that is not iconic, detached or associative, but material and embodied and known intimately through localised engagement with place.

The young adult novels under consideration engage in scientific-phenomenal debate over the ontological properties of the earth by exhibiting tension over what Mann (2005: 57) terms the 'discursive turn' in postmodern engagement with place that dematerialises the planet and leaves no access to the earth except via language. Post-apocalyptic rhetoric is particularly well poised to interrogate postmodern discourses of dislocation in place of human–earth symbiosis since it envisages a world in which the potential for human embeddedness within nature is already seriously if not irreparably compromised. In apocalyptic narratives that envisage radically ruptured cultural normativities, the discursive evocation of planetary blind space signals the existential threshold on which humanity teeters and from which it must pull back if a sustainable life on earth is to be achieved. In each of these novels, authorial preoccupation with the workings of history on the local landscape turns the abused body of the earth into a discursive site of otherness rather than belonging: a post-natural landscape viewed through an ecophobic lens. These novels are caught in tension between discourses of control that advocate dominance over an increasingly unruly planet and counter-hegemonic narratives, influenced by ecofeminism, of a phenomenal earth that must be known intimately and nurtured back to health.

In what follows I situate my analysis of the young adult novels' apocalyptic renderings of a degraded earth within the context of contemporary narratives of crisis and explore the degraded post-natural landscapes of the apocalyptic sensibility. I take individualist neoliberal ideologies to epitomise the self-advancing rhetoric of the war on climate change that offers technological progress as a fail-safe solution to crisis. I signify the planetary consciousness that signals an 'overview' of planetary exigencies as a controlling ideology predicated on surveillance and visual containment (White, 1998). In response to Greta Gaard's (2010: 658) assertion that '[t]he resonant detachment of both ecoglobalism and the whole earth image offers fruitful ground for feminist ecocritical explorations', I denote phenomenal belonging a discursive strategy to interrogate this planetary consciousness and to foster place-based attitudinal change. I suggest that phenomenal belonging inheres in the surprising possibilities for growth and renewal offered by the post-apocalyptic landscape, suggestive of a comparable restoration of human community after apocalypse. The novels discussed caution their readers to take responsibility 'for what we learn not to see, what our knowledge-generating practices shield us from knowing' (Gatens-Robinson 1994: 218). With their manipulated post-natural landscapes, these novels invoke such shielded knowing to dramatise a western tendency to turn a blind eye to encroaching crisis.

Beyond the tipping point: crisis narratives and blind space

In post-apocalyptic texts, an acute moment of crisis frequently provides the tipping point, or global rupture, that leads to the novels' given state of social and environmental degradation. According to Kearns and Keller (2007: xi), the phrase 'tipping point' indicates 'the transitional moment when small changes make huge differences, when predictable processes give way to nonlinear and irreversible amplification'.

Moments of sudden amplification function to provide the apocalyptic conditions that lead to the erasure of cultural normativities. These moments are positioned to have occurred either within the reader's own historical period or in his or her immediate future, in a narrative formulation that John Stephens (1992: 126) argues is typical of its genre:

> [P]ost-disaster fiction evokes a deep past which usually approximates to the reader's present, and hence its moral and political lessons are cast back to the moment at which the text is being *read*. ... [B]ecause the message of such a book applies at the moment of reading, then the possibility of a new beginning is also displaced into the moment of reading, so that history always begins *now* rather than *before*.

Opportunities for narrative didacticism as warning, intimation or moral lesson are overt, albeit usually treated with a relative amount of subtlety; as Clare Bradford (2003: 112) argues, the implied child readers of books with environmental themes 'carry significances over and above those involved in the narrative processes, because they represent various versions of our environmental future'. In novels in which a single moment of crisis is held responsible for planetary decline, the crisis, as tipping point, is discursively formulated to dramatise the linear inevitability of environmental crisis, and is couched in a discourse of ethical responsibility directed towards the reflexive reader.

The popular apocalyptic motif of a material brink, edge or threshold underscores the urgency of the novels' call for climate action. In the various tipping points responsible for the novels' new social orders, a few key words arise as powerful referents for current societal ills – oil, coal, petroleum, nuclear, atomics, war, viruses, governments, economies; in Scott Westerfeld's *Uglies* trilogy [2005–2006], Tally questions her forebears' use of '"oil for everything"' whilst Katniss in Suzanne Collins' *The Hunger Games* trilogy [2008–2010] muses that '[s]omehow it all comes back to coal' (Westerfeld 2005a: 346; Collins 2009: 50). It is clear blame lies not only with western neoliberal ideologies built around unsustainable discourses of capitalism, consumerism and self-advancement, but also with the governments' failures to respond to humanitarian crises when economic 'progress' pushes the environment beyond the brink of collapse. With an ecological stimulus as trigger for social upheaval, the disasters around which societies rally are both environmentally and culturally imbricated. For young readers positioned on the brink of adulthood and soon to be called upon to maintain, or reconstitute, existing ontological frameworks, such a brink positions them on a further threshold – or tipping point – preceding entry into adult systems of political and social responsibility. Unlike child readers, whose potential for effective social responses to climate change is limited, young adults await the imminent transgression that will see them affirm, or refute, the social systems that regulate them. The delineation of climate crisis as tipping point, edge or brink, thus forces the young readers into affirmation of, or resistance towards, current standpoints for ethical engagement with the earth. If the novels are similar in rendering planetary transgression a favoured motif, they differ in the level of redemptive agency they finally allocate to the average human in his or her critical response to disaster.

Climate crisis is commonly portrayed not simply as a warning for the future but as a graphic element of present existence, enacted on the world's most vulnerable people and landscapes. Julie Bertagna's *Exodus* [2002], a novel set in 2099 in a world drowned after the melting of the polar icecaps, employs a discourse of immediacy to foreground human complicity in environmental disaster. Its prologue ends: *'Now retrack to the dawn of the world's drowning. Stand at the fragile moment before the devastation begins, and wonder. Is this where we stand now, right here on the brink?'* (Bertagna 2003: prologue). Jenny Robson's *Savannah 2116 AD* [2004] similarly recounts a past in which *'[h]alf of Africa teetered on the brink of famine'* (Robson 2004: 63). An existential brink is tacitly envisaged in the far-future world of Philip Reeve's *Mortal Engines* quartet [2001–2006], whose tipping point is engendered by the 'Sixty Minute War' – several millennia before the events portrayed – in which 'the Ancients destroyed themselves in that terrible flurry of orbit-to-earth atomics and tailored-virus bombs' (Reeve 2002: 7). A nuclear catastrophe of planetary proportions, the Sixty Minute War recalls the Cuban Missile Crisis of 1962 in which the world was similarly poised for imminent destruction. The rhetoric used in media coverage of the Cuban Missile Crisis has been shown to resemble that of current media speculations about climate change; political, media and social discourses engendered by the crisis envisaged an edge or brink as the final standpoint against planetary disaster.[1] Like the brink on which *Savannah 2116 AD* imagines the developing world to teeter and the brink on which *Exodus* imagines its readers to now stand, this historical edge is deemed a fragile one: a threshold in danger of being transgressed.

In *Exodus*'s sequel, *Zenith* [2007], a single voice transmitted forever across the internet-like 'Weave' discursively dramatises, and constantly enacts, '*the edge*' on which humanity is poised (Bertagna 2007: 206):

> '*...ice caps melting twice as fast as feared...*' *A disembodied voice crackles in the ether then fades. ...*
> '*...we may be on the edge...not much time left...*'
> *The voice seems to be coming from one of the satellites marked NASA. This one hangs above the northern hemisphere.*
> '*...all countries must stabilise emissions of carbon dioxide...can't wait, must act...flooded Earth would be an alien planet...armadas of icebergs, rising oceans...the end of civilisation...how long have we got?*'

The speed and immediacy of the earth's decline is couched in the language of linear crisis; with the world moving towards a projected end, the *non*-linear moments of sudden amplification provoke a panicked delineation of temporal markers: '*twice as fast*', '*not much time left*', '*can't wait*', '*how long have we got?*'. With scientific projections failing to delineate the extent of climate crisis, this final question – '*how long have we got?*' – might well be directed towards the earth itself. The '*alien planet*', defamiliarised and made hostile – alienating its human inhabitants – is discursively formulated as a weapon of war ('*armadas of icebergs*'). From an embattled subject position metonymic of wider planetary dislocation, the '*disembodied voice*' of the lone reporter prefigures the humanitarian catastrophe to which such planetary alienation leads. Mara's response – '"*They could've done something but they didn't. They knew. They didn't think about the future, did they? They never thought about us*"' – foregrounds the failure of those who '*knew*' to take epistemic responsibility for the world's escalating crisis (206). That the voice of the reporter eventually '*fades*' to remain forever on loop in the virtual reality of the Weave suggests that the apocalyptic rhetoric of linear crisis is an ineffectual stimulus for societal change.

In Bertagna's novels, the post-disaster earth instantiates a divide between the pre-modern isolated island on which the protagonist Mara has grown up and the hypertechnological society of the sky city of New Mungo in which her lover, Fox, resides. This latter society cocoons the elite few in self-enclosed sky cities built to tower above the rising oceans. The devastating sea surge that wiped out the whole of Europe engenders the radical manoeuvring of humanity as far away from nature – in both a physical and ideological sense – as humanly possible, whilst engendering a socially stratified society based on the segregation of the 'best' human beings from the subordinate remainder (2003: 196). Such a society actively expels the socially 'useless' from its utopian dreams of a future human race dislocated from, and untainted by, the degraded natural world. Segregated living spaces here invoke the imbalanced geographic systems of privilege that currently see non-western societies bear the brunt of climate crisis. Whilst the past has invariably become lost to the villagers of Mara's island through the inexorable infraction of the rising tides, the past in New Mungo has *purposefully* been forgotten. Deletion of the past constitutes a purposeful strategy for delimiting any lingering guilt, anguish or longing for the drowned world of the previous social order or hope for an embodied and embedded return to the earth. Environmental crisis here renders societal collapse in the language of apocalypse: the *'end of civilisation'*. The world has been pushed beyond the brink and entered a state of existential uncertainty. The question of whether – and how – to refute the epistemic validity of the masculinist ethos that has led to societal upheaval in favour of the embodied knowledges of ecofeminist engagement underpins the crisis rhetoric of the novel.

In much young adult fiction, apocalypse as tipping point is shown to result in environmental change, but more radically, perhaps, it is shown to target the very values, relationships and social structures on which human life as we know it is based. Dramatised moments of crisis are shown to result in radical ruptures to civilisation and technological losses of staggering proportions, correlative with Lovelock's (2006: 10) famous argument that 'it would take more than the predicted climate catastrophe to eliminate all breeding pairs of humans; what is at risk is civilisation'. The novels' readers – variously labelled 'ancestors' (Bertagna), 'Ancients' (Reeve) and 'Rusties' (Westerfeld) – have been rendered extinct: wiped out through apocalypse and reconstituted in new, posthuman forms. A prevalent use of narrative blind space indicates that epistemic ignorance is a concomitant factor in, and consequence of, apocalypse. The split societies of Bertagna's novels are metonymic of the common narratological device employed in young adult apocalyptic fiction of imagining either pre-technological societies or contrastingly hypertechnological societies to evolve out of cataclysm. Whilst the protagonists of the pre-modern societies actively struggle to forge an agential identity within the circumscribed framework of a post-disaster landscape, their ideological frameworks – their inclusive community values and desire to recuperate the past, for instance – are generally represented as capable of engendering a responsible mode of ecological engagement. It is conversely the hypertechnological societies of the post-apocalyptic landscape that delimit humanity's potential to become a truly integrated and sustainable societal species; technological advancement here functions to hinder intersubjective growth even whilst it cocoons its beneficiaries from the worst effects of crisis. In novels in which a refuge is sought in technology, young people are offered unlimited superficial pleasures at the expense of a reduced capacity for agency, thereby obligating a narrative trajectory demanding both environmental *and* ideological reappraisal. If the hypertechnological societies of these novels are a teleological manifestation of contemporary 'progress', pre-modern societies, like Mara's, are contrapuntal in their refusal to sustain this trajectory.

A matter of perspective: a planetary overview

For the first time in human history, Archibald MacLeish reflected grandly in the *New York Times* on the day after the *Apollo 8* photographs were first released to the public, men have seen the earth in its wholeness: beautiful and small.[2] This whole earth perspective in which 'men' can comprehend the earth in all its beauty, fragility and sublimity renders the earth a feminine platform for male relationships and obscures those gendered discourses that systemically oppress both women and the environment in favour of triumphalist discourses of earthly transcendence. Planetary feminisation is bolstered by what Yaakov Garb (1990: 272) terms a 'God's eye view' of the earth. Such an image, Garb (272) contends, is the product of 'an oversized literalisation of the masculine transcendent idea' and 'an attempt to achieve selfhood freed not only from gravity but from all it represents: the pull of the Earth, of matter, dependence on the mother, the body'. The Mother Earth imagery that has sustained the human imaginary for centuries bolsters a metanarrative of propriety over 'feminised' peoples, groups and spatialities, including the earth itself. Brotherly love and a common humanity invoke a macrolevel contemplation of the earth that fails to account for the specificity and particularity of human and nonhuman relationships and the multiplicity of systemic relations through which women and the environment alike experience marginalisation. The novels demonstrate tension over this masculinist trajectory towards planetary alienation by invoking the whole earth image both as a discursive site of male symbolisation and as an ecofeminist standpoint against dislocation.

Both Julie Bertagna's *Exodus* trilogy and Philip Reeve's *Mortal Engines* quartet speak to a feminist interpretation of planet earth. The whole earth image of the planet functions in each to dramatise not belonging but alienation in the protagonists' interactions with their post-apocalyptic landscapes. The literary technique of an expanded and contracted viewpoint allows both novelists to experiment with perspective as they attempt to negotiate sustainable livelihoods for their protagonists; the limits of planetary symbolisation are brought to bear in a reading attuned to the spatialities of earthly existence. In *Zenith*, the whole earth image is engendered to negotiate interlocking discourses of alienation and belonging, materiality and embodiment. Guided by Fox, with whom she communicates via the Weave, Mara enters a virtual space in which she can look down at the earth as if from space (203–4):

> *The Weavesite crackles and Mara gasps as she's sucked into the whirl of a cyberstream. ... She draws breath, swallows, blinks.*
> *Looming up before her is a vast glowing gem.*
> *'Planet Earth,' says a voice in her ear.*
> *They are floating in black space. Mara wants to grab Fox's hand then remembers she can't. She stares up at the amazing vision.*
> *'This is Earth?'*
> *She can hardly breathe as she takes in the beauty of the glowing, gem-like planet: the stunning blue of the oceans, the brown and green of its lands and ice-crusted mountains and white ice caps, all wrapped in swirls of cloud...*

A poetics of planet here renders the earth a thing of beauty: an ethereal 'vision', 'glowing' in the blackness like a precious 'gem'. Wrapped protectively in 'swirls of cloud', the earth engenders nostalgia for a lost sense of earthly belonging in counterpoint to the detachment and dislocation inherent in Mara's own relationship with the earth. Mara's experience of the planet, however, is anti-sensory and unmediated by human touch; it literally takes her breath away (*'gasps'*, *'draws breath, swallows, blinks'*, *'can hardly breathe'*) and leaves her feeling alienated, wanting but unable to reach out for Fox's hand. Fox's fairy tale register as he relates man's successes at landing on the moon – '*"Once upon a time"*, says Fox. *"In a time out of mind"*' – intimates the illusory nature of planetary belonging; the earth becomes simply the backdrop or setting against which dreams of escape constitute a universal metanarrative (204).

From Mara's aerial perspective, the whole earth view is found to be deceptive in its symbolisation. From the calm of space, Fox *'zooms in closer and now the occasional shock of noise, an image or a disembodied voice flashes up from the planet below'* (205). The closer Mara and Fox move towards the Earth's surface, the more hostile the planet becomes: *'A mushroom cloud billows up. In the distance, a tidal wave crashes on a raft of islands, obliterating the land. Ahead, cracks appear in the mountains and the Earth shudders'* (205). As Fox continues to adjust his perspective, these disembodied voices discursively narrate the earth's ecological decline. Reading the flags that mark each event – *'[n]uclear bomb, tsunami, earthquake'* – Fox imbricates human and natural phenomena in the earth's destruction such that the *'great wail of despair'* that *'rises from the smoking remains'* could come from the lips of a dying humanity or be rent from the earth itself (205). Zooming out from the ruins, Fox returns to a view of the planet that *'looks calm and beautiful once more'* (206). This outwards movement, abnegating responsibility for environmental crisis or human suffering, deems planetary engagement simply a question of perspective and finally a matter of choice: *'"It's not all like that," says Fox. "I promise. We must've just been at the wrong altitude and picked up all the bad stuff"'* (206). The whole earth image, then, whilst seductive in its beauty, nevertheless denotes a disengaged controlling ideology that leaves Mara feeling queasy. A view that engenders a sense of alienation by denying humanity's phenomenal interaction with the earth, the whole earth perspective fails to nurture the empathetic values of care and reciprocity that underpin Mara's quest for a new home. If Mara is to negotiate an embodied and embedded relationship with the earth, it is not – the text implies – one that can be modelled on a planetary image of material dislocation.

The whole earth view of the world evoked in Reeve's *Predator's Gold* [2003] and *A Darkling Plain* [2006] is, by contrast, one that *already* communicates earth oppression, foregrounding humanity's disengagement from the planet: 'Tom realised that he was seeing what no human had seen for millennia; the world from space. ... Oddly, it was not very impressive' (Reeve 2009b: 507). This 'not very impressive' planetary perspective had previously been evoked in *Predator's Gold* in which a usually unobtrusive narrator accords the reader to 'look down on the world from somewhere high above' (Reeve 2004: 215):

[I]f you were a god, or a ghost haunting one of the old American weapon platforms which still hang in orbit high above the pole – the Ice Wastes would look at first blank as the walls of Hester's cell;

a whiteness spread over the crown of the poor old Earth like a cataract on a blue eye.

The 'God's eye view' noted by Garb (1990: 272) is here appropriated both to acknowledge, and lay blame for, the earth's distress under a formulation that clearly implicates the novel's readers. The 'old American weapon platforms' are semantically linked to the 'cell' that represents the earth's imprisonment, rendering earth oppression a product of American expansionism. The 'blank' walls of this cell – unreadable, non-communicative, unvoiced – are subject to ideologies of control. The 'poor old earth', couched in a patronising discourse of false endearment, is an aged and blinded entity whose green kingdom has been dethroned.

A planetary consciousness in Reeve's novels tacitly acknowledges humanity's complicity in the earth's degradation. Such complicity underpins the Tractionist mentality of the novels' post-apocalyptic societies in which humans live above the ground in tiered mobile cities. Municipal Darwinism – a mechanised version of Darwin's survival of the fittest – has seen the cities uprooted onto giant caterpillar tracks in order to hunt each other for human and mechanical resources. Gouging open the earth to expand their hunting grounds, the mobile cities clearly manifest humanity's physical and metaphysical displacement from the earth's surface. An aerial view of the degraded landscape evoked in *Mortal Engines* foregrounds the cities' planetary dislocation (78–9):

> Down, and down, and then the cloud thinned and parted and Tom saw the vast Out-Country spread below him like a crumpled sheet of grey-brown paper, slashed with long, blue shapes that were the flooded track-marks of countless towns. For the first time since the airship lifted away from Stayns he felt afraid, but Miss Fang murmured, "Nothing to fear, Tom."
>
> He calmed himself and gazed out at the amazing view. Far to the north he could see the cold glitter of the Ice Wastes and the dark cones of the Tannhäuser fire-mountains. ... To the south-east there... [was] a dingy layer of mist above a tract of marshland, and beyond that the silvery shimmer of water.

Unlike the whole earth view in *Zenith*, this decaying natural landscape is not glowing or iridescent, but 'dark' and 'dingy'. Suffering visibly from human manipulation, the earth has become a human waste product ('a crumpled sheet…of paper'), physically abused by its human inhabitants. The referent of Tom's fear is ambiguous: readers might question whether it is the vastness of the Tractionist hunting grounds or the strange Aviatrix, Anna Fang, whose anti-Tractionist ideologies position her in opposition to Tom and render her an angry spokesperson for the degraded natural world. Readers might question, indeed, whether Tom's fear in fact arises through contemplation of the degraded and gaping earth itself. By advocating an expanding view of the earth as she brings her flying ship down to land, Anna Fang provides Tom with a powerful counter-hegemonic symbol of feminine care to replace his acculturated ideologies of distant planetary control.

In the final novel of the series, the whole earth view that Tom finds 'not very impressive' is employed as a metaphor for the tragic breakdown of human relationships engendered by environmental collapse. Like Fox in *Zenith*, the Stalker Fang (the cyborg incarnation of Anna Fang) expands and contracts her perspective as she moves the eye of the satellite across the earth's surface until she finds Tom and Hester's daughter, Wren (510):

> Odin zoomed again and there was nothing on the screen except their daughter's face. Tom went closer, pushing past the Stalker Fang, reaching out to touch the glass. At such close range the image started to grow vague; Wren's face broke down into lines and specks and flares of light; this smudge of shadow an eye, that white smear her nose. He traced with his hands the curve of her cheek, wishing he could push through the screen somehow and touch her, speak to her.

If the long-range image of the planet from space has engendered no more than a disengaged sense of planetary responsibility, this close-range view of Wren's face by contrast awakens in Tom his love, fear and hope for the future. Failing, however, to 'touch her, speak to her', Tom is denied phenomenal engagement with his daughter such that his experience of 'watching her' becomes a form of spatial containment through visual surveillance. Tom's experience of the planet is, like Mara's, *anti*-sensory and alienating; unable to make Wren 'feel' anything, Tom fails to affect an emotional connection with his daughter.

Not simply, then, does the whole world image foreground earth dislocation, it also labels technological innovation a screen inhibiting human communication. The closer the image zooms in – the more fully technology interpellates the human subject – the more 'vague' this communication becomes. Separating Wren's face into constituent parts – 'an eye', 'her nose', 'her cheek' – the satellite lens produces a view of the human as an object of empirical assessment made up of 'lines', 'specks', and 'flares', rather than an embodied being of felt sensitivities. The whole earth view reveals humanity's incapacity to formulate embedded and embodied relationships with one another and with the earth when circumscribed by a planetary consciousness. This planetary consciousness delimits human belonging by inscribing the earth as an anti-sensory space of failed and ineffectual human relationships. If Tom's desire to 'push through the screen' is a metaphor for more intimate and embodied phenomenal engagement, the poetics of planet engendered by the satellite images in both Reeve's and Bertagna's novels must be replaced by an ecopoetics of earthly attachment. These novels are hopeful in imagining a future for humanity despite overwhelming ecological devastation, but this future – they suggest – will come at the expense of the planetary.

Post-natural nature: a trajectory towards hope

The toxic landscapes that constitute a re-formed and re-shaped post-disaster world are visible manifestations of anthropogenic manipulation. These tainted landscapes render an *im*pure ecology the new baseline for planetary appraisal and urge 'the expansion of "nature" as an operative category' (Buell 2001: 45). Rebecca Raglon (2009: 66; 61) further points to the decidedly less glamorous aspects of our current ecological context, such as 'areas of exclusion, wastelands, garbage dumps, cramped suburban refuges, ecological hotspots'; 'What confronts contemporary nature writers in contrast to past writers', she argues, 'is an understanding of nature as thoroughly anthropogenic'. In the novels discussed these toxic landscapes render the earth an abject site on which human abuses are enacted. As overt manifestations of climate crisis, they offer a graphic warning to current generations to direct attention to the exigencies of the planet. Despite engendering alienation, these post-natural landscapes demonstrate a melding of the urban, suburban and rural under a hybrid formulation suggestive of ecological resilience. Instances of toxicity or impurity in the natural landscape are often tempered with a hopeful show of nature's persistence or adaptability to anthropogenic manipulation. In these new post-natural circumstances, nature's adaptability becomes a metaphor for human resilience in the face of environmental crisis; a robust and enduring earth offers a model for human resistance to planetary dislocation. In the novels, a trajectory can be recognised from planetary alienation to – potential or tentative – earthly belonging through recognition of the earth's capacity to withstand oppression. This narrative trajectory is correlative with an increasingly embodied connection between humans and the natural world predicated on the rejection of a disengaged planetary consciousness and the affirmation of an embedded engagement with the earth. Ecoconscious renegotiation unfolds alongside a discourse of ecological growth and renewal; the image of a bud, flower or weed blooming despite the toxicity of the post-natural landscape is a common metaphor for this earthly restoration.

In an ironic appropriation of the imagery of environmental flourishing, the bud that initially blooms in *Mortal Engines* is one that poses a deadly threat to the remnants of a surviving ecology. MEDUSA, an ancient super weapon unearthed by Pandora Shaw whilst 'digging for Old-Tech', has been buried for millennia – like a dormant bulb – in the soil of the Dead Continent of America (44). Appropriated by London's Mayor for use against the Anti-Tractionist League, this weapon becomes a violent symbol of environmental imperialism. Concealed within the dome of St Paul's cathedral aboard the city of London – one of the last remaining remnants of the former imperial social order – MEDUSA is described using a sustained metaphor of a 'bud blooming' (174; 181; 183):

> Slowly, like a huge bud blooming, the dome of the ancient cathedral was splitting open; Katherine watched, transfixed, as the dome of St Paul's split along black seams and the sections folded outwards like petals; [t]he metal orchid was open to its full extent now, casting a deep shadow on the square below. Only it was not an orchid. It was a cowled, flaring thing like the hood of some enormous cobra.

Not an innocent flower but a hooded snake recalling the snaky tendrils of the mythological female figure from which it takes its name, MEDUSA emerges from the dome of London's most institutionalised church; the weapon is overtly positioned as the tempting serpent in the Garden of Eden, threatening to seduce humanity into destroying the sanctity of the earth's remaining green places through technological expansion. In this symbolic instantiation of the destructive consequences of unsustainable consumerism on a battered ecology, the 'bud blooming' is in fact more analogous to the mushroom-cloud of nuclear warfare whose toxic radiation retains an effect on the environment long after the bomb is detonated.

In the mangled remains of London when MEDUSA self-implodes and destroys the city, the lingering radiation of the bomb blast engenders a post-natural landscape that reminds Tom of 'another country' (Reeve 2009b: 190). In this alien landscape, the earth is 'completely hidden' and 'so twisted, so jumbled-up, so distorted' that it seems antithetical to human belonging (188; 191). However, despite manifest alienation, the post-natural landscape is surprisingly '*beautiful*', as Wren notes in her diary (226):

> *You wouldn't think there would be beauty in a great smashed-up heap of rubbish, but there is. In all the clefts and stretches of open earth, trees and ferns grow, and in every soil-filled nook among the debris too. Birds sing here; insects buzz about. Angie says that in another month the scrapheaps above Crouch End will be pink with foxgloves.*

The post-natural world is both resilient and exuberant, growing in '*all the clefts*' and '*in every soil-filled nook*'. Here, '*trees and ferns*' cover over the man-made '*rubbish*', '*debris*' and '*scrapheaps*' of London's ruin and foreground the capacity of the natural world to resist human manipulation. Metaphorically relegating humanity's violent actions against the planet to the 'scrapheap' of history, the post-natural ecology negotiates a future at the intersection of the manmade and the natural. The plants growing in tainted soil thus highlight the regenerative potential of earth embeddedness. Wren herself begins to experience a sense of belonging in this new '*secret*' London, wishing that she were a native Londoner herself (226). With the surviving London community learning techniques for growing food, the society that evolves out of London's catastrophe is feudal, self-sufficient and dependent on sustainable engagement with the earth. The buds that now bloom in London's soil – unlike that which prefigured London's end – are indicative of an ecologically embedded future for humanity predicated on ecofeminist values of care and community.

As in Reeve's *Mortal Engines* quartet, the post-natural landscape in *Exodus* is initially – shockingly – alienating. In the toxic seas surrounding the refugee boat camp anchored at the foot of New Mungo, the 'putrid, stomach-turning stench of sewage, sweat and sickness' pervades the atmosphere (70). This alliterative list of human waste products designates the natural world humanity's dumping ground. In this toxic landscape, emphasis is similarly placed on nature's surprising capacity for growth and renewal (93; 137):

> [A] solitary spider...is weaving a web in a small crack of the bridge leg. Weeds and wildflowers sprout there, and the toxic green algae that breed on the water reach up towards it too. And there's a single blue forget-me-not. It's a tiny miracle, all that life bursting out of such a barren little space. ... Mara climbs through the rubble of bones and bottles and weeds that lie inside the ruined building. In the middle of the room with no walls or roof sits a smashed television set, its innards overgrown with chickenweed and dandelions. A kitten cries like a lost child in a wasteland, but as Mara clambers through to get up to Wing she sees it's not really a wasteland at all. The place is teeming with wildlife – birds, bluebottles, beetles, cats, goats, a wild dog, chickens, wasps, worms, slugs, spiders and ants. Nature has reclaimed the ruins of the human world.

Like the 'solitary spider', the natural world is invested with the potential to weave the possibility of a future out of the destruction of the past; even the 'toxic algae' that is a victim of anthropogenic tampering is not a passive entity but actively 'reach[es] up' towards the sun. If the 'tiny miracle' of 'life bursting' from a world previously deemed 'barren' relegates planetary destruction to the past, the 'forget-me-not' functions as a still-present reminder of the apocalyptic conditions that spawned planetary collapse. Actively re-weaving a more ecologically embedded relationship between humans and the earth, the plants replace defunct technology with overgrown 'chickenweed and dandelions'. If the crying 'kitten', like a 'lost child', demands human compassion and protection, the 'teeming' wildlife implies that nature, in its post-natural guise, is in fact capable of taking care of itself. In this 'wasteland' that is 'not really a wasteland', nature is found to exceed human expectations. Having 'reclaimed the ruins of the human world', it enacts its own spiritually-inflected resurrection in an exuberant demonstration of natural agency.

In the far-future America of Anderson's *Feed* [2004], the manipulated environment has become, by contrast, the ecological norm. Here, the show of hopeful natural recovery is decidedly more ironic since it centres on monstrous or grotesque reincarnations of 'the natural'. In this society with no past, nostalgia for a lost ecological purity ironically centres on an *already* anthropogenically adapted suburban landscape (Anderson 2004: 94):

> *I remember seeing the hawks perched on street lamps, during those last days of the American forests...I miss that time. The cities back then, just after the forests died, were full of wonders, and you'd stumble on them – these princes of the air on common rooftops – the rivers that burst through city streets so they ran like canals – the rabbits in parking garages – the deer foaling, nestled in Dumpsters like a Nativity.*

Here, juxtaposing pairs of natural and man-made have instantiated a new set of post-romantic dualisms: hawks/street lamps, rivers/city streets, rabbits/parking garages, deer/Dumpsters. Anthropocentric appropriation has created a secular dystopia in which 'deer' in a 'Dumpster' constitutes the new, ironic '*Nativity*'. In a world in which whales are laminated to mediate the effects of the toxic seas, butterflies have scales and slugs are large enough for toddlers to ride, human-induced ecological adaptation has seen the intrinsic properties of the natural undergo substantial alteration. Whilst unnatural nature in excess is distasteful to our contemporary sense of natural balance, the will to survive exhibited by the nonhuman world foregrounds the subversive capacity of the natural world to exhibit agency in the face of anthropogenic oppression. Hayles contends that 'although some current versions of the posthuman point towards the anti-human and the apocalyptic, we can craft others that will be conducive to the long-range survival of humans and of the other life-forms, biological and artificial, with whom we share the planet and ourselves' (1999: 291). It is this form of tempered discourse that many young adult novels adopt, at least in part, to allay the bleakness of a post-natural future.

Disembodiment and transcendence: a thing of beauty?

Through a discursive foregrounding of 'natural' beauty, these novels explore the ways in which an embodied connection between humans and the natural world is adapted to accommodate the abstract systems integral to the technologically hybrid post-natural landscape. If beauty in nature signals embedded growth and renewal, a contrasting move *away* from the earth through an escape into abstract modes of 'natural' symbolisation is visible in these novels as a strategy to redistribute emphasis to a disembodied sense of natural worth predicated on artificial aestheticism. In promulgating a vision of transcendence over human embodiment, the novels interrogate the possibility of a human identity embedded not in the earth's ecology but in a technological nexus predicated on mind control and scientific mastery. The ethereal beauty of artificial cyberscapes is achievable through transcendence of natural constraints; its appeal stems from sensual appreciation of conceptual technologies rather than embodied communion with the earth. This counter-narrative that refutes ecological embeddedness hinges on the allure of virtual reality in a context of worsening environmental crisis; the question becomes, how can a disembodied conception of beauty that foregrounds human–earth dislocation negotiate a more agential subject position for the inescapably embodied human actant? The narratological strategy of directing attention away from the ontological properties of the natural world itself and towards what are thought to be specifically *human* qualities such as the desire for, and willingness to apprehend, beauty, quietly bypasses ecoconscious appraisal of this failure to negotiate the protagonists' ecological embeddedness.

In *Mortal Engines*, Shrike's inexplicable fondness for Hester centres on achieving his 'heart's desire', a desire to see her scarred face made 'beautiful' through posthuman technology (177):

"CROME WILL RESURRECT YOU AS AN IRON WOMAN. YOUR FLESH WILL BE REPLACED WITH STEEL, YOUR NERVES WITH WIRE, YOUR THOUGHTS WITH ELECTRICITY. YOU WILL BE BEAUTIFUL! YOU WILL BE MY COMPANION, FOR ALL TIME."

In his repeated human-machine pairings – flesh to steel, nerves to wire, thoughts to electricity – the disembodied machine is conversely re-embodied to become a replacement for the weak and defective human body. The desired resurrection can only take place through the death of Hester's human body, and her rebirth as a human-machine hybrid. Such reincarnation lacks spiritual implications (Shrike is quick to point out that Hester's feelings – her humanity – will be forfeit) yet since Shrike's request is a plea for companionship, such reincarnation does not lack emotional resonance. Shrike's 'heart's desire' becomes more poignant still considering the impossibility of its fulfilment: the 'Old Tech' components out of which Shrike and the Stalker Fang are made – the mechanical equivalent of mental reasoning, subjectivity, memory and cognition – are lost to the Traction Empire's engineers and thus such a human-machine melding cannot be realised. In finally dismantling the human (heart, desire, emotion) from the mechanical (brain, memory, cognition), the human *within* the posthuman is ultimately recentred.

Whilst in Reeves' texts the man-machine hybrid is envisaged as an enhanced and superseded form of human embodiment, the intangibility of internet-equivalent technology in Anderson's and Bertagna's novels suggests an electronic alternative to embodiment that seeks to naturalise an almost complete reincarnation of the human actant. In *Feed*, in which a chip implanted in humans' brains feeds them an advanced version of our modern internet, the total interpellation of the teenagers' lives by technology is in infrequent moments, and in a way that appears almost subconscious, described as a blissful heightening of awareness, made possible only through technological progress (70; 106):

> And the feed was pouring in on us now. ... It came down on us like water. It came down like frickin' spring rains, and we were dancing in it. ... It was like they were lots of friendly butterflies, and we were smeared with something, and they kept coming and coming, and their wings were winking beautifully, and more and more came.

Here, natural images – spring rains, butterflies – are used to describe otherwise ineffable sensations, sensations that are artificially constituted. The natural imagery used here accomplishes a certain naturalising, and familiarising, of such artificiality. In a post-natural world in which nothing grows unless anthropogenically planted, such attempts to naturalise the internal lives of the human beings whose external lives are so severely compromised can be seen as an effective mythologising of nature to keep the *idea*, rather than the reality, of the natural world alive. If nature is something to be cherished, cyberspace now constitutes the new baseline for natural sanctity.

In *Exodus*, an artificial natural world is constructed within the towering sky cities as a placebo for humanity's earthly dislocation. Within the man-made nexus of tunnels, a bridge spans a pond under a blue sky whilst a disembodied voice oozes from the bridge and charges Mara to rest and whisper a secret into the wishing well. Here, 'nature' is imbued with magical powers, capable of healing a weary soul through wish fulfilment. In a society revolving around sensory perception – of a hedonistic and artificial, rather than embodied, nature – such weariness comes from the malaise associated with constant shallow pleasure seeking. Artificial nature is here used to compensate for a lack of *real* nature, and the natural embodied connections between people and places that such a lost nature has come to signify. Turning her gaze away from the glimmering lights of this oasis in the city at the thought of the slaves used to build such a paradise and the refugees such a paradise excludes, Mara 'looks at the pond with clear eyes. The fish are fake and swim in endless electronic circles. The tree and its bird, the crystal sky and sunset, are all fake too. Even the bridge is made of mock-stone. It's false enchantment' (227). Here, manipulated nature is not beguiling or seductive but 'fake' and 'false' and an inferior replacement for the lost reality of the drowned natural world. Mara's success at turning her gaze away from the artificial landscape constitutes a metaphoric rejection of such 'false' aestheticism.

If this gesture towards earth embeddedness is predicated on an acknowledgement that the artificial landscape is a product of inter-locking discourses of environmental imperialism and social injustice, Mara's failure to resist the artificial landscapes of the 'Noos' suggests that aesthetic standardisation is differentially interpellated. The high-tech Noos of 2099 ostensibly offers humanity the potential for emancipation via its assimilation of artificial technologies into organic ecosystems. Like the feed in Anderson's novel, the Noos is an advanced version of our current internet that similarly demands complete sub-servience from its human users. Living in sky cities that distance their inhabitants both physically and conceptually from the natural world, the users of the Noos have been conditioned to perceive their internal lives as more fulfilling than their embodied relationships; as Mara wryly comments, real life bores the Noosrunners since they only 'come alive' when entering the Noos (237). As in *Feed*, whilst an apathetic willingness to turn the natural world into a blind space is overtly critiqued as anti-utopian, a noticeable emphasis is neverthe-less placed on the seductive beauty of the internal landscapes inspired by the Noos. The quasi-spiritual language used to describe the archi-tecture of the *Cybercath* ostensibly suggests that the Noos offers its users a form of divine transcendence: 'this cathedral-like place seems to be created out of light and air, glass and crystal and mirror – and yet more light. And wide open space. And soaring walls and ceilings that make you look ever upwards' (222). As Mara herself qualifies, such an uplifting atmosphere is remarkably successful in dissuading the enclosed city inhabitants from looking 'down and out', both lit-erally and figuratively (222). A prevalence of natural images, similar to those found in *Feed*, is used to describe the network of sky cities that have risen out of the dying planet. In a globe that charts the sky cities' positions, Mara finds that a 'crystal tree' represents each city, making a 'forest of crystal that glitters around the globe' (224). Inside the cities, the cubicles in which the Noosrunners lose themselves in cyberspace are described using the metaphor of a honeycomb: a thriving, organic community based on natural order and precision. Here, such technological innovation is naturalised to the point of being made beautiful.

More beguiling yet is the Noos itself, through which Mara gains access to another world entirely (239):

> In realworld she stops breathing as she spins out of her cupule in the cybercath, far away into another dimension, into a world of utter beauty, grace and chaos. ... All around, above and below, as far as she can see, the godgems of the New World have merged to create an organic frenzy of colour and pattern. Fractals and feathers, frosts and ferns and flowers, crystals and corals, constellations and cloudbursts and galaxies, shells, stars, strata, streamers and spirals, bird flocks and bubble clusters and butterfly wings, roses and acorns, loops and spheres, lichen, rainbows and honeycombs, fungus, snowflakes, spheres, pyramids and prisms, webs and jungle weaves, knits and knots and so much, much more. Everything imaginable and beyond. All of it linked by an endless pattern of connections. A living world of info and data within each pattern. All of it endlessly changing and mutating and repatterning. All dying and recreating every microsecond.

The artificiality of the cyberworld is naturalised not simply through repeated references to organic, living forms and the long alliterative lists of natural systems like constellations and cloudbursts, but also through references to the correlative patterns found in both mathematical systems and the natural world, patterns that underpin the structural design of a fractal and a snowflake and a human genome. These correlative patterns connect the dying natural world to the new cybertronic world and subvert the pessimism of the world's drowning by foregrounding the regenerative capacity of such systems: that death and rebirth, flux and flow are an integral part of our evolving world.

Both earthly – 'wild and savage' – and celestial, the Noos offers humanity an entire universe to replace the old (239). Immersion in such a world allows for constant wish fulfilment ('Everything imaginable and beyond'). The enchantment that the Noos provides takes Mara's breath away, quite literally, since in this electronic world the Noosrunner becomes an avatar of any description. Noos, the reader is informed, is the Ancient Greek word for mind or intellect and, in this future world, this 'global Supermind' is accessed via the head-gem that constitutes the 'mind's eye' (237). The new world sprung from the drowned remains of the old is thus an entirely disembodied one, requiring neither physical presence nor lived experience, corroborating Hayles' contention that '[h]ere, at the inaugural moment of the computer age, the erasure of embodiment is performed so that "intelligence" becomes a property of the formal manipulation of symbols rather than enaction in the human lifeworld' (1999: xi). Mara, in fact, likens the Noos to 'a genie let loose from a bottle': an ethereal entity of smoke and mirrors designed to grant wishes that, in a metafictive nod to tales of the Arabian Nights, rarely bring true happiness (240). Realising that the Netherworld from which she came, rooted within the earth, feels more alive than this artificial reconstruction of natural beauty, Mara is confronted with the total integration in the New World society of a technological landscape that has 'wrapped itself invisibly, powerfully, around the Earth' (240). In this disembodied world of beauty and escapism, the Noos has become a hangman's noose for the natural world.

Conclusion: the blind space of apocalypse

Environmental crisis narratives have been enthusiastically embraced by the media in service of what Tom Hillard (2009: 688) calls 'a nearly ubiquitous cultural fascination' with the hostile and deadly elements of the natural world and the threat they pose to human life. A fascination that sees crisis narratives move seamlessly from newspaper headlines to popular entertainment leads to what Simon Estok (2009: 207) terms near universal 'ecophobia', which he defines as 'the contempt and fear we feel for the environment'. Ecophobia, Estok (2009: 208) argues, is 'an irrational and groundless hatred of the natural world, as present and subtle in our daily lives and literature as homophobia and racism and sexism'. A prejudicial discourse invoked whenever nature is represented as an opponent that poses a threat to our safety, ecophobia is 'rooted in and dependent on anthropocentric arrogance and speciesism, on the ethical position that humanity is outside of and exempt from the laws of nature' (Estok 2009: 209; 217). Extending the disjunction between culture and nature that characterises normative engagement with the natural world, many of the novels invoke an ecophobic discourse to portray the planet as vengeful and vitriolic, lashing out at the humans who have engendered widespread ecological devastation. The earth is not the redemptive, sublime entity of the romantic tradition, but a deadly threat to humanity in its fragile state of recovery after disaster or apocalypse, or simply an unintelligible entity with which the human population must battle for territorial supremacy. A 'scapegoat for social problems', the planet becomes a by-product of the technological master narrative of relentless human progress (Estok 2009: 211). Ecophobic renderings of the environment reveal an anthropocentric failure to invest in nature the intrinsic qualities ecofeminists deem necessary to engender respect or reciprocity; the irony inherent in ecophobic rhetoric lies in its capacity to displace or obscure the fact that humanity itself is responsible for planetary retribution.

In questioning when crisis thinking might shift from being 'a progressive politics of hope to a reactionary politics of fear', Sarah Amsler (2010: 129–30) signals the 'crisis of hope' that often accompanies climate change rhetoric (132). Such a crisis revolves around the premise that normative neoliberal social systems are inherently isolating and dehumanising and therefore breed apathy and scepticism rather than encouraging the traditionally underplayed values – such as empathy and compassion – that are central to ecofeminist advocacy for change. In positioning climate change as impending peril, crisis narratives can have the unwanted effect of denying agency and inducing an excessive sense of despair, paralysis or disempowerment. The teleological implications of such a nihilistic trajectory, couched in distinctly narratological terms, cause Stefan Skrimshire (2010: 233) to warn that 'we may have reached a point at which the idea of human agency – the ability to act – has also become swallowed up in some larger meta-narrative in which the end of the story is beyond people's control'. Post-apocalyptic fiction questions the extent to which apocalyptic rhetoric produces human fear and delimits human belonging by engendering planetary alienation and dislocation, and to what extent such rhetoric conversely empowers people to fight for change.

Climate change rhetoric hinges on the linearity often attributed to environmental crisis. Kearns and Keller (2007: xi) argue that the climate change 'tipping point' that is envisaged to push the earth beyond the brink of collapse will be met by a 'green shift' towards a 'tipping *counter*point':

> [H]ope for a sustainable earthling future – for a *green shift* – may depend upon a dramatic nonlinear transition as well. All effort on behalf of ecosocial justice thrives on the hope that the achingly small beginnings of movement may precipitate a "butterfly effect" of change, a tipping *counter*point, an avalanche of responsible action. The green shift seems to require a root change of human

outlook, a mutation of collective philosophy, a spiritual phase transition. Certainly the ecoapocalyptic rhetoric of threat alone will not do the trick.

If the ecoapocalyptic rhetoric of climate crisis and the ecophobic metanarratives underpinning current understandings of climate change will 'not do the trick' then one is forced to ask what will. As Greenway warns in the quotation used to preface this discussion, novels for young people are unlikely to come up with a solution to ecological crisis. Yet, the strength of these novels lies in rejecting existing ideologies to make room for new, and different, world orders. The post-apocalyptic landscape becomes the standpoint for an ecofeminist environmental ethics and newly envisaged interrelationships between humans and the earth; as Greta Gaard (1998: 4–5) puts it, 'a space for future generations to work out their relationships with the rest of nature'. The blind space that is opened up through the dismantling of the old world order is discursively radical and transformative in its potentiality.

The novels that are most successful in engendering a sustainable mode of earth engagement do so by evoking planetary dislocation – on a worldwide scale – only to refute such alienation and negotiate a more embedded relationship between humans and the earth. Such novels look to the post-natural landscape not as a space of threat but as a potential space of human belonging. In finding in nature's resilience and adaptability a restorative model for human–earth interaction, these novels advocate the rejection of a disengaged planetary consciousness and the affirmation of a reflexive ecoconsciousness. If the blind space of the earth has previously engendered discourses of abuse and oppression, it is here re-envisaged as a space in which to nurture an embedded discourse of growth and renewal. By resisting the abstraction of the planetary and the artificial aestheticism of the virtual, the novels seek to re-materialise the planet and ground their human protagonists within the earth. Metaphorically 'zooming in' towards the earth, these novels offer a future predicated on place-based values and ecological embeddedness.

2
Ideologies of Advancement: Writing on the Body

Ecofeminist appraisals of the effects of global processes at a local level can be useful in addressing the monopolisation of global capitalism in much of the world and the current and future effects of such a monopoly on the human body and the body of the earth. The feminist agenda implicit in such a reading – an agenda that acknowledges the hierarchical distribution of power, wealth and privilege in political and monetary systems designed to benefit the few rather than the many – sees the planet as an embodied entity similarly subject to uneven distributions of power and privilege. The naturalisation of human advancement in the contemporary western imagination centres on the notion that progress and particularly technological progress can provide an on-going solution to crisis. Ideologies of neoliberal individualism place market value on the progressive self-advancement of the autonomous subject or on what Hickel and Khan (2012: 224) term 'the "sovereign consumer" [as] the principal agent of change'. Capitalism, as a product of the neoliberal free market, rewards the self-actualising individual and marginalises discourses of dependence, community or collective empowerment to produce what Douglas Vakoch (2011: 24) labels 'the self-conscious, radically alienated, self-contained, sovereign subject of market theory'. Such radical alienation and self-containment reveals itself in the young adult novels in the fraught relationships of the young protagonists with the institutional regimes that regulate them. The self-advancement lauded by such regimes is enacted not simply at the level of subject but at the level of the body so that beautification, bodily modification or self-erasure become both a symbol of, and resistance to, the 'rampant individualism' that neoliberalism produces (Worden 2009: 221). The planetary consciousness engendered through apocalypse that has seen humans dislocated from a degraded earth thus frequently results in the alienation of human inhabitants from their own embodiment. Whether this alienation is engendered through technological advancement or post-natural degradation, or enacted through a drive towards consumerist self-actualisation, it becomes physically written onto the skin. Under the auspices of self-advancement, the female body and the earth body are similarly denoted a blind space, subject to constructivist discourses of neoliberal individualism.

The environmental implications of a globalised consumerist economy are neatly summed up by Max Oelschlaeger (1991: 287) in his critique of resource conservationism, an environmental policy that sees 'the wilderness in whatever guise...effectively reduced to an environment, a stockpile of matter-energy to be transformed through technology, itself guided by the market and theoretical economics, into the wants and needs of consumer culture'. Estok (2009: 211) echoes these sentiments by pointing to the paradigmatic shift occasioned by the Industrial Revolution that saw nature redefined as 'pure object, a machine that ideally could be intimately and infinitely controlled and forced to spit out products in the service of an increasingly utilitarian capitalist economy'. Defining nature as 'stockpile of matter-energy' or 'machine' denies the natural world organic agency in and of itself, thus paving the way for its commodification in light of human wants and purposes. Oelschlaeger's contention that resource conservationism sees the natural environment 'reduced *to an environment*' (my italics) resembles both the literary relegation of the natural world to the ontological status of 'setting' and the colonial sanctioning of foreign soil as *terra nullius*, or empty land (Buell 1995: 85). Val Plumwood (1993: 4) argues that the designation of nature 'as the "environment"' signifies the natural world as the 'invisible background conditions against which the "foreground" achievements of reason and culture (provided typi-cally by the white, western, male expert or entrepreneur) take place'. Plumwood identifies such 'backgrounding' as an element of oppres-sion in the establishment and maintenance of gendered, sexualised, racialised and class-bound hierarchies. Backgrounding centres on the simultaneous dependence and denial of dependence of the oppressor towards the oppressed. Such a dependency is threatening to the stable identity of the oppressor since 'the master more than the slave requires the other in order to define his boundaries and identity'; the oppressor thus undervalues, or relegates to the background, the qualities of the oppressed (Plumwood 1993: 48).

Ecofeminists have been quick to extend this insight to their engage-ment with environmental politics and to identify the backgrounding of female voices within the language, theory and praxis of normative ethical theorising. Their focus extends to the co-constitutive ways in which globalisation 'depends on both gendered processes of marginalisation and emergent processes of gendered resistance' (Nagar *et al.* 2002: 262). The challenge ecofeminists extend to the systems of power that produce individual subjectivities interrogates the inadequacies of normative ethical standpoints for dealing with environmental problems and more pertinently the epistemological foundations on which these standpoints rest. By investing agency in the natural world, ecofeminists argue for the necessity of transformative social and political action to re-conceptualise humanity's relationship with nonhuman others, as a relationship based not on degrees of seperation but on mutually agential cohabitation. The discursive and material constitution of the body has been the subject of much theorising, particularly as a key site for understanding power formations (Foucault) and the workings of gendered performatives (Butler). Arguing against social constructivist theories of the body by theorists who posit, like Judith Butler (1990: 136), that the body has 'no ontological status apart from the various acts which constitute its reality', ecofeminists attempt to reconstitute the body as a product of the material environment. In doing so they acknowledge the ways in which human embodiment is mediated by neoliberal processes.

The emergent discourse of posthumanism in young adult fiction usefully examines the 'toxic discourses' of globalised oppression that Giovanna Di Chiro (2010: 200) argues produce the necessity for an '*embodied* ecological politics':

> Thinking of the body as home/ecology, especially in consideration of those bodies, communities, and environments that have been reviled, neglected, and polluted, provides an apt metaphor and material grounding for constructing an *embodied* ecological politics that articulates the concepts of diversity, interdependence, social justice, and ecological integrity.

The degraded post-natural landscapes of the novels discussed are occupied by advanced and abject incarnations of the posthuman being on whose bodies are written the effects of environmental toxicity and an ethos of unlimited human progress. Whilst much innovative critical work has been undertaken on the analysis of the representational strategies employed to critique biotechnological advancement, genetic engineering, cloning, cyborg technologies and so on, I shall narrow my focus here to the novels' representation of posthumanism primarily in light of its capacity to interrogate the discursive site of the 'natural' human, and particularly female, body. I concur with John Stephens' (2010: 205) premise that one can recognise a common narrative progression in environmentally-aware young adult fiction in which 'parallel narratives [are] underpinned by a metonymic interrelationship, whereby threatened or damaged nature is matched by threatened or damaged lives'. In moving from an analysis of the ways in which individual subjectivity is unfolded against an ecological backdrop, I here explore the interface between subject and object – human and nonhuman, human and machine – in novels in which the validity, or very existence, of such individual subjectivity is in question.

In what follows, I accord key importance to the texts' dramatisation of the ways in which 'bodies may function in the construction of socialities – places, spaces, and processes of all kinds, whether cultural, political, or economic – in conjunction with the natural world' (Bradford *et al.* 2008: 87). Concerns over human embodiment, or *dis*embodiment, underpin the protagonists' struggles to negotiate their embedded sense of self within the degraded post-natural landscapes. In a formulation that resembles the disengagement engendered by a planetary consciousness, the rhetoric of posthumanism produces bodies that are dislocated from natural constraints. I work from the premise that one can recognise what Buell (2005: 109) terms the 'double paradox' of '"nature" having been androcentrically constructed as a domain for males...yet at the same time symbolically coded as female – an arena of potential domination analogous to the female body'. I therefore read the reincarnations of the female body and the posthuman body, as imagined in my focused novels, not simply as sites of male symbolisation but as loci of resistance – successful or failed – to hegemonic control. Under a framework of aesthetic enhancement, sexualisation, animalisation, commodification and vilification, natural bodies, female bodies and posthuman bodies are rendered blind spaces subject to masculinist discourses of physiognomic control.

Emancipation from nature: the body beautiful

In post-disaster novels for young adults, tension can be perceived between the common construction of subjectivity as a stable, autonomous category and an acknowledgement that the visibly decaying landscape must nevertheless impact upon the identity formation of its inhabitants. A desire to emancipate the human body from nature, or the natural, under the auspices of anthropocentric superiority can be perceived in the institutionalised efforts of the novels' political regimes to manipulate, undermine and reject human evolution as a normative ontological standpoint. Such manipulation arises from an ecophobic contempt for natural human embodiment, underpinned by the premise promulgated by Enlightenment humanism that a distinct and separate humanity is in essence divorced from his ecological embeddedness. Such institutional repression of natural embodiment is targeted at the female body, and the cultural norms of femininity become a particular locus of control. The novels exhibit tension over the paradoxical nature of self-advancement: that it is couched in the language of individual empowerment yet simultaneously engenders the collective standardisation of the female body under discourses of regimental control. In interrogating the socialisation of female and posthuman bodies, I work from the premise promulgated by Joel Dinerstein (2006: 473) that 'the Enlightenment utopia of the mind – as the rational host of self-control, self-mastery, and perfectability – has shifted to the body'.

In Suzanne Collins' *The Hunger Games*, a novel set in a far-future America in which a rigid class system circumscribes the lives of Panem's inhabitants, the surgical enhancements of the people of the central Capitol are predicated on a class-conscious effort to emancipate the elite from natural constraints. The beautification of the upper classes is overtly critiqued as a manifestation of class privilege that renders only the posthuman form capable of perfectability. Such perfection is ironic in the light of the lower class protagonist's narration; Katniss' consciousness of the oppressive social injustices on which the Capitol relies to maintain its stranglehold rule over Panem is communicated through her critique of Capitol aestheticism. Upon arrival in the Capitol, Katniss' surprise that her stylist, Cinna, looks 'normal' – with hair that appears to be its natural shade of brown – accounts for the friendship Katniss develops with him since the other stylists are 'so dyed, stencilled and surgically altered they're grotesque' (77). To Katniss, normal is correlative with natural and the artificial is a grotesque instantiation of non-normativity, in a formulation replicated in contemporary discourses of health and wellbeing ranging from household hygiene to breakfast cereals. To the people of the Capitol, however, Katniss' normal is substandard, and the lengthy beautification process imposed upon to her to meet the Hunger Games' requirements is testament to class-differentiated baselines for aesthetic categorisation. Katniss' disgust at Capitol fashion reveals itself in the dehumanising metaphors she uses to dramatise her stylists' distance and difference from herself: 'oddly coloured birds' with garish colours that remind her of the 'flat round discs of hard candy we can never afford to buy at the tiny sweet shop in District 12' (76; 72). Katniss' supercilious attitude towards the vacuous lifestyles of the rich – sugary and lacking in substance – discloses a deep-seated anger against the systems of privilege that allow a few to have plenty whilst the many starve whilst lauding the surgical operations that mask such plenty through a duplicitous emphasis on looking 'younger and thinner' (150).

In Scott Westerfeld's *Uglies*, a novel also set in a far-future America in which urban societies are marked by aesthetic standardisation, bodily perfection is not only attainable but anticipated and thus – in an inversion of the aesthetic focalisation of *The Hunger Games* – the natural body is perceived as freakish and unnatural. Standardisation takes the form of a series of surgically-enhanced appearances that mark each stage in human aging: 'uglies' (natural children) become 'new pretties' after their first operation, then 'middle pretties' and finally 'late pretties', nicknamed 'crumblies'. As a result of an operation in which 'they grind and stretch your bones to the right shape, peel off your face and rub all your skin away, and stick in plastic cheekbones so you look like everybody else', all marks of individuality – scars or birthmarks for instance – are removed under the strictures of physical conformity (50). An intertextual reference to the popular English folktale 'Jack and the Beanstalk' in which the giant threatens to grind Jack's bones to make his bread, this allusion serves to caution the natural child against the corruption of those who purport to protect. The inferiority with which natural embodiment becomes associated is clearly demonstrated in Tally's inability to communicate with her best friend, Peris, after he has undergone his 'pretty' operation: '"I just...", she sputtered. Now that she was facing him, she didn't know what to say. All the imagined conversations had melted away into his big, sweet eyes' (17). Tally's awkwardness inside her own body hinders her ability to express herself when confronted by Peris' physical perfection; physicality here emerges as a master narrative capable of silencing alternative discourses.

In positing the grotesque a property of childhood rather than old age, and beauty the property of maturity, the socially-instigated standards of beauty provide a counter to natural female aging. Ecophobia here manifests itself in politically-motivated contempt for natural embodiment, the natural aging process and the female body in particular. Whilst male subjects undertake the same kind of beautification, as is the case for Peris, its implications are explored primarily through the focalisation of the female characters, Tally and Shay, and thus provide a more thorough critique of our oppressive contemporary cultural obsession with feminine beauty. In interrogating the 'marking out of particular bodies' in western discourses of rationality and aesthetics, Richard Twine (2001: 33; 39) notes that only particular types of bodies have historically been thought to 'master their "burden of embodiment"'. In the west, Twine (2001: 34–5; 39) goes on to suggest, 'there are well-established gendered and racialised regimes of aesthetic judgement' through which 'literal marking [of the body] performs the role of identification, classification, and control simultaneously'. Such classification and control is visible in Westerfeld's 'pretty' society in which the successive operations imposed on individuals mark them as collective by-products of a standardised physiognomy. Difference, here, is erased not simply from physical appearance but also from personality, with the suggestion that such overt standardisation of looks is simply the outward manifestation of a socially-implemented mental standardisation. Homogenisation here takes the form of a streamlining of desire and preference in the construction and manipulation of female subjectivities.

A schema for naturalness is carefully unfolded in the text and centres on a physiognomic discourse revolving around an ambiguity: whether standards of beauty are evolutionarily prescribed or whether they simply constitute subtle and flexible means of cultural control. The authorities use Darwin's theory of evolution as a justification for anthropogenic change and maturation to promote physical standardisation as a natural stage in human evolution. Tally's response to Shay's claim that a desire for beauty is not instinctual but 'programmed' into children, is to suggest conversely that a positive response to beauty is 'just a natural reaction' and primitive in its basic evolutionary function (83; 16–17):

The big eyes and lips said: I'm young and vulnerable, I can't hurt you, and you want to protect me. And the rest said: I'm healthy, I won't make you sick. And no matter how you felt about a pretty, there was a part of you that thought: *If we had kids, they'd be healthy too. I* want *this pretty person...*

'A trick' – as Shay realises – to 'make us hate ourselves', the operation exploits concerns over human embodiment in order for children to be more effectively controlled by a system that demands regimented behavioural patterns and frowns upon individual autonomy (82; 44).

Shay's determination to keep her own face even under intense peer pressure demonstrates a fear that biological and technological enhancement will compromise the diversity of the human condition: that to change her physiognomy will be to erase her subjectivity. That the operation to make uglies pretty is found to do just that – manipulating aspects of the patients' brains to compromise their natural humanity – is an indication of the novel's nostalgic conceptualisation of natural human embodiment as an outward sign of inner autonomy.

This anti-posthumanist stance is problematically unfolded since a discourse of fairness undercuts such posthumanist critique by arguing for an egalitarianism grounded in aesthetic standardisation. The reasons for the original development of the pretty operation – as taught in the school curriculum – centre on the humanitarian efforts of those in control to put a stop to prejudicial judgements based on appearance, racism-inspired violence and weight-related diseases such as anorexia. The text's critique of sameness and standardisation as a product of post-human innovation is therefore complicated by the ostensible validity of the reasons for its implementation. In a totalitarian social system in which the operation is obligatory, however, the protagonists' lack of choice in the construction of an egalitarian society effectively renders any concomitant possibilities for agency unattainable and standardised beauty meaningless. The underlying dynamic of the text thus centres on the fear that physical sameness will lead to a concomitant mental standardisation and an inability of future humans to think outside of the cultural, political or technological systems that interpellate them. The naturalisation of this underlying dynamic marks the embodied female subject as a manipulatable entity divorced from her material, ecological context.

A highly ordered and standardised cityscape is evoked as a metonymic representation of this aesthetic standardisation. The trees that line the river are 'generic carbon-dioxide suckers that decorate[] the city', both functional (reducing global warming) and attractive (decorating the city like icing on a cake) (56). The river itself is 'dignified' and 'stately' whilst it meanders slowly through the city, yet turns into a 'snarling monster' upon entry into the forest (56). Nature, within the cities, is highly cultured; outside the cities, nature is monstrous and wild. Clearly, ecology is here being used to make a concomitant statement about human nature: whilst the population is kept within city boundaries, it is civilised, decorative and harmless to the planet (functional and attractive), yet outside of the cities, it is dangerous, wild and potentially monstrous. An ecological symbol of femininity – the white orchid – is subject to this discursive merging of beauty and monstrosity. Once valued at the price of a house, the orchids are, in fact, '"the ultimate weed"' after undergoing genetic modification (181–2):

> 'They crowd out every other species, choke trees and grass, and nothing eats them except one species of hummingbird, which feeds on their nectar. But the hummingbirds nest in trees.'
> 'There aren't any trees down there,' Tally said. 'Just the orchids.'
> 'Exactly. That's what monoculture means: Everything the same. After enough orchids build up in an area, there aren't enough hummingbirds to pollinate them. ... So the orchids eventually die out, victims of their own success, leaving a wasteland behind. Biological zero.'

A metaphor for the human population now in its 'pretty' incarnation, the orchids – 'so beautiful, so delicate and unthreatening' – are indicative of the mapping of human standards of aesthetic categorisation onto the natural world (182). Reminiscent of the germ that devastated the planet's human and nonhuman populations, reducing the diversity of the Earth's ecology to a point just short of '[b]iological zero', these orchids embody the effects of aesthetic manipulation on the nonhuman body. Biological simplification, according to Ynestra King (1989: 19), has overtly social implications, akin to 'reducing human diversity into faceless workers, or to the homogenisation of taste and culture through mass consumer markets'. The rangers' failure to destroy the orchids with poison, predators or diseases and their eventual decision to simply contain the weeds with fire, echoes the mind-altering policies adopted by the authorities to contain the new pretty culture within the ideological boundaries of the cities through aesthetic – and mental – homogenisation. That the orchid was once a unique and valuable entity and has been reduced, devalued and standardised through centuries of biological engineering, suggests that the sorry history of the orchid prefigures a similar narrative trajectory for both nature in general, and (post)human nature in particular.

The 'sexism/speciesism nexus' and the consumable body

If an ecophobic desire to emancipate the body from the natural for reasons of self-actualisation manifests itself in body modification and artificial body enhancements, it is a desire borne out in the personal hygiene and cosmetics industries which 'cite nature's "flaws" and "blemishes" as objects of their work' (Estok 2009: 208). Since the hygiene and cosmetics industries are primarily marketed towards the female consumer, such ecophobic contempt for the natural adheres to what Gaard (2010: 645) terms the 'sexism/speciesism nexus' that links women and animals as comparable objects of (sexual) abuse and exploitation.[1] This blurring of the woman-animal boundary, reminiscent of Deleuze's deployment of the notion of 'becoming-animal', supports what Stacy Alaimo (1994: 140) terms 'the historically ingrained position of women and animals as Other to a male subject, roles that easily fit misogynist narratives of oppression'. Under the sexism/speciesism nexus, the female body becomes a locus of abuse and consumption. Masculinist discourses here materially dispossess both the earth and the natural female body through the imposition of hierarchies of female aestheticism onto women's bodies.

The sexism/speciesism nexus is interrogated in *The Hunger Games* through a sustained use of animal imagery that represents Katniss as vacillating between the animal and the human. Handed over to her stylists to be readied for the Hunger Games opening ceremony, Katniss surrenders her body to the Capitol's beauticians in order to reach a level of physicality acceptable to their aesthetic standards. The process is couched in sacrificial language, leaving Katniss feeling 'intensely vulnerable' (75):

> [The process] has included scrubbing down my body with a gritty foam that has removed not only dirt but at least three layers of skin, turning my nails into uniform shapes, and primarily, ridding my body of hair. My legs, arms, torso, underarms and parts of my eyebrows have been stripped of the stuff, leaving me like a plucked bird, ready for roasting.

Like a 'plucked bird', Katniss' female nakedness is open for voyeuristic consumption, as her male stylist 'walks around my naked body, not touching me, but taking in every centimetre of it with his eyes' (77). Whilst Cinna in fact disputes such sexual objectification by treating Katniss' vulnerability with sensitivity – averting attention away from her nakedness to thoughts of her mother – the beauticians conversely foreground Katniss' animalistic embodiment, associating her with dirt, filth and hair. When Katniss' beautification is complete, she is deemed to be 'almost' like a human being: 'now that we've got rid of all that hair and filth', they proclaim rapturously, 'you're not horrible at all!' (76). In negatively declaring Katniss to be 'not horrible' and qualifying her humanity by proclaiming that she is 'almost' like a human being, the stylists employ an ecophobic discourse constituted at the intersection between the human, the animal, and the female in which the grotesque is sexualised and the sexual made grotesque. It is a discourse specifically reserved for the lower classes whose 'humanity' is already compromised.

In scrubbing her body, removing layers of skin, ridding her of hair and stripping her naked, the stylists enact a dismantling process whereby Katniss' human self is discovered beneath her animalistic outer self. Yet, despite this stripping away of layers, Katniss interprets her beautification as a process of objectification predicated on her animal nature. Left 'like a plucked bird, ready for roasting' she expects of her stylist 'someone who viewed me as a piece of meat to be prepared for the platter' (78). This interlinking of sex and consumption, whereby Katniss becomes simply body/flesh/meat offered up for sacrifice, prefigures her entry into the arena where she is forced to wait in a room described as a cage before moving to a room nicknamed the Stockyard: '[t]he place animals go before slaughter' (175). Tellingly, however, such a cannibalistic discourse of animal sacrifice/female sexual abuse is subverted by Katniss' own appropriation of the animal as a metaphor for her oppression. When demonstrating her skills in front of the Hunger Games' judging panel, whose attention is almost entirely taken up by the arrival of a roast pig on a platter, Katniss allows her instincts to take over (124):

> Suddenly I'm furious, that with my life on the line, they don't even have the decency to pay attention to me. That I'm being upstaged by a dead pig. My heart starts to pound, I can feel my face burning. Without thinking, I pull an arrow from my quiver and send it straight at the Gamemakers' table. The arrow skewers the apple in the pig's mouth and pins it to the wall behind it. Everyone stares at me in disbelief.

Overtly linking her own plight with that of the animal about to be ingested, Katniss lets her body, rather than her head, do the 'thinking', foregrounding her embodied agency within the interlocking discourses of sacrifice and animal/woman oppression. An action that she thinks will have her arrested, but that in facts sees her receive the highest score of any of the tributes, Katniss' skewering of the apple in the pig's mouth – in a distinctly phallic gesture – deems the Gamemakers accountable for female/animal abjection.

Whilst Katniss initially undergoes a process of objectification whereby her animal body becomes alien to herself, she thus succeeds in reclaiming her animality as a subversive gesture against oppression. The interviews that take place before a live audience, however, serve to unsettle her self-identification once again by instantiating a dual act of erasure: of both her appearance and her subjectivity. In practising for the interviews she attempts a variety of personas – cocky, witty, funny, sexy, mysterious – until '[b]y the end of the session, I am no one at all' (143). This nihilistic dismantling of Katniss' personality is configured as the adoption of the various 'people' she thinks Haymitch wants her to be (147). The instantiation of a singular and autonomous selfhood here serves to resist mental dissolution even whilst Katniss' body undergoes a physical version of the same: '[t]hey erase my face with a layer of pale make-up and draw my features back out' (145). That Katniss succumbs to such aesthetic deconstruction and reconstruction suggests that the text places higher importance on the maintenance of autonomous subjectivity than on the dismantling of aesthetic categories of female embodiment.

Having rejected sexual appropriation via the image of meat on a platter, Katniss is overtly sexualised for the televised interview with Caesar. No longer a human but a 'creature' through her own focalisation: Katniss is not simply animalised but made alien, self styled as 'from another world' (145). Adopting a previously unseen girlishness ('my dress, oh, my dress'), Katniss embraces the persona of the desired female (145). In becoming an 'object of love' through Peeta's public declaration of his feelings for her, Katniss is further sculpted into an acceptably desirous subject according to the Capitol's aesthetic standards (165): 'there I am, blushing and confused, made beautiful by Cinna's hands, desirable by Peeta's confession, tragic by circumstance, and by all accounts, unforgettable' (167). In this series of makeovers in which she is 'made' beautiful, desirable and tragic by male hands at the behest of a male social system, Katniss is quite literally designated an 'object' within the sexism/speciesism nexus to be transformed, ultimately, into *'easy prey'* in the Hunger Games arena (88). In the eroticisation of Katniss' animal body, only the 'tongues of fire' embroidered into her dress signify her buried voice: that she is more than simply a consumer item in a posthuman marketplace, validated by the audience's applause (145).

The ecophobic contempt for natural human embodiment that underpins the consumer-based politics of *Feed* is unfolded via a graphic representation of *un*natural degradation. The deterioration of the body is here appropriated into the realm of female beautification through an unnatural eroticisation of the grotesque. Lesions – welts that spread across the body – have been appropriated as a fashion trend and commodified into a marketable product. When lesions become popular fashion accessories, Titus' friend Quendy appears at a party having undertaken the expensive operation to cover herself in them: 'She raised her arms. The cuts were like eyes. They got bigger and redder when she moved. "Do you like them?" she said, laughing' (191–2). The group's reaction to Quendy's appropriation of the grotesque for sexual purposes varies from disgust to approbation. Designed to increase Quendy's sex appeal, the lesions are a product of a male discourse that posits the woman as consumer and the female body as consumed, through a process of objectification that sees money literally bartered for flesh. Such a bartering is enacted under the male gaze, yet tellingly the lesions, looking 'like eyes', appear to stare back at the male voyeurs in accusation, implying that the female body offers both pliancy and resistance to masculine control.

This eroticisation of bodily disintegration echoes Efrat Tseëlon's (1995: 117) claim that artificial modification of the body is undertaken to mask a fear of natural decay and eventual death, since 'the beautification of the living…[is a] defensive strateg[y]…designed to protect the person from realisation of some lack by creating an illusion of wholeness and immortality'. Masking a collective fear of social extinction, the commoditisation of the lesions enables environmental pollution – the cause of the welts – to gain some level of social acceptance. The damaging industrial causes of such pollution, and the governmental policies that approve them, are thus quietly bypassed, as the narratological marginalisation of the following brief feed bulletin suggests (85):

"[W]e shouldn't think that there are any truth to the rumours that the lesions are the result of any activity of American industry… Okay, we need to remember that America is the nation of freedom, and that freedom, my friends, freedom does not lesions make."

Bodily disintegration is clearly accompanied by linguistic deterioration, as the American president's muddled discourse – a mishmash of biblical and popular culture references – signals discursive atrophy. Such deceptive rhetoric works alongside consumer branding to mask the plausible cause of the lesions and their medical implications, and underpins the consumerist push to turn civil unrest into a fashion trend. The commoditisation of the degraded (female) body averts attention from any political implications such degradation might have and the mental conditioning such bodily disintegration clearly signals.

Violet's disability – as her malfunctioning feed gradually worsens – marks her body as un-commercial and thus socially useless: a disposable waste product of consumerism. The explicit link between nature-as-product and woman-as-product is voiced by Violet's father when he berates Titus for his apathy towards the consumer culture that justifies the existence of the feed: '"We Americans," he said, "are interested only in the *consumption* of our products. We have no interest in how they were produced, or what happens to them" – he pointed at his daughter – "what happens to them once we discard them, once we throw them away"' (290). The instantiation of consumerism as a form of female cannibalism ironically echoes the plotline of a soap opera fed into Titus' brain earlier on in the novel in which a clone struggles to save her liver from her original who attempts to farm her organs, voicing the anguished cry: *'I'm not a product, but a person!'* (26). The irony, here, comes in the readers' acknowledgement that it is neither the female clone who fights so hard for her autonomy or Violet who resists the streamlining of her corporate consumer profile in order to retain her individuality who are 'products' rather than 'people', but that Titus and his friends are the real products of global corporate practices they neither wish nor know how to challenge. The feed thus becomes a metaphor for a posthuman society literally consuming itself, a social dynamic that can only end in the extinction of both the human race and the planet itself, via the degradation of the female body; in the words of Violet: '*"You don't have the feed! You are feed!"*' (202). No longer a human being but a 'monster' and a 'creature', the abject posthuman of Anderson's dystopic fantasy is animalistic in her lack of humanity (202).

Regimes of difference: discourses of female animalisation

As has been well-documented, human and animal bodies are not simply embedded in biological systems but also in complex social processes. Following the work of the early ecofeminist theologian Rosemary Radford Ruether, Twine (2001: 38) contends that bodily 'markings' are implicated in the production of gender difference:

> [A] wide set of discursive markings...have accentuated the embodiment of others, while leaving the centralised master-identity in certain ways 'unmarked'. This has projected a sense of uncontrolled flesh and desire out from the master-identity and onto marked others whose essence or identity is regarded primarily as being "bodily" rather than rational.

Identified with the nonhuman, these 'bodily' humans are expelled from the hegemonic identity in 'a process of agency-stripping which is comparative with that experienced by nonhuman animals'; with the 'human/animal boundary...conveniently shifted', these 'animalised *humans*' are rendered abject (Twine 2001: 38). With uncontrolled flesh and desire and irrational behaviour, these animalised humans are also, clearly, feminised so that this process of expulsion inheres in ideological productions of gender difference. In the novels here discussed, animalised portrayals of the female protagonists serve to link the treatment of women with the treatment of nonhuman animals, denoting the female body a contested site subject to discourses of animal consumption.

As delineated in the previous section, *The Hunger Games* explores representations of female animalisation through the purposeful eroticisation of Katniss' animal body. It also, however, invokes the dehumanised female body as a discursive site of political dissent and subsequent material punishment. The Avox who waits upon Katniss in the Capitol is a traitor whose crime against the government has resulted in her literal silencing: the removal of her tongue. Animalised through her inability to communicate her oppression, the girl is neither named nor voiced, giving her the ontological status of the 'bodily' human noted by Twine. Her maimed body, like those of the nonhuman animals contemporary western society neatly removes from our daily lives, provokes in Katniss feelings of anxiety and guilt. In subsequently narrating the girl's story to Peeta – since the Avox can no longer do so herself – Katniss describes the girl and the boy who fled with her through the woods outside District 12 as 'animals...at bay' (100). Hunted, abused, silenced: the Avox with her tattered clothes and dark circles under her eyes discloses the dangers of political dissent against an intolerant totalitarian system by becoming a symbol both of resistance and the *failure* to resist. It is in fact the 'idea of the girl with her maimed tongue' rather than the girl herself that frightens Katniss since the sight of her reminds her of her role in the games: to die a bloody death in front of the crowds (97). A locus of Capitol control, the girl's animalised body prefigures those of the tributes in the Hunger Games arena who are similarly animalised and objectified under Capitol rule.

In the sporting event that sees child tributes forced to hunt each other to the death, the dynamics of the animal food chain are unnaturally imposed onto the network of human relationships with the stronger, better trained 'careers' of District 1 occupying a higher level in the food-chain than the starved and weakened tributes of District 12. In her enforced vacillation between hunter and prey, and her attempts to work her way up the food chain, Katniss struggles to adapt to her changed ethical context. Whilst Peeta is wounded in the Games, with his weak and passive body becoming a similar locus of Capitol manipulation, his ostensibly unwavering love for Katniss (gleaned through Katniss' naïve focalisation) and his courageous desire to not let the Capitol turn him 'into some kind of monster', resists the dehumanisation accorded to Katniss (171). Katniss – a hunter by nature, whose arrows have ended the lives of countless animals – is however forced to discover upon killing a boy from District 1 that the hunting of humans is surprisingly similar 'in the execution' but devastatingly different 'in the aftermath' (294). It is only in picturing the body of the girl whose death this boy caused – a body that in death reminds Katniss of a baby animal curled in a nest – that Katniss can force herself to address the question pertaining to hunting animals and hunting humans: 'How different can it be, really?' (285). Plumwood's (2000: 286) objection to 'scientific and hunting ethics' is, in this scenario, worryingly apt:

> [S]cientific and hunting ethics…treat animals (but not, or not yet, humans) in abstract, mass general terms as replaceable members of species and populations, to ignore, discount, or oppose individual life and justice perspectives for nonhumans, and to identify humanity closely with a glorified predatory ecological role which is only too readily given the lineaments of mastery and managerialism.

In a society that has crossed the threshold from the hunting of animals to the hunting of humans, the lineaments of such mastery and managerialism are written onto the children's bodies. In banishing the boy she has killed from her mind, Katniss banishes the implications of such human-animal defamiliarisation from emotional appraisal.

In its instantiation of human-animal isomorphism whereby both categories are mapped onto the same referent, *The Hunger Games* critiques anthropocentric attitudes towards nonhuman others, particularly as objects of consumption. The accusing gaze of the Avox is metonymic of the guilt that underpins a failure to undertake a converse *humanisation* of the animal that would bind the animal to the human through fellow feeling. That the animalised Avox provokes hate in Katniss for her 'reproachful eyes' suggests a failure of empathy towards the nonhuman other, precluded by a deep-seated cultural anxiety that desires to maintain the alienation underpinning animal objectification (144). Carol Adams (2010: 304) argues that:

> [A] process of objectification, fragmentation, and consumption enables the oppression of animals so that animals are rendered

being-less through technology, language, and cultural representation. Objectification permits an oppressor to view another being as an object. Once objectified, a being can be fragmented. Fragmentation is the hidden aspect in the production of meat – that about which we are not to speak. Through fragmentation the object is severed not only from its body but its ontological meaning.

Both the Avox's and Katniss' identities undergo such fragmentation, with their bodies rendered 'being-less' to ready them for consumption by the Capitol regime, the hunter tributes and the viewing public. In simultaneously hating the mute Avox and wanting her protection, Katniss desires a communal strength in marginalisation – the hunted against the hunters – and a denial of her cowardice, even whilst acknowledging that she 'was wrong' (144). In imagining that her own death will make up for the death of the Avox's loved one, Katniss misunderstands the justice system under which she must perform as an animalised female and thereby underestimates the Capitol's success at 'divid[ing] [us] among ourselves' in order to delimit social retaliation (16). On Katniss' animalised body is written both the abjection of the hunted and the guilt of the hunter making Katniss' female body a particularly subversive locus of critique.

Robson's *Savannah 2116 AD* institutes a woman–animal connection not to interrogate the (sexually) abusive sexism/speciesism nexus but in a similar bid to dehumanise (make animal) the resistant female subject. In the South Africa of 2116, an inverted human–animal dualism sees the lives of wild animals valued above those of the lowest class of Africa's human inhabitants who are known derogatorily as Homosaps. Not only have the Homosaps been corralled into small reserves on the outskirts of wide open spaces of Wilderness where elephants, lions, giraffes, kudu and other mammals roam free, but they have also been organised into a hierarchical class system through which the elite few – the Cons – live in luxury in safari ranches in the Wilderness whilst the lower orders are kept under strict guard behind electrified fences along its margins. Environmental disaster has segregated wilderness and urbanity under a racialised ethic of human subordination that offers up 'humanity' as a sacrifice on the 'Altar of Green' (26). Since the novel is focalised by the teenage Homosap, Savannah, the animalised female body is reconfigured as a discursive site of resistance to patriarchal oppression.

Oppression centring on race, class and species is enabled, in this novel, by linguistic defamiliarisation. In her analysis of Robson's novel, Elsie Cloete (2009: 52) suggests that '[t]he act of corralling all other non-human sentient beings into the single concept, animal, leads rapidly to the metaphoric representation of the human other or alien in terms of animality'. The consistent derogatory labelling of the female orphans by the guards as smelly and mindless – living in their own 'filth and stink' – is a manifestation of the successful linguistic defamiliarisation and hyperseparation of the animalised other from the human self (31). The animality assigned to these lower class girls is linguistically instigated and occurs in what Groves (2009: 37) labels 'those semantically unstable spaces where adjacent but radically distinct meanings of a word meet, oppose, and often change positions with one another'. Linguistic substitution aids the Cons in their attempts to naturalise the Homosaps' oppression; orphan children have 'keepers' and subordinate humans are 'zooed' (imprisoned) and 'put down' (executed) as punishment for dissent whilst animals are raised to a position of 'majesty' (26).

If Melody Dora Halifax, the keeper of the girls' orphanage, lives in 'constant danger of epidemics' from the female Homosaps, the contamination she more overtly fears is that of the pure and pristine wilderness by the animalised Homosaps and the overthrow of class hierarchy such an epidemic would entail (31). Melody Dora Halifax's comment is racially-inflected; in a society in which the girls are named after natural phenomena – Rose, Savannah, Dune, River, Breeze, Valley, Everest – or else given traditionally Afrikaans names – Naledi, Blommetjie – the distinctly English name of the girls' keeper exhibits what Alaimo (1998: 124) terms a 'displacement' of 'corporeal connections' from the white woman to the black woman: 'even though "the body" has been persistently coded as female in Western culture, white women have fled from corporeal connections with a debased nature by displacing that nature onto the bodies of African Americans and others'. We might infer that Melody Dora Halifax's fear of epidemics masks a darker fear of the ostensibly 'black African' disease of HIV/Aids.

Semantic ambiguities over the meaning of humanity arise through a new world order underpinned by the dictum: '*On the Altar of Green we will lay / The sacrifice of our humanity*' (26). As Cloete notes (2009: 56), 'humanity' refers either to the qualities inherent in human beings that render them honourable, just and altruistic and therefore *willing* to sacrifice their freedom, comfort and pleasure for the good of the Earth, or suggests more cynically that honour, justice and altruism are the very qualities of the human that will be sacrificed – a necessary price to pay for a greener earth. Here, the meanings assigned to humanity and animality are destabilised and collapsed in a purposeful bid to produce a radically ruptured society without the core ethical framework necessary for social welfare. Popular dissatisfaction with the circumscribed lifestyles available to the human population on account of ecological asymmetries manifests itself in the orphan Dune's preference for 'people stories' rather than animal ones: 'interesting stuff' compared with 'stupid animals' (28). Here, the desire for a narrative teleology with emotional resonance situates the circumscribed lives of lower class girls within the limited epistemic framework accorded animals.

In response to the radical destabilisation of meaning that redistributes the boundary-line of the human and the animal, the female Savannah with her rural upbringing and the male Ged (Genetically Engineered Donor) D-nineteen attempt to define and separate the two opposing categories in a prolonged debate over the intrinsic values and inherent properties of the human and the animal (58; 59; 70–1):

'You can explain things to humans; they have minds you can reason with. But not animals. All they have is instinct – dumb, blind instinct';
'It is only human eyes that can see the beauty';
'[A]nimals don't kill their own kind. They only kill for food, not out of hatred';
'There's no such thing as courage in your animal world. Only human beings understand courage';
'[A]nimals don't turn the earth ugly';
'[Animals] can't imagine a world any different from the one they are born into. It's only humans who won't accept things as they are, who strive to change what they don't like'

D-nineteen's hatred of animals manifests itself in what he terms 'doing the animals' with the young P-six, an activity that sees the two boys stab, slash and rip a canvas painting of animals with knives (51). In the discursive formulation of the animalised female, such an attack is metonymic of the rhetorical abuse directed towards the female body. Such semantic linking of the female and the animal manifests itself in the Geds' nonchalant channel hopping between a pornographic movie of women undressing to an action movie with '[p]lenty of blood and gore and dismemberment' (47). Such sexualisation of the animal and animalisation of the feminine adheres to what Adams (2010: 304) identifies as 'an overlap of cultural images of sexual violence against women and fragmentation and dismemberment of nature and the body in Western culture'. The debate that sees Savannah defend animals against D-nineteen's contempt – reflective of their differing levels of embodiment – is metonymic of Savannah's larger struggle against female animalisation and her re-appropriation of her own body as a site of feminist resistance.

The objectification of the Geds' male bodies takes animalising discourse one step further. Forced to undergo a 'brain-death' in the 'harvest ward' presided over by Dr Retta, the Geds are bred to be killed at the age of eighteen so that their auto-immune organs can be transplanted into the bodies of endangered animal species (130; 129). These posthuman Geds undergo selective breeding, farmed – like animals – until ready for xenotransplantation; their numbered labellings (D-nineteen, C-two, P-six and so on) constitute 'a countdown to death' that renders the operating theatre a slaughterhouse (141). A hierarchy of animal worth sees the gorilla for which D-Nineteen's heart is intended – named Anastasia Tricia-Leigh – raised to the status of an 'ancient wise woman' who reminds Dr Retta of his grandmother whilst the human Geds are conversely dehumanised – labelled Genetically Engineered Donors – and yoked to the animal bodies of meat production which are similarly farmed for consumer supply and demand (100). That the Geds' organs are in fact being harvested to supply old Cons – monied high class citizens – with new lungs and kidneys instead of the animals for which they were intended configures the objectification undergone by the Geds' animal bodies a racially-inflected manifestation of radically unequal power and privilege. The 'dumping' of the boys' bodies in the Wilderness once harvested – 'an unexpected feast for hyenas and vultures' – interrogates the consumer-politics that sanction over-production within the economic free market and that imbricate natural worth and commodity use-value (130).

In the discursive materialisation of the Geds' bodies, the Cons figure as absent referents – a standardised, white, male, upper class collective – benefitting from the labour, pain, abuse and sacrifice of those who are marginalised under systems nominally enabling development and progress. The Geds' young bodies – 'straight and healthy and whole… [and] perfect' – are circumscribed within discourses of ownership and propriety that naturalise the old Cons' desire to 'live on and on' (130; 129). Dr Retta's perverse voyeurism as he 'gaze[s] down the rows of naked young Geds', stroking their arms and legs and whispering 'my boys' over and over, eroticises the boys' naked bodies in a formulation that could signal either paternalistic ownership or homoerotic desire and plays into the racial stereotype of the virile black male (130). Under an abusive ethical framework that reduces the boys to body parts, this discursive eroticisation functions within the 'sexism/speciesism nexus' noted by Gaard to situate the boys' bodies within the interlocking discourses of sex, consumption and abuse normally reserved for females. Dr Retta's sense of power in the operating theatre as he assumes the position of 'ultimate master', reveal the Geds' further function as stimulus for massaging the ego of the lame surgeon; the Geds' sacrifice acts as confirmation of his virile masculinity within the 'sterile readiness' of the operating theatre (126). Having failed to save C-two's 'unblemished' body from slaughter through disinclination to 'buck…the system and interfere…with routine', Dr Retta enacts the routine abuse of the eroti-cised and animalised subject in a discursive instantiation of masculinist oppression.

The female body: an unreliable economic investment

The marginalised positioning of the female subject – through whom discourses of biological essentialism naturalise 'feminine' traits such as sexuality and animality – serves to foreground biological as well as discursive productions of gender difference in socio-political systems. In advocating an 'embodied materialism', Ariel Salleh (2005: 10) contends that '[o]ur bodily energies are artificially configured and constrained by gender, and those dissociations, in turn, deform economic practices, social institutions, and cultural beliefs'. In the novels, female protago-nists experience alienation from their own selves through a process of inscription predicated on a masculinist ethos of capital accumulation through which female bodies are accorded monetary value. According to Susan M. Roberts (2004: 135), such a formulation works to further the neoliberal mentality that posits women as 'units of human capital' that 'can be developed (through education, training, health care, and so on) so that they may more productively participate in (formal) labour markets'. The link between capitalism, women and the body in service of western economics manifests itself in these novels in representations of the female body as a marketable resource and economic investment. In its discursive formulation, the female body acts as currency, subject to, and a product of, the interlocking monetary discourses of a glo-balised consumer culture.

In *Zenith*, in which Mara leads the struggling refugees on a long and dangerous sea voyage to the shores of Greenland where they attempt to make a home, Mara is dehumanised in service of an economic superstructure that deems her a capitalist resource rather than a human actant. In a racially-inflected allusion to colonial slave trading, Mara is surveyed by prospective buyers at the marketplace who designate her a commercial resource by literally branding her skin with the dollar sign (138):

> She can't believe what is happening. They are being branded like cattle. ...
> Mara feels unreal, as if she's been shocked out of her own self. '*Mara.*' She murmurs her own name because for a petrifying moment she can't remember who she is. She has lost herself in the herd. '*Mara*', she repeats, and concentrates on the pain of her arm. The pain is the only thing that feels real. Mara eases the clothes from her shoulder to let the icy air cool her burned skin, and sees the symbol that's been branded on her arm.
> A snake coiled on a stick.

Unable to name the instrument of her oppression and thus unaware of the larger symbolism of the 'snake coiled on a stick', Mara nevertheless becomes defined and delimited by the monetary economy, with her marketability literally carved onto her skin. Animal imagery ('branded like cattle', 'lost...in the herd') compounds Mara's ontological status as an economic resource, to be bartered or traded under the American emblem of phallocentric supremacy. That she becomes 'shocked out of her own self' through such branding signals the dehumanising effects of a consumerist hegemony which alienates the subject from her own sense of self in a denial of female agency and a corresponding erasure of subjectivity. Mara's naïve description of the dollar sign accords dual significance to this symbol of monetary power; it both reflects the seductive materiality of consumer culture – a seduction akin to that of Eve by the tempting serpent – and also the natural (nonhuman) victims of consumerist expansionism who (like the snake trussed up on a phallic 'stick') are similarly subject to discourses of economic instrumentalism.

Mara's economic commodification is metonymic of the wider commodification of the earth itself; her branded body is in fact discursively associated with the degraded earth since both are labelled currency in the power-plays of a globalised economy. A wall painting in the cave in which the escaped refugees shelter to survive the Arctic winter renders this connection vivid (210):

> The carving shows a vision of the sun beating down on what must have been a great city. ... The city seems unaware of what is rolling

towards it – a wave, seething with people and animals and the debris of a destroyed city. Mara peers into the wave. Carved into the great swirl of water are what look like bits of paper, each one marked with (Mara peers even closer to be sure) the very same sign that is branded on her arm.

The snake on a stick.

In pictorial rendition of environmental apocalypse, the cave painting clearly posits the monetary economy, and particularly the American dollar, as the cause of the world's drowning. Forever marked by their economic commodification, Mara and the earth nevertheless survive the economic meltdown that has seen the old world global networks fail. Mara's reclamation of her branded body, not as a product of the oppressive conceptual frameworks of a dying consumer culture but as a newly embodied locus of material resistance, sees her identify herself with the earth in service of an alternative ecofeminist ethic predicated on a non-exploitative and non-monetary interrelationship between humans and the planet.

In *Feed*, the 'Global Alliance' – an oppositional political organisation – advocates environmental justice for the voiceless peoples whose political and geographical marginalisation sees them bear the brunt of industrial disaster, placing blame on American corporations for environmental pollution. As Violet tells Titus (241; 242–3):

> *Have you heard about this Central American stuff? Two villages on the Gulf of Mexico, fifteen hundred people – they've just been found dead, covered in this black stuff... The Global Alliance is blaming the U.S...*[:] *"the physical and biological integrity of the earth relies at this point upon the dismantling of American-based corporate entities, whatever the cost."*

In the drive to extend its capitalist stranglehold, America is portrayed as having commodified the natural world, including those people with more 'natural' lifestyles, to the point at which the earth and marginalised peoples have been similarly erased ('covered in this black stuff'). '[W]hatever the cost' is a poignant reminder of the imbrication of economic factors in environmental crisis, calling attention to the ways in which uneven distributions of wealth often mean that environmental damage is disproportionally borne by marginalised peoples (Mies and Shiva 1993). The 'industrial disaster' that kills fifteen hundred people is one that the sheltered American citizens of the novel (cocooned not only within their artificial ecosystems but also within their limited epistemological frameworks), may or may not have 'heard about'.

In a society in which 'everyone is like, *da da da, evil corporations, oh they're so bad*', the general response to the total interpellation of human identities by the feed is 'it's no good getting pissy about it' (48). Only Violet makes the explicit connection between the feed and the homogenising effects of mass marketing, through the attempts of conglomerates to make the market conform to simpler and less varied consumer types for easier marketing. In this process of simplification, humans *en masse* are the target market; personal preference is subsumed and appropriated so that individual desire in fact replicates that of the population as a whole. A process of defamiliarisation of oneself *from* oneself – like that experienced by Mara – sees the feed's streamlining enacted metonymically on Violet's posthuman body after her feed is hacked by a protester on the moon. A locus of resistance, struggling against consumer profiling, Violet's body ultimately fails to 'resist the feed' and becomes instead a consumer waste product and an abject site of failed resistance (298).

Prior to the corporate erasure of her body as a marketable product, Violet herself tellingly undertakes a process of self-erasure, attempting to create a consumer profile 'that's so screwed, no one can market to it' (98). In making herself 'invisible', Violet refutes the master model of economic control upon which the capitalist system relies and effectively declares herself uneconomic (98). Subject to masculine discourses of control revolving around the three male figures who have shaped her identity – her father, her boyfriend and the hacker who triggers her feed's malfunctioning, all three working within, or against, an overarchingly masculine system – Violet attempts to resist interpellation even whilst such discourses preclude effective resistance. In a class-conscious allusion to systems of privilege in light of Violet's malfunctioning feed, her father admits that he '"skimped"' when buying the feed (289). Told that if he had bought a better feed model, Violet's feed might have been more adaptable, he defines his daughter's condition in monetary terms, underpinned by the guilt of capitalist accumulation (289). In this process of erasure whereby Violet is alienated from her own agency and subjectivity and from her ontological status as currency, she is made the subject of male discourse, to be used and defined by men.

Titus' reaction to Violet's bodily deterioration in fact compounds Violet's own attempts to make herself invisible, declaring that the feed 'was making her not herself' and wondering how close she was to the girl who had previously alienated his friends (211). Standing beside her bedside when her feed function is nearly down to zero, Titus finds that '[i]t didn't feel like you were in the room with anyone. You could stand there and you would feel completely alone, like you were just in a room with a prop' (286). Dehumanised to the point of becoming a wooden prop against which Titus' weighs up his previous fantasies of wanting 'to kiss it and feel it up', here Violet's female body is de-gendered (made an 'it') and her subjectivity erased (286). Violet's father defines such a dehumanised condition as a form of embodied imprisonment: 'in a statue like the Sphinx' (287). A merciless female figure in Greek mythology, the mute Sphinx functions as an ambiguous referent for Violet, whose rebellious nature is rendered traitorous. Entrapped, bewildered: Violet is an abject figure imprisoned within a larger cultural metanarrative of patriarchal progress through capitalist consumption.

It is ironic in light of such a masculine hegemony that the mouthpiece of the conglomerate culture which shapes her – *'Nina, you're FeedTech customer assistance representative'* – is in fact a woman; in turning down Violet's request for assistance, the corporate entities force a female voice upon masculinist oppression (246). Designated an unreliable investment, Violet lacks the consumer profile necessary to engender corporate interest. Violet's body becomes the site on which her punishment is enacted, with her limbs and vital organs gradually shutting down. Yet, in spite of her graphic bodily disintegration, Violet fails to segregate herself entirely from the consumer market having been 'sketched demographically' according to her taste in requiem masses (262). In 'trying to resist' yet ultimately caving in, Violet demonstrates that the corporations and data servers, far from being 'really close to winning', had in fact already won from the moment the feed became an integral component of the human body (262). In a tragic inversion of the more common schema in young adult fiction for the hopeful confirmation of agency in response to crisis, the active resistance whereby Violet designates her female body uneconomic within a prevailing capitalist economy is shown to have only ever been futile.

The post-apocalyptic condition: bodily erosion

In the emerging discourse of posthumanism in young adult fiction, the discursive materialisation of the body primarily takes the form of a melding of 'natural' bodily systems with nonhuman or artificial technologies; as Hayles (1999: 35) suggests:

> The posthuman implies not only a coupling with intelligent machines but a coupling so intense and multifaceted that it is no longer

possible to distinguish meaningfully between the biological organism and the informational circuits in which the organism is enmeshed.

The posthuman condition as technological coevolution suggests a decisive break from the 'natural' human condition, with the result that '"[p]ost," with its dual connotation of superseding the human and coming after it, hints that the days of "the human" may be numbered' (Hayles 1999: 283). To allay the sense of the human as a finite entity, the posthuman is often alternatively envisaged not as a definitive break from a previous incarnation of the human but as a continuously evolving human-machine or human-nonhuman hybrid. In the various instantiations of post-apocalyptic hybridity explored in these novels, the smoothly contoured human body is often subject to an interplay of hegemonic forces and left broken, open-ended and grotesque in its lack of proper containment. Such bodies adhere to the premise that 'the categories of nature and culture, the natural and the cultural continue to constitute each other not so much by their apparent stability but by their flexibility, their erosion and redifferentiation' (Castree and Nash 2006: 501). Key to an ecofeminist reading of contemporary young adult fiction is an interpretation of this 'erosion' as a gesture towards the anthropogenic redistribution of borderlines - where the categories 'continue to constitute each other'. Like the melding of rural, urban and suburban in post-natural landscapes, this erosion is less a dismantling of dualisms and more a syncretic evolution 'in which the "after" surpasses in the same breath whatever went "before"' (Whatmore 2004: 1360).

Several generations prior to the start of Carrie Ryan's *The Forest of Hands & Teeth* [2009], set in what we imagine to be a future United States in which only one known village remains hidden deep within the Forest, 'the Return' has seen human biology irrevocably mutate and produce the first living dead. These zombie figures – human beings who have died and risen again – are naturalised as non-sentient and ontologically inhuman. Discursively formulated as closer to the natural than the human, these Forest-dwelling creatures are predicated on an ecophobic rendering of a debased and degraded natural world. Life in the village, perpetually surrounded by the Unconsecrated and their threat of infection, has given rise to the protagonist Mary's failure to securely negotiate the parameters of her body. Experiencing moments of felt erosion, Mary's uneasy preoccupation with the ends and limits of her own embodiment leaves her – at moments of tension – 'feeling as if everything that I ever was is draining out of my body and leaving me' (24). Overpowered by her emotions, Mary desires 'to curl in on myself' and hide from engagement with the world (302). Experiencing a split between 'I' and 'me' – a disjunction between subject and object, signifier and signified – Mary performs, or enacts, her own erosion. With the body understood as a receptacle for the self rather than an integral part *of* that self, bodily dissolution equates to a loss of the secure parameters of Mary's selfhood. This loss parallels that of the Unconsecrated in the Forest whose hollow skin and gaping wounds are a constant reminder of the proximity of death and the ease with which a body can be divested of its 'human' component and transformed into a grotesque and inhuman remnant of itself. Here, erosion does not signal an intersubjective melding of self and other, but a disempowering lack of control over the boundaries of one's body and an inability to negotiate one's subjectivity, leading to a complete loss of identity in response to trauma.

If Mary's erosion of bodily boundaries is psychological rather than actual, her mother undergoes an overt and grotesque bodily trans-formation after being infected by the Unconsecrated. Such infection is graphically inscribed as a punishment on the female form, and denoted a sickness that renders its owner nonsensical; Mary narrates: 'I sit nearby, listening to her pop her jaw and clack her teeth like a cat lusting after a bird as the infection roars through her body. She is too sick to talk now, too ravaged to even understand' (11). Female decay enacts a grotesque exaggeration of the cultural norms of femininity through the association of Mary's mother with the animal ('like a cat'), the sensual ('lusting after'), the voiceless ('too sick to talk'), the grotesque ('ravaged') and the uncerebral ('too ravaged to even under-stand'). Penned inside a cage that separates her from the villagers, able only to crawl on hands and knees, Mary's mother is portrayed as an animalistic and supplicate figure trapped within a system that must banish her beyond the boundaries of hegemonic control to prevent her from infecting the village, both physically and ideologically. In this formulation, women are associated with the natural, the irrational and the counter-hegemonic, yet are powerless to challenge a matriarchal system that strictly enforces boundary markers. Whilst Mary herself manages to escape the confines of the village, her mother is dismissed as irreparably marked by bodily perversion and forever expelled from the public sphere.

The blonde, green-eyed tribute from District 1 in *The Hunger Games* who dazzles the audience in the public interviews with 'her body tall and lush' undergoes a similarly grotesque bodily transformation under the masculinist gaze of the viewing public (151). With her 'sexy' femininity overtly linked to her investment potential, Glimmer is subject to violent discourses of sexual appropriation; the more convincingly she performs her feminine sexuality in the arena, the more likely she is to remain alive (151). Glimmer's death, when stung repeatedly by a swarm of genetically modified 'tracker-jackers', is one that enacts a debased and accelerated form of feminine erosion: her beautiful body bloats, oozes and disintegrates, '[h]er features eradicated' (233). The eradication of cultural markers of acceptable femininity here renders Glimmer not simply inhuman but radically a-feminine. The smoothly defined contours of her erstwhile body, veiled tantalisingly in her see-through dress, are ruptured such that her fleshy nakedness becomes a debased inversion of her earlier sexual mystique. The erosion of bodily boundaries here equates to the Capitol's success at quashing autonomous displays of selfhood or agency by the district inhabitants in service of retaining a population of quasi-automated citizens whose broken spirits render resistance futile.

The transformation of Glimmer's body from contained to ruptured is accorded further significance in its converse re-containment as a genetic 'muttation' towards the end of the games. These 'muttations' – half-wolf and half-human creatures made from the genetically engineered and re-animated bodies of the human tributes who have died earlier in the Games – are grotesque instantiations of human-nonhuman coevolution. The Glimmer-mutt with 'silky waves of blond fur' and 'unmistakably human' eyes is abject in its sexualised animality (404; 405). A weapon designed by the Capitol to ensure the deaths of Katniss and Peeta, Glimmer is reconstituted in a new posthuman form in whose smooth and enclosed surfaces can be read the violent mechanisms of Capitol control. Contained, ruptured, and contained once more, Glimmer's body becomes a graphic manifestation of the interplay of competing feminine discourses. The grotesque melding of human and nonhuman – prefigured by the animalism attributed to Katniss in her stylistic overhaul – is in this dystopian world 'the final word in entertainment' occasioned by a radical loss of subjective agency and a renewed insistence on the post-natural body as an ecophobic construct (412).

Conclusion: the resistant female body

In these novels, female bodies are puzzled over, dismantled, made animal or alien, made-up and made-over, and reconstituted by those in authority. Katniss in *The Hunger Games* is metonymic of this discursive bodily materialisation. Forced to hunt for her survival – both prior to, and during, the Games – Katniss puts herself in physical danger, labouring to feed her family and raise her young sister, in a stratified social hierarchy in which such unpaid female labour goes uncelebrated. Upon entry into the Games, Katniss becomes a marketable product, a commercial investment whose odds of winning (or investment potential) are hotly debated by the faceless sponsors. Playing up her female wit, charm and skills in front of an invisible audience to engender economic support, Katniss is forced to balance her actions against her economic value. Eroticised and animalised by her stylists with a view to the buyers' market, Katniss' body is a product of interlocking discourses of female aestheticism instigated by a voyeuristic male culture; as her mentor, Haymitch, wryly comments: '"[o]h, oh, oh, how the boys back home fall longingly at your feet. Which do you think will get you more sponsors?"' (164). Starved and maimed within the arena itself, Katniss' body is further marked out as abject by the ruling patriarchy whose control remains physically scarred onto her skin (until tellingly erased by the Capitol beauticians once the Games are over). Fetishised throughout the Games, her body finally becomes a locus of resistance against the Capitol's hegemony and, in the two following novels of the trilogy, inspires the social revolution that sees the Capitol falter and finally fall.

In these variously imposed unnatural subject positions – Katniss is simultaneously desired and made abject, empowered and disempowered – Katniss is dislocated both from her sense of self and from her natural embodiment. In each of these novels the (female) body – resistant, discursive, transformative – is correlative with the blind space of the earth, subject to interlocking discourses of capitalism and consumerism: a potentially radical site of challenge to the ruling hegemony and a space in which to renegotiate a more caring relationship between humans and the natural world. The posthuman body is a similarly contentious site of symbolisation: a blind space subject to humanist fears over man's slippage from his ontological supremacy. In each of these human and posthuman incarnations, the human–earth connection is lost, reformulated and subsequently re-invoked in the new, alternative human-nonhuman relationships arisen through apocalypse. Mary Mellor (2000: 120–1) contends that a '[f]ailure to comprehend the materiality and material consequences of the human condition occurs where dominant social groups use the labour and resources of others (human and nonhuman) to mediate between themselves and their biological/ecological conditions'. With their bodies functioning as mediatory spaces, the female protagonists of these novels are valued for their materiality even whilst such material labour is institutionally denied. Like Violet in *Feed*, Katniss becomes essentially invisible with pervasive male discourses written onto her skin. Yet if Violet fails to survive her erasure, the success of Katniss in retaining her embattled agency despite her interpellation by male discourses posits the female body as a locus of political resistance potentially capable of subverting neoliberal control.

Donna Haraway's seminal 'cyborg' figure, or cybernetic organism – an organic-technical hybrid – has the potential to reconfigure the human subject through a contestation of bodily boundaries. Haraway's (1991: 152) cyborg appears 'precisely where the boundary between human and animal is transgressed', in the space 'between animal-human (organism) and machine' and in 'the boundary between physical and non-physical' (153). The cyborg thus functions as a symbol of liminality and subversion, interrogating humanist narratives of bodily autonomy. It is an embodied entity yet embodied *differently*, since such embodiment transgresses normative categories of stable selfhood. Represented by Haraway as capable of dismantling dualisms, the cyborg is a useful figure for ecofeminist appraisal since it moves analysis of human–earth interaction into the sphere of the mechanical, the technical and the cybernetic, and directs attention to the differing notions of human embodiment that such transference must necessarily entail. As Chris Cuomo (2002: 3) puts it, cyborgs 'can help us understand the dynamics of interimbrication, and the relationships between conflicting discourses and complex identities' and thus are useful 'precisely because they are so open to interpretation'. Resembling the post-natural landscape in its imbrication of human and nonhuman, the cyborg is a resistant figure with similarly counter-hegemonic potential.

The post-natural hybrid is evoked, in these novels, to unsettle normative dualisms in a way that furthers an ecofeminist call for environmental and social re-appraisal. However, the posthuman and post-natural figures as discussed fail to live up to this call for boundary dissolution; posthumanism here appears to result in a heightened anthropocentric sense of suspicion or paranoia towards the nonhuman world and a defensive lashing out at those whose 'unnatural' bodies threaten the stability and autonomy of the human actant. Unable to offer more than implicit resistance to hegemonic social structures, these posthuman figures are envisaged as a means to perpetuate a sexist model of female commodification, disembodiment and dislocation from nature. 'So long as cyborgs are imagined as...*male* technological society's *man*-made technological saints', contends Dinerstein (2006: 589) with emphatic italicising, 'then the posthuman dream of evolving into cyborgs both perpetuates the mythic triumphalism of progress and constitutes a refusal to acknowledge the limits of an individual human body and an individual life'. The novels' purposeful refusal to engender such mythic triumphalism – Anderson's *Feed*, for instance, is overt in its lack of resolution – intimates that utopian endings in futuristic fiction often lack political feasibility. If posthumanism is associated with female perversion and embodiment with the grotesque, the gendered systems of power that laud progress as the desired endpoint of societal engagement will need to be countered by what Twine (2001: 50) terms 'an alternative construction of embodiment which is less easy to exploit as a means to negative symbolic marking'. In order words, if an embodied relationship with the earth will require a mode of being that Patricia Gunn Allen (1990: 52) lyrically calls 'staying in your body, accepting its discomforts, decayings, witherings and blossomings and respecting them', a discourse not of transcendence but of immanence will need to define an embodied ecofeminist ethic.

3
Regimes of Gender Difference: An Ecofeminist Ethic of Care

In analysing the commonly-used slogan 'saving the world', Andrew Bowman (2010: 189) pauses to ask the pertinent question: 'what kind of world is being saved? Whose world?'. Bowman's intimations of ownership in his questioning of whose world we might preserve, underpin the ecofeminist premise that current political and social systems are predicated on a metanarrative of propriety and oppression over peoples, groups and spatialities deemed to embody the qualities of the 'feminine', including some men, many women, and the earth itself. Ecofeminists advocate a reconceptualisation of the epistemological and ontological frameworks underpinning ethical enquiry by attempting to re-signify traditionally feminine values as conduits for empowerment and care, and to re-appropriate such values into a largely masculinist history of philosophical thought. If a feminist ethic is to re-envisage environmental thinking – most ecofeminists argue – it must do so by establishing conceptual frameworks that are non-oppressive and non-subordinating and effectively freed from oppositional thinking. Such an ethical re-visioning must confront the cultural normativity of a masculinised public sphere and a feminised private sphere, and interrogate the political context and conditions of knowledge production. Analyses of systemic imbalances of power and privilege at the macrolevel delimit the potential for acknowledgement of gendered power-plays at a smaller scale – within the family, household and the body – and the crucial ways in which such microlevel systems of gender difference impact the formal sphere.

The language of neoliberalism that actively rewards individualism and self-advancement, as denoted in my previous chapter, places little value on opposing notions of self-sacrifice, dependence or caring for others. Such notions have traditionally been coded as feminine and relegated to the informal sphere of 'women's work'. Caring for others is an often unvalued and unwaged activity occurring within the home and operating counter to the neoliberal principles of market efficiency, competition between individuals and personal responsibility. An ethic of care, as promoted by contemporary feminism, argues for the centrality of care activities to the formal sphere and so 'reframes responsibility' for the giving and receiving of care within social systems that currently feminise and privatise care-based activities (Lawson 2007: 5). In contrast to the autonomous sovereign subject of neoliberal discourses, the subject of feminist theorising is relational, contextual and a product of particular places, societies and relationships. Such a relational self cannot but view care as 'integral to being and subjectivity' since interdependency is a precondition of human existence (DeFalco 2011: 239). Suzanne Gordon *et al.* (1996: xiii) provide a useful definition of care as 'a set of relational practices that foster mutual recognition and realisation, growth, development, protection, empowerment, and human community'. This set of relational practices has been extended productively by ecofeminists to encompass the needs of the ecological other and to reconceive the environment as 'the extension of the body, the household, and the community' (Abbruzzese and Wekerle 2011: 140).

Historically or traditionally undervalued practices such as care, friendship, trust, kinship and love are thus key to the formulation of an 'ethics and politics of mutuality' based on a relational view of self and an understanding of human and nonhuman community (Plumwood 1993: 52). Such an understanding promotes situated knowledges and plural perspectives rather than individual epistemologies, and takes affective relationships and emotional connections as serious conduits for ethical thought. In moving care-giving into the formal arena and promoting, rather than demoting, hitherto privatised care practices, feminists politicise their engagement with care discourses and demand the recuperation of 'feminine' values within social welfare practices. Yet, if foregrounding the political nature of the private destabilises the ostensibly stable categories of formal and informal, it 'remains unclear', to quote Patricia Martin (2004: 19), 'that dissolving such boundaries is either desirable or possible'. Since the production of gendered identities is 'tightly bound up' in the 'construction of political subjects, their power, and their capacities', such destabilisation risks naturalising the processes of subordination and dependency that are still clearly located within discourses of femininity and associated with women's capacity to care (Staeheli and Kofman 2004: 11).

The validation of an ethic of care or care-sensitive ethics is therefore problematic on a number of accounts. Sherilyn MacGregor (2004: 57) questions whether 'care is a wise choice of metaphor around which to create a feminist political project for social and ecological change' when care itself has been so problematically linked to female oppression. This critique has much in common with that directed towards the ontological or essentialist association of women with nature, namely that it situates 'feminine' values and female bodies within gendered ideologies of power. The question directed towards those tasked with formulating a new and alternative ecofeminist ethic then becomes (MacGregor 2004: 57):

> How can societal expectations that women be caring or the exploitation of women's unpaid caring labour under capitalism be challenged at the same time that the specificity of women's caring stance towards the environment is held up as an answer to ecological crisis?

If care is to retain its legitimacy, many theorists contend, it must be situated within a care ethic freed from gendered and sexualised hierarchies and made 'fully political' (Wekerle 2004: 249). The tendency in justice ethics towards the abstract and universal is critiqued by ecofeminist theorists as lacking awareness of the specific conditions that produce the need for care, including that of our ecological embeddedness.

A politicised ethic in which the specificity of the object of discourse belies any potential opportunities for the abstract imposition of gendered ideologies can extend care-giving beyond normative notions of justice to encompass the multiplicity of systemic relations in which women and the environment alike experience marginalisation. A politicised care stance is particularly useful in interrogating the power relationships enmeshed in notions of citizenship, itself a term frequently offered in place of care since citizenship is a concept accorded value within the construction of political subjectivities.[1] Defined in opposition to the masculinist universal citizen, the citizen of feminist theory is an un-predetermined political agent in an egalitarian arena, without the pejorative associations of the feminised and privatised maternal subject often associated with female carers. Such a citizen can achieve 'membership, standing, and inclusion in a political community' through a non-gendered and relational affinity with others whilst interrogating the systems of gender difference that institutionalise 'feminine' roles and marginalise care practices (Staeheli and Kofman 2004: 7). Citizenship, according to Macgregor (2004: 64) thus strikes 'a balance between an ethic of care and an ethic of justice' and can engender responsible political engagement in service of the exigencies of marginalised peoples and an institutionally silent, dependent and feminised natural world.

In what follows I read the abused bodies of the female protagonists – as delineated in my previous chapter – as subject to discourses of gendered power that devalue care as a response to environmental crisis and fail to recognise the female protagonists as political and ethical actants. My interrogation of masculinist modes of representation centres on the limited 'feminine' subject positions available to the novels' protagonists under the auspices of neoliberal individualism. My analysis focuses on exclusionary practices that polarise gender differences with the result that social relations are inimitable to those deemed to occupy the position of the 'feminine'. My reading centres on the giving and receiving of care, and the ways in which the development of an ethic of care either fails or succeeds to re-envisage the systems that produce gender difference. In exploring interlocking discourses of femininity, agency and care, these novels advocate a politics of resistance to neoliberal individualism and open up possibilities for alternative ecofeminist ethics predicated on values of community and mutuality. These alternative ethical stances delimit hegemonic interpellation and write the female body back into the narrative in ways that are transformative and counter-hegemonic. I thus venture some suggestions as to what an ecofeminist ethic might encompass in light of the environmental concerns of contemporary young adult literature.

Narratives of exclusion: productions of gender difference

A dualistic construction of gender is a recognisable element of the novels here discussed, revolving around a set of gendered behaviours, characteristics and identities. Such a radical polarisation works in the text as a manifestation of unsustainable gendered relations. The identities of the male and female characters are neatly encapsulated in what Alison Jaggar terms (1983: 316) 'gendered definitions' of humanity:

> To the extent that women and men conform to gendered definitions of their humanity, they are bound to be alienated from themselves. The concepts of femininity and masculinity force both men and women to overdevelop certain of their capacities at the expense of others. For instance men become excessively competitive and

detached from others; women become excessively nurturant and altruistic.

A failure to integrate competing elements of experience results not simply in self-alienation but also in a disregard for non-normative genderings. The idealisation of hegemonic masculinity and the relegation of care practices, empathic engagement and emotional connection to 'women's experience' serves to position certain women and 'feminised' men as 'less eligible subjects' (McDowell 2004: 156). Hyper-masculine and hyper-feminine identities are implicated in power-plays over the appropriation of gendered subject positions and act – in these novels – as the precondition of new, less polarised, social orders.

In *Exodus*, regimes of gender difference operate to produce starkly opposing masculine and feminine traits. The two very different responses to climate crisis exhibited by Cal and Candleriggs are a result of highly gendered behavioural patterns, predicated on exclusion of the gendered qualities of the other. Neither ethical model serves to successfully negotiate crisis since both are based on radical polarisation of opposing traits rather than dialogue or integration. Cal prototypically exhibits what Plumwood (1993: 28) terms 'the highly valorised traits' of masculinity; he is objective, impartial and rational, and considered brilliant yet callous by his colleagues. Candleriggs prototypically exhibits the historically devalued traits of the feminine; a nurturing figure of care and emotion, she epitomises the values radically excluded from Cal's sky cities. Any possibility for mediation between the poles of the masculine and feminine is restricted through Cal and Candleriggs' inability to see beyond the limits imposed by such systemised gendered definitions.

The New World sky cities over which Candleriggs' former lover, Cal, presides offer an overt critique of gender difference, predicated on the expulsion of the qualities of the feminine, the natural and the collective. Cal's phallic cities display a hubristic desire for transcendence over, and distance from, the natural world. The blueprints and sketches Mara discovers in Cal's office, underscoring the sky cities' design, show patterns adapted from nature, inspired by worm tunnels, termite nests, honeycombs, spiderwebs and hive and ant-like structures, yet no *actual* or material manifestation of the natural world is anywhere present. In this disembodied space that privileges mindscapes over landscapes, nature has instrumental, rather than intrinsic, value. Under a neoliberal framework, Cal places individual survival above empathetic engagement in an act of disregard that engenders the New World's blindness to the 'mass of poor souls' outside the city walls (196). The towering sky cities are underpinned by a hierarchical entry system on the rational premise that a more inclusive mentality would make 'the system...collapse' (Bertagna 2003: 197). An intelligence test is set for the world's flood refugees that allows entry only to those who scored highly and leaves everyone else regarded as 'an alien, an outcast' (196). Such alienation is experienced by Cal's lover, Candleriggs, whose rebellion against the sky cities sees her expelled by the New World hegemony in much the same way that the dead and dying natural world is expelled from human consciousness. In restructuring his cities around neoliberal principles, Cal internalises a patriarchally-instituted use-value mentality and denotes the suppression of emotion a means of control over the feminine traits of alienated others.

Candleriggs, on the other hand, not only speaks out on behalf of those disadvantaged by Cal's hierarchical entry system and thereby reinvests value in altruism, emotion and empathic engagement, but also valorises community by presiding over the establishment of the Treenesters' alternative society. Whilst Cal looks towards space to accommodate a new era of superior human beings, Candleriggs looks to the earth as a localised space of situated beliefs in which to nurture the domestic values that Cal's society excludes, principle among which is care-giving. Candleriggs connection with the land is written onto her skin: she is 'as gnarled as a tree with a face as pale as the moon' and wears earthen clothing woven from grasses and leaves (107). This connection is spiritually inflected since the place names the Treenesters adopt allow them, in animistic reverence, to remember the names of the drowned world and to resemble 'the living limbs of the lost city' (132). An alternative epistemological framework to that offered by Cal's hegemonic model sees Candleriggs place her faith in the 'stone-telling', a prophesy believed to be written into the stones of the drowned city of Glasgow in the form of a mantra or story by which the Treenesters are to live their lives (132). Nesting in trees, telling bedtime stories and invoking the spirits of those who have drowned to keep the Treenesters safe, Candleriggs takes on a maternal role as substitute for the emotional attachment offered to, and rejected by, Cal.

The elision between the ontological categories 'man' and 'human' that underpin the New World hegemony fuels the New World's bid to build an empire based on segregation of the purportedly 'human' from the undervalued rest. Whilst these social asymmetries are condemned within the text, Candleriggs nevertheless confirms her status as not fully human under the representational strategies available to her. In her alienation, she concurs with a model of biological essentialism and performatively adheres to the patriarchal representational framework that links women with irrationality. She exhibits an unfounded fear of learning and forbids the Treenesters from touching the books in the university library (one of which Mara eventually uses, secretly, to negotiate the Treenesters' exodus from the Netherworld), and thereby conforms to a gendered stereotype of the un-cerebral feminine. In a series of conditional clauses, Candleriggs herself questions whether the human tragedy could have been averted if her own behaviour had been less irrational (197):

> 'Maybe if we had had more time to argue our cause, if we had been less hot-headed and rash and had spoken calmly to people about their fears, maybe we could have convinced them that reaching out to help others needn't devastate their own future…maybe then more people would have joined us and we would have spoken as the voice of the people.'

As Candleriggs herself narrates when reflecting upon her alienation, her 'hate was all mixed up with love'; the 'savage war raging inside' her prevents her from successfully negotiating her pejorative female subject positioning (198). The text's oppositional positioning of Candleriggs means that her ideologically preferable ethic of care for an alternative world order is therefore prevented from being perceived as a viable alternative to Cal's dominant hegemony. Spurned for her beliefs, exiled and alone, Candleriggs is undoubtedly a sympathetic character, yet her gendered stereotyping effectively maintains her subordination. Her failure to challenge the radically polarised dualisms of Cal's society inheres in a feminine connection with nature that is not liberating and transformative, as it will be for Mara in the following book in the series, but becomes instead an 'instrument of oppression' or 'relic of patriarchy' – terms used by Plumwood (1993: 20–1) to delineate the woman–nature connection when perceived as pejorative to a liberal feminist agenda.

Whilst Candleriggs – a figure of old age and resignation – is thus truly a product of her oppression, the much younger Mara exhibits the key traits necessary to challenge the limits imposed by the 'gendered definition' of her humanity. It is Mara who explicitly raises the need for an alternative ecofeminist ethic when she defies Candleriggs' orders to avoid the university and searches for a record of the world's 'great dreams-women' from which to construct a 'theory of dreams, of the missing women in the mosaic of creation' (175). Mara's concern identifies the failure of history to invest value in female voices and the corresponding lack of feminist ethical standpoints with which to avert the world's social and ecological decline from 'dream' to 'nightmare' (175). Gorbal's subsequent well-meaning celebration of motherhood – '[b]ut women grow the living dreams, the human ones' – advocating a female role predicated on biological essentialism, unwittingly compounds Mara's contention that women's achievements in the formal sphere have been devalued in preference for their nurturing capacity (175). The language of dreaming employed by Mara to illuminate the gender bias of western history alludes to the alternative ethical visions of indigenous peoples, such as the 'dreaming' of Australia's aboriginal peoples, and gestures towards the establishment of a feminist ethic based on the language of poetry, dream and lore rather than on discourses of empirical, impartial or objective knowledge. If Candleriggs is unsuccessful in delineating a community-based ethic of care to replace Cal's hegemonic individualism, Mara is conversely capable of uniting the Treenesters in resistance against the New World superstructure precisely through her refusal to work within the limits imposed by Cal's hierarchical social system and her corresponding drive to establish a new (feminine) language for politics.

Death and the zombie: gendered sexualities

In the social and discursive materialisation of the body, the zombie is a creature of pure appetite and bodily desire. A profane figure instantiating an unsettling conflation of categories, the zombie is a manifestation of the fear occasioned by human mortality: an abject figure existing on the threshold between the living and the dead, containment and excess, embodiment and dissolution. Its instinctual and relentless hunger has given rise to its cinematic and literary materialisation as a metaphor for first world consumerism (Lauro and Embry 2008). Since consumerism is often coded as feminine, such a metaphorical figure has deeply social implications for ecofeminist theorists. Andrea Friedman (2001: 159) argues that:

Since Western nations began building consumer economies, the consuming woman has been constituted as an object of dread and ridicule, fear and desire, a figure whose wants and needs some seek to suppress, others to incite. At the same time, consuming women have ranged between home and marketplace, crossing boundaries that demarcate private and public, self and family, production and reproduction, and feminine and masculine. These two aspects of consumption—how women are constituted as objects and constitute themselves as subjects—are not unrelated.

The female consumer's borderline identity, conflating categories pertaining to home and marketplace, subject and object, renders her transgressive. In *The Forest of Hands & Teeth*, consumerism is inescapably associated with abjection and discursively coded as feminine. The insatiable figure of the zombie is employed to interrogate the ways in which the desire to consume becomes written onto the body of the young female protagonist. Whilst transgression is valorised as an agential female prerogative in response to the strictures of village life in the Forest, such transgression discursively ties Mary to the zombies and circumscribes her choice within interlocking discourses of female embodiment, sexuality and consumerism.

Ryan's zombies, or 'Unconsecrated', are grotesque instantiations of boundary crossing, forever defying limits and 'pulling at the...fences' (2). They are quintessentially abject figures, corresponding with Kristeva's (1982: 3) designation of the corpse as 'the utmost of abjection...death infecting life', that enact a debased inversion of human reproduction, playing into global fears over viral epidemics and sexually transmissible diseases. The survival skills that ensure the villagers' safety delineate care a subversive response to the threat posed by the Unconsecrated; the giving and receiving of care must end at the moment a loved one 'turns' or such care becomes fatal to the care-giver. Such a denigration of care renders Mary's refusal to surrender her own embodied needs and desires a paradoxical form of female solipsism. If – as Friedman (2001: 159) contends – 'consumption remains uncontained and uncontainable within the ideological boundaries of Western capitalist societies', Mary's similar refusal to remain contained within the ideological boundaries of the village renders her subjectivity problematically circumscribed within the abject consumerism of the Unconsecrated.

Mary's physical desires and needs make fallible the religious teachings of the Sisterhood by foregrounding the inescapable embodiment of the human subject. The reader is made constantly aware of the physical effects of Mary's love for Travis on her body: separation is 'like ripping my own flesh from my body' (183). Like the Unconsecrated with their own ripped flesh, Mary associates physical need with a 'fierceness' that overrides sentience (182). Yet the physical demands of Mary's love are condemned by the Sisterhood as inappropriate to the needs of the village in which commitment is valued above love and desire. Mary's betrothal to Travis' brother Harry, and her best friend Cass' betrothal to Travis himself, signals that marriage in this village is a perverse failure of love, disregarding embodied experience and privileging the needs of the community over the desires of the individual. Reacting against matrimonial conscription, Mary conversely posits embodied desire as the very thing that makes her human; a life without such desire is 'not a life' and no better than the half-lives of the undead shuffling along beside the fences (50). If the Sisterhood has kept a totalitarian hold on the village by deny- ing the physicality of its inhabitants and thereby severing the roots they share with the Unconsecrated, Mary conversely values the moments at which she can acknowledge such common roots since these moments foreground the ontological embeddedness of human existence.

The enigmatic nature of Mary's multiply-coded female body defies its safe containment. Her aggressive female sexuality has the effect of enfor- cing a link between femininity and death – an association that Kathryn James (2009: 14–16) recognises as common in historical and contempo- rary representations of death – with its roots in a psychological fear of the sexually active female. As Bronfen and Goodwin (1993: 14) argue, 'death and femininity have formed two possible axes of negation and enigma in relation to masculine subjectivity and culture'. Mary's desire for Travis manifests itself in a discursive foregrounding of the nihilistic 'hunger' she shares with the Unconsecrated: 'I am angry at all that sepa- rates us and that I can't consume all of him at once, his whole being. For a moment I understand the craving of the Unconsecrated, the need for the flesh of a living soul' (182). This instantiation of female irrationality and excess, pitted against the masculine subjectivity noted by Bronfen and Goodwin, is left uncritiqued since Mary's strong inclination towards the Forest and the threat of danger and death it encapsulates replicates other female instances of emotion-driven irrationality throughout the novel. When Mary swaddles an undead infant, hugs the baby to her chest and tries 'to give her comfort' despite the baby's ashen skin and sickening smell, she does so under the gendered performative that she 'should feel something inside me tugging me toward this helpless child, some sort of dormant maternal instinct' (194). This non-rational death drive, couched in a discourse of biological nurturance, is posited as distinctly feminine. According to the masculinist ideologies of Mary's brother, Jed, such an 'unnatural' association between women and death is to be condemned as 'sick and horrid and evil' (23). This semantic association of femininity, death and 'evil' engenders a pejorative representation of female solipsism, a fear that finds its most significant object in Mary, whom Sister Tabitha critiques for being unable to 'love outside yourself' (117). In the eyes of the Sisterhood, it is Mary, more so than the Unconsecrated, who constitutes the monster in the sense proposed by Halberstam and Livingston (1995: 27): 'a cultural object whose role is to articulate the presence of impurities – those aspects of the community that need to be expelled in order to support and sustain economic, social, and sexual hierarchies'. Foreseen by the Sister to be 'the end of us' – her inquisitiveness and desire being too strong for the safely demarcated physical and ideological barriers surrounding the village – Mary is desired sexually by both of the brothers, Harry and Travis, and hated by her best friend for being so desired, and yet even Travis whom she loves in return is eventually 'not enough' for her (65; 208).

In light of the subversiveness of female desire, the parallels made between Mary and Gabrielle – the only 'Outsider' to enter the village – is an eerie one: 'My breath hitches – it is like looking at a reflection in the water. The same age, same dark hair, same questions in our eyes...' (71). An allusion to the biblical Angel Gabriel who signified to Virgin Mary the existence of a realm outside her known world, Gabrielle similarly acts as messenger for Mary, investing hope in a life outside the enclosed perimeters of the village. The fate of this girl whom the Sisterhood secretly releases into the forest to be bitten by the Unconsecrated is positioned as correlative with Mary's own; both Gabrielle and Mary must be radically expelled so that their 'hunger' cannot disturb the fragile balance of life in the village. Mary's obsession with this girl vies with her love for Travis, and eventuates in a fatalistic and eroticised desire to capitulate to Gabrielle's craving: 'I think about slipping a finger through the fence and into her mouth. Letting her consume me and infect me' (167). Mary and Gabrielle's similar desire to 'consume' until death those whom they crave (Travis, after all, dies in order to save Mary's life), and not simply to consume but to be consumed in a nihilistic affirmation of mortality, reaffirms patriarchal fears over female sexual appetite and thereby numbers this novel amongst those which James (2009: 7) suggests 'reaffirm hegemonic ideologies pertaining to gender and sexuality' insofar as 'they function to enable a transgression of those boundaries, [while] at the same time...generally work towards restoring them too'. This discursive association of death, sexuality and femininity renders abject the sexualised female consumer.

Motherhood and madness: a failure of care

In the novels discussed a maternal propensity towards love, care and trust is couched in a discourse of biological essentialism rather than agential choice. A woman's failure to care or be cared for under hierarchies of gender difference is configured as a form of female madness and explored through the archetypal figure of the mother. Motherhood – an ontological state intimately associated with care – is rendered lacking when the protagonists' mothers fail to develop an ethic of care in response to trauma. Female madness is here naturalised not in service of a narrative of resistance to dominant ideological constructions of the feminine but in order to foreground the disempowering effects of sexualised hierarchies on the female person, and particularly the female body. The novels' portrayals of female madness associate mothers with feminine characteristics traditionally deemed inappropriate, ineffective or undesirable within society, including irrationality and – as seen in the previous section – a nihilistic inclination towards death. Such 'natural' feminine characteristics are portrayed as a response to an irreconcilable lack: in *The Hunger Games* and *The Forest of Hands & Teeth*, the death of a husband, in Franny Billingsley's *The Folk Keeper* [1999], an inability to return home to the sea. It is the women's daughters, in fact, who are perceived to be more successful at retaining female agency in the face of social oppression, and through whom the texts validate a more successful ethic of care. The resistant characterisation of the women's daughters denotes care a vehicle for female empowerment, even whilst revealing the limitations such a care ethic imposes on non-agential constructions of the feminine.

Female madness in *The Hunger Games* is explored through the lens of an angry and resentful daughter looking back on her mother's grief-induced madness after the death of her husband. Deemed by Katniss an unnatural, or at best excessive, response to grief, such madness underpins Katniss' attempts to remember that her mother 'must have really loved' her father (10). Female emotion, in this case love, is problematically devalued as a form of madness: an excessive response to another human being. Katniss' mother herself describes her madness as a result of sickness, curable with the help of the right medicine. This interpretation of female madness as clinical depression – the encouraged response to the text – is, however, an interpretation that Katniss herself refuses; she insists, with monetary inflection, that such sickness is 'one we can't afford' (43). Situated thus at the intersection between the interlocking discourses of irrationality, irresponsibility and illness, madness is configured as an inappropriate feminine response to grief. Female strength, on the other hand, is correlative with the ability to act caringly in the face of oppression. Whilst Katniss' blame very specifically centres on her mother's inability to care for her daughters during her distress, the roots of her mother's madness lie in the oppressive social asymmetries of the Seam that render a father's death in a mining accident and the subsequent starvation of the family left behind 'not an uncommon fate' (33). A general helplessness to challenge the hegemonic system in which such oppression is engendered is the all-pervasive response to social deprivation. The victimisation of those towards the lower end of the social hierarchy extends beyond women to the 'socially useless' of all kinds, including the elderly, the incapacitated and children whose parents cannot afford to feed them. Katniss' anger at her mother's madness is metonymic of her anger towards the stratified social hierarchy imposed by the Capitol and serves to challenge the resignation displayed by the majority of the populous. If such anger interrogates the ethical implications of such a naturalisation of gender difference, it also has the effect of devaluing care as a responsible reaction towards another's grief; Katniss can more successfully undertake her heroic quest if she herself remains unmarred by any inclination towards care-giving.

In *The Forest of Hands & Teeth*, the portrayal of female madness similarly centres on a mother's total absorption in grief. Mary's mother's death-in-life – constantly waiting for her dead husband to come home – is comparable to that of the Unconsecrated who roam the Forest in a similar state of suspended decay. Mary's mother's response to her husband's 'turn' constitutes a refusal to function within the social structures that have allowed for such a tragedy, and manifests itself in her reversion to a child-like state; her children 'never allow her to approach the fence line unaccompanied' under a very deliberate and careful ethic of care (3). Such a response is juxtaposed with other instances of female madness evoked throughout the text including a mother who set herself, and half the village, on fire upon seeing her son infected by the Unconsecrated. Female madness – it is implied – is destructive to both self and wider community; its association with childishness and irrationality deems it apposite for increased social strictures even whilst such strictures constitute its underlying cause. A split is manifest between the self-denial, rationality and reason enforced by the Sisterhood to ensure the village's survival, and the excessive emotional responses of village women unable to abide by such a 'masculine' hegemony. It is a widow who establishes the moral and ethical structures surrounding the villagers' dealings with the infected, pleading with the Sisterhood to be allowed to fulfil her marriage vows to the man she loves by joining him in the Forest to roam forever amongst the undead. Mary's mother's similar plea sees her knowingly enact her own abjection. The text's portrayal of female madness thus foregrounds the care values that are lacking in the enforced ideologies of the sisterhood, under whose 'masculine' rule the feminine characteristics of commitment, inseparability and love are problematically devalued.

In Billingsley's *The Folk Keeper* – a novel set in a world akin to the old Ireland or Scotland of folklore but which suffers from an apocalyptic disjunction between the human world above ground and the nonhuman world of the monstrous Folk below – female madness centres on the mysterious figure of the Lady Rona, a selkie figure or Sealmaiden (both human and nonhuman), who died long before the start of the novel. The Lady Rona's piecemeal introduction foregrounds the fragmented nature of her mental state: her name is first a password to ensure Corinna's acceptance into the household of Marblehaugh Park, then the name of a ship, then a name carved repeatedly into the walls of the cellar, and finally a name on a gravestone. It is only after these several pieces of information have been gathered by Corinna that readers learn she was also Lord Merton's first wife, and finally that she was Corinna's mother. The Lady Rona's protracted introduction – whilst she herself remains voiceless – is testament to her mythic role within the Marblehaugh household: a woman whose whispered name echoes down through the generations. An element of chaos within the otherwise ordered Park, Lady Rona constitutes a presence much like the words she carves on the cellar walls which had 'been whitewashed over' long before, yet 'you could see them easily when you knew to look' (Billingsley 2001: 43). Her words – 'Poor Rona: take pity on her' – carved over and over again, protest the practices of domination that have seen her seal self subsumed into her human self through enforced and landlocked marriage, and constitute the Lady Rona's repeated attempts to inscribe her identity into the oppressive patriarchal system that have attempted to deny it (42). Here, the absence of an ethic of care results in the Lady Rona's unanswered plea for empathy within a system that constrains and delimits female emotion.

Madness is conceived as a consequence of the Lady Rona's failure to retain an integrated identity after her husband burns her sealskin. Prevented from giving full expression to her dual selves as both woman and seal, the Lady Rona interiorises the death of her seal self by refusing to look at the sea. Tellingly, it is through her daughter's narrative, rather than her own, that such oppression is brought to light and Lady Rona finally given a voice (127):

> I cannot cease my weeping, Sire,
> I'm chilled unto the bone.

> I've lost my lass, my tiny babe,
> I've lost my ancient home.
> The singing sea is far, yet near;
> I'm locked in solid stone.

In the rhyme's dialogic structure, the Manor is denoted a masculine space lacking empathy or warmth ('chilled unto the bone') in which Lady Rona's female voice falters until finally silenced in death (the 'solid stone' in which she is forever entombed), whilst the 'singing sea' is denoted a feminine, nurturing space ('lass', 'babe', 'home') to which she is forever denied entry. This polarisation of masculine and feminine space results in a naturalising of female madness as the only available response to patriarchal oppression.

In each of these portrayals of female madness, a sense of physical entrapment within a condition, space or mentality represents the female figure's conceptual entrapment within the oppressive gendered hierarchies underpinning her society. Such madness is naturalised through the conventional association of women with the irrational, bodily and emotional, an association that appears to leave no outlet for female expression except madness. That Katniss in *The Hunger Games* retains some degree of hate for her mother that obligates her to 'put up a wall to protect myself from needing her' suggests an eroded sense of generational – and particularly matrilineal – trust and a refutation of the centrality of care to the female experience (64). Conversely raising her father to heroic levels after his untimely death – a masculine glorification that is comparable to that which Mary exhibits towards her brother and Corinna to her soon-to-be husband Finian – Katniss deems female weakness a traitorous perversion of motherhood. The ineffectuality of these maternal figures has the effect of shifting the focus to the younger generations and their need to make sense of a world in which they receive no guidance from those who are normally perceived as care-givers. In the post-natural landscapes of the novels it foregrounds the strength and agency desired by the novels' young protagonists who have the responsibility of challenging the controlling social systems that privilege gender difference over caring feminine values.

Intersectional language: power and resistance

As has commonly been noted, language is implicated in the maintenance of gendered hierarchies; as Patricia Martin argues (2004: 16): 'Discursive practices link language with materiality and point to ways in which legitimacy and truths are produced in relationship to unequal distributions of power'. Acknowledging the materiality of the written word, Jim Cheney (1989: 132) argues for a language that 'grows out of experience and articulates it, language intermediate between self and world, their *intersection*, carrying knowledge of both'. Yet, language in these novels fails to live up to this promise of intersectionality and is instead implicated in systemic power imbalances. Often subject to decay and lacking in intrinsic meaning, language can simultaneously oppress and be oppressed. Such ambiguity is implicit in the word 'earth' in *Zenith* which, for the seafaring gypsea peoples of Pomperoy, has devolved into the curse word 'Urth'. '*Earth*', Tuck remembers his grandfather to have insisted, '*Not Urth. Earth! A good old word. It's you youngsters who've made it a curse*', to which Tuck's father would respond: 'It's you oldsters who cursed it' (33). Both cursed and a curse, Earth/Urth indicates the fragility of the semantic bonds that constitute a word's material embeddedness. Here language, particularly in its capacity to name and categorise, is implicated in the systemic underpinnings of oppressive social hierarchies and denoted an instrument of power. Care is here a vehicle for de- or re-gendering the language used to maintain such social hierarchies.

In *Feed*, language is one of the many human faculties that has undergone deterioration as a result of the evolution of the feed and has become implicated in masculinist discourses of power and agency. In a society in which people now communicate primarily through unspoken 'mchatting', and text, image and memory downloads direct from brain to brain, spoken language has been severely compromised and is suffering from the same kind of decay as that visible in the planet's ecology. The parallel instances of decay in language and environment are called forth in the epigraph to the novel – a fragment from W.H. Auden's 'Anthem for St. Celia's Day' – which conceives of a decaying world in which the image of a misunderstood language dwarfing children at play invokes a sense of nonchalance and complicity in the face of ruin. Sarah Beckwith (2006: 210) explores the dual images invoked by what she terms the 'landscape of ruin' in archaeological discourse:

> One insists on void, on absence; the other insists that even in the horrifying new landscapes formed by the sheer contingency of destruction, new meanings are made out of old ones. In the landscape of ruin, the survival of a past monument is a work in progress in which every finding is a refounding: not obliterating the present in the past, but giving to the past a new and transformed meaning.

In *Feed*, whilst isolated individuals such as Violet's father attempt a 'refounding' of meaning in the languages and discourses of the past, the general populous denotes history a 'void' or 'absence' and is content to obliterate not the present but the past in favour of discourses of immediacy and desire.

In the novel's post-apocalyptic landscape, consumer profiling has resulted in vastly reduced modes of expression and a devolving language of passive desire rather than an evolving discourse of agency and choice. Taking pleasure in debate, Titus unwittingly illuminates the empty signifier that now resides at the heart of language: 'I said this thing, and Calista said this thing, and it was like, *da da da da da, da da da da da, da da da da da*, all day' (76). 'Desire', suggests Patrick J. Murphy (2000: 83), 'is bound with the alienated objectification of the natural world as a commodity, and the concept of the commodity is the foundation of consumer societies'. In Titus' world, the desire to consume subsumes the protagonists' means of expression; 'I was trying to talk to Link', Titus narrates when first landing on the moon, 'but I couldn't because I was getting bannered so hard' (8). Consumerist discourses here serve as a barrier to communication, dislocating Titus not only from his friends but also from his own subjectivity since the ontological properties of his dreams and desires are shaped by the slogans of advertising. In regretting that 'I would have liked to have been able to take the opportunity to check out these great bargains' when his feed shuts down on the moon, Titus demonstrates that his very means of expression has also undergone such linguistic manipulation (50).

The differing language use of Titus' and Violet's fathers respectively signals their internalisation of, and resistance to, linguistic entropy. Titus' father's inarticulateness is foregrounded in his failure to communicate with his son after the hacking of Titus' feedware on the moon. Despite being perceived as 'very powerful and businesslike', Titus' father fails to provide his son with either practical information or emotional support, leaving him staring at the walls in a manner that replicates the inarticulateness of his parents (55). 'Power' in western society, suggests Mary Mellor (2000: 112) 'is defined by the ability of certain individuals and groups to (temporarily) free themselves from embodiedness and embeddedness.' Titus' father's language use demonstrates just such freedom or dislocation from linguistic embeddedness to the point at which the question inevitably becomes: 'If words are untethered from the material world, how do representations gain a foothold?' (Barad 2008: 130).

Attempting a converse 'tethering' of words to their material referents, Violet's father aims to reinvigorate a degraded language by reclaiming older linguistic structures; as his daughter tells Titus: 'He says the language is dying. He thinks words are being debased. So he tries to speak entirely in weird words and irony, so no one can simplify anything he says' (137). Extending care towards language as if it were an oppressed and dying individual, Violet's father questions the ontological properties of human language within a world in which the human itself has been superseded by the posthuman. Upon meeting Titus for the first time, he states: 'I am filled with astonishment at the regularity of your features and the handsome generosity you have shown my daughter' (136). The awkwardly formal nominalisation 'regularity of your features' works alongside the use of the adjective 'handsome' to refer to Titus' 'generosity' rather than his appearance (a linguistic misplacement that constitutes an ironic reminder that in this society babies are 'made' rather than 'conceived') to engender linguistic defamiliarisation. Such defamiliarisation serves to denote language a historical construct capable – like the culture from which it springs – of distortion, imprecision and eventual extinction; as Titus admits to Violet, '"I didn't understand a single thing he said"' (137). The 'powerful' model of masculine control that Titus' father fails to live up to is, however, appropriated by Violet's father precisely through his command of a more authentic language. In Violet's memories of her father teaching at the university, focalised through Titus (140):

> He looked all his students in the eye, like he was challenging them to a fight. He leaned towards them and said, "In object-oriented programming, discrete software objects interfaced more freely, in a system of corporate service provision that mirrored the emergent structures of late capitalism." Who the hell knows what he meant, but suddenly, he seemed kind of powerful, like someone who shouldn't necessarily be wound up in a cocoon of pink insulation and hidden in a basement somewhere.

Using language as a weapon ('like he was challenging them to a fight'), Violet's father demonstrates the capacity of language to determine social hierarchy. The integration of linguistic constructs in the epistemological frameworks structuring *Feed*'s dystopian society closely allies the death of language with the death of civilisation, and linguistic re-appropriation an instantiation of care and a mode of challenge to the ruling hegemony.

Whilst it similarly portrays language as both an instrument of control and a mode of resistance against the ruling patriarchy, *The Folk Keeper* rejects a 'powerful' model of male dominance over language as delineated in *Feed*, to envision instead a distinctly female re-appropriation of language in service of expression. In a novel in which the human population attempts to subdue the Folk, language functions as a means of mediation between the human and the non-human, and becomes a powerful weapon of control over the Folk. From the start, the young protagonist Corinna (masquerading as the male Folk Keeper, Corin) takes delight in the subversive potential of linguistic competency. Using language to refute the authority of the Great Lady, Corinna acknowledges the power of words to engender an epistemic framework of resistance against authority. In her dealings with the Folk, Corinna attempts a form of containment through language that would see the Folk incapacitated by 'the Last Word': sets of rhyming couplets that cause the Folk physical pain (9). Prior to the acknowledgement of her maternal origins, Corinna can only produce a rhyme with 'a hole in its middle, right where the heartbeat should be' (9). Such a linguistic failure, in which the 'heart' or essence of language remains elusive, renders Corinna unable to maintain power over the nonhuman Folk with the result that the Folk that strain against the boundaries of Corinna's candlelight also transgress the further boundary of Corinna's own subjectivity and 'mix[] me all together with myself, my insides turning outward to meet my own translucent skin' (47).

As a repository for the truth, language plays a key role in the formation of Corinna's identity since it is in 'reading backwards' through the pages of her Folk Record – piecing together fragments of conversation – that she realises something 'that makes my heart squeeze in on itself': her true identity as a Sealmaiden (112). Corinna's linguistic piecing together of her identity accords language an active discursive role ('now my words are coming back at me, mocking me'); language can influence the course of events rather than simply record them (102). That Corinna can only appropriate the power of the Last Word once she has acknowledged her own nonhuman maternal origins suggests that the patriarchal strictures of control that have delimited her identity have similarly maintained practices of human dominance over the nonhuman. Using words to create 'a net of rhythm and rhyme' in which to entrap the Folk, Corinna accords narrative the power to wrest agency from the Folk (126). Envisioning a lack of words as cultural stagnation or paralysis, Corinna uses her newfound linguistic prowess as a means of empowerment to tell her own story rather than to record that of others: 'it is no longer a Folk Record: I relinquish my duties! Call it instead Corinna's Journal' (112).

Corinna's full linguistic appropriation of her new dual selfhood enables her to refute language as a patriarchal mechanism of power and instead to use it as an expressive tool for exploring her newfound subjective agency. Yet, her transformation from human to seal is accompanied by a parallel transformation of her linguistic capabilities since only her human self can use and value language (159):

> The Sealskin crept up my side, wrapped round my middle. And then, when I was more seal than human...
> My words vanished. I could no longer shape an image of inky wetness, spitting up pearls. I could no longer name Finian, couldn't even pretend I didn't love him.
> An aching desolation overcame me. Gone was my new power of sculpting images with rhythm, welding rhythm to rhyme. Gone, too, was my newest power: saying those three words Finian had coaxed from me. My hands moved of themselves, pulled at the Sealskin. I couldn't go on before I knew I could retrieve my words.

Here Corinna's embodiment comes at the expense of her linguistic expressivity; as her Sealskin 'wrap[s] round' her middle, her 'words' concomitantly dissolve away into the 'inky wetness'. Such linguistic dissolution is accompanied by an immediate, embodied response: an 'aching' desolation that sees her hands 'move[] of themselves'. Her love for Finian – acknowledged, tellingly, through her body as an instinctual, animal emotion – is both the cause and means of her linguistic retrieval since it allows her to recognise her 'new power' to 'sculpt[] images' of a newly integrated identity as Sealmaiden in which she is both human *and* seal.

In beginning the first page of 'my new book, my new life', Corinna invests narrative with the ontological status of reality so that her story constitutes the life she can now go on to live (156). Integrating both the 'wet' ink of the sea and the land's 'air to dry it', Corinna accords language the capacity to carve out an unimpeded future in which her dual selves can both find expression (156). Language, then, is appropriated by Corinna both as a means of control over the Folk in order to test the limits, or boundary-line, of her selfhood, and in service of self-expression, to shape her agential, dual identity as both human and seal. Whilst language in *Feed* is denoted an oppressed and oppressive construct – invoked for its power or revoked for its patriarchal interpellation – here language is transformative when re-appropriated as a means to formulate a resistant female subject position. If Cheney (1989: 132) denotes the appropriateness of a 'language intermediate between self and world', it is in the intersection between Corinna's human self and seal self that language can enact its transformative potential, opening up a mediatory space for the nurturance of intersubjective relationships between humanity and the natural world. Corinna's integrated identity – both voiced and embodied, human and nonhuman – constitutes an empowering model upon which to base an alternative ecofeminist ethic of care.

Ideological rehabilitation: developing an ethic of care

The integration of Corinna's dual identities through language in a formulation that melds care for the self and care for the other adheres to Victoria Lawson's (2007: 4) designation of care as a 'relational social ontology' based on mutuality and trust rather than on differentiated modes of dependence. The subject positions available to the female protagonists are limited by social systems that designate care a privatised activity, particularly when – as suggested previously – a woman's, or mother's, capacity to care privately is compromised by grief or loss. In what follows I analyse the ways in which care is positioned as a contested response to crisis and finally rehabilitated as a public responsibility and as a means to engender a meaningful collective response. In *The Hunger Games* trilogy and *Mortal Engines* quartet, care-giving is expanded outwards from the private sphere and employed instead to engender community safety. Care practices are here circumscribed within wider practices of citizenship and politicised in their transition into the formal sphere. Such practices gain the potential to transform 'the terrain of participation' in care practices by challenging the power relations that underpin systematised productions of gender difference (Marston and Staeheli 2004: 884).

In the second novel of *The Hunger Games* series, *Catching Fire* [2009], Katniss undergoes a shift in attitudes towards female care-giving that results in her 'trying hard to mend my relationship with my mother' (Collins 2009: 38). Having vilified her mother for emotional weakness after her husband's death, Katniss now watches her mother undergo a transition outwards into the formal sphere that enacts her rehabilitation as a useful member of society. Katniss' mother – unnamed within the text – performs the role of District 12 healer, a role that allows her to extend the care she failed to give her daughters to the wider community in a gesture that both recuperates the collective into the private care-giving practices of the home and also resituates care-giving within the public sphere. Katniss' mother's medical competency, hampered by the minimal and rudimentary materials available to her, works in the text as a sign of the emotional strength deemed lacking in her earlier relationship with her daughters: 'She's gone into that special zone that includes only herself and the patient and occasionally Prim. The rest of us can wait' (137). This 'zone' – a removed space akin to that induced by grief in the first novel of the series – is not a space of blindness, solipsism and weakness but a productive space of care. The inclusion of Prim and not Katniss in this caring space is significant insofar as Katniss' earlier rejection of her mother now results in her heightened capacity to acknowledge her mother's own exclusionary tactics, leaving Katniss 'clearly not a priority' (136).

Katniss' growing respect for her mother in this novel and its sequel, *Mockingjay* [2010], leads not to an overt recognition of love or affection but instead to a disengaged sense of 'awe': 'I'm filled with awe, as I always am, as I watch her transform from a woman who calls me to kill a spider to a woman immune to fear. When a sick or dying person is brought to her...this is the only time I think my mother knows who she is' (135–6). Katniss' mother's metamorphosis – perceived as an actual and physical 'transformation' – centres on her capacity, clearly shared by her daughter, to reject fear in the face of trauma or crisis. With fear here constituted as a debilitating emotional weakness, Katniss' mother's increased selfhood ('the only time...my mother knows who she is') associates such a refutation of fear with a strength of purpose clearly linked to her emotional capacity to withstand oppression. Such a correlation equates care with social struggle, rendering care-giving a political act of resistance against the Peacekeepers who violently maintain the social hierarchies that lead to class-based oppression. Care in this novel is not a privatised emotion-driven response to a loved one but a disengaged interaction with alienated, disadvantaged and incapacitated individuals who attempt to function within a violent social system that generates the need for care-giving practices at a public and collective level.

In Reeve's *Mortal Engines* quartet, care practices and their conflation within the private and public sphere are explored through a discourse of posthumanism, reconceived in light of an ethic of care that renders the human *in* the posthuman capable of affective relationships with human and nonhuman others. Such a strategy recentres the human actant not in service of reinstating the autonomous Enlightenment individual but in the hopeful assertion that humanity can be reinscribed within an ethic of care that collectively encompasses the nonhuman other. Myra Seaman (2007: 270) defines the 'contemporary posthuman' as a being who 'defends the beauty of the singular human by deliberately retaining, within its machinery or altered physical state, the weaknesses and vulnerabilities that result from the memories of its old, historical, body and hence, its all too affected and affective self'. This layering of human and posthuman – both physically and ontologically – is a representational strategy to retain selected and valorised traits of the erstwhile human being. Since human emotion constitutes the weakness posthuman mechanical innovation is often designed to counteract, these valorised human traits are those that attain a privatised and feminised space within the posthuman condition. The validation of an ethic of care centring on the private and the feminine conflates the traditional categories of public and private in a transformative move towards care-based empowerment.

The traditional dichotomy that associates the human with care-giving and the machine with an incapacity to care is complicated in Reeve's quartet through the internal war waged between the stalkers' buried human selves and their superimposed mechanical subjectivities. For Shrike this war manifests itself in his inexplicable fondness for the badly scarred orphan child Hester and in fleeting memories – that both comfort and plague him – of a previous life. Hester herself complicates the purported association of the human with emotion and the machine with the potentially monstrous by designating monstrosity instead a property of the disfigured female body. Hester's self-labelled monstrosity finds expression in her all-consuming drive for revenge and her 'hideous' face which she imagines denies her the opportunity to play a more feminine role (Reeve 2002: 26). Yet it is precisely Hester's inability to adopt a more acceptable feminine subject position that awakens the care-giving capacity of the stalker Shrike (95):

> The only sign of tenderness she ever saw in him was when he busied himself with his collection. ... [H]is favourites were all women or children: beautiful ladies in moth-eaten gowns and pretty girls and boys with porcelain faces. All night long Shrike would patiently dismantle and repair them, exploring the intricate escarpments of their hearts as if searching for some clue to the workings of his own.
>
> Sometimes it seemed to Hester that she too was part of his collection. Did she remind him of the wounds that he had suffered on the battlefields of forgotten wars, when he had still been human?

That Shrike's nostalgic fascination with women and children of the past denotes a form of 'feminine' weakness is clearly suggested in later books when the engineer Oenone Zero successfully disables Shrike's killing instinct by coercing him into feeling 'guilt and shame' for 'every terrible thing he had done since he became a Stalker' (Reeve 2009a: 295). If Hester calls forth a schema for feminine lack that revolves around marginalisation, exclusion and the unnatural, this man-machine conversely develops caring responses integral to 'natural' femininity on behalf of the girl who lacks them.

For the Stalker Fang, the correlative of human-machine manifests itself in a schizophrenic juxtaposition of two personalities: the dead Anna Fang and the resurrected battle leader who uses the memories of Anna 'to understand the world' (Reeve 2009b: 505). When unmediated by the care-giving capacity of Anna, the monster-machine demonstrates the consequences of complete mechanistic subservience to rationality and reason, at the expense of natural human emotional engagement. In advocating misanthropy as an answer to ecological crisis, the Stalker Fang adheres to the nihilistic premise that planetary health will demand the annihilation of the human race, rendering the human population expendable – or manipulatable – in an effort to 'make the Earth green again' (Reeve 2004: 67). In an effort to protect 'the good earth', the Stalker Fang structures ecological rehabilitation around 'the long view' of human life on earth (Reeve 2009b: 504):

> 'You have to take the long view, Tom. It isn't only Traction Cities which poison the air and tear up the earth. All cities do that, static or mobile. It's human beings who are the problem. Everything they do pollutes and destroys. ... If we are really to protect the good earth we must first cleanse it of human beings.'

In desiring to 'cleanse' the earth of human beings, the Stalker Fang instantiates a schema for planetary health that is religiously inflected; the removal of humanity from the earth's surface is tantamount to the removal of earthly sin and guilt through expulsion of that which defiles it.

The planetary ethic of care instituted by the Stalker Fang is set against the far more intimate care practices undertaken by Tom to keep his daughter safe. With his weak heart failing, Tom watches his daughter through the lens of the satellite: 'He traced with his hands the curve of her cheek, wishing he could push through the screen somehow and touch her, speak to her' (511; 510). This desire to 'push through the screen', as delineated in my first chapter, communicates a desire to break down the inhibitive filter of technology in order to extend care towards his child. This intimate and affectionate instantiation of care is set against Stalker Fang's misanthropic validation of life in general over human lives in particular: that '[t]he life of a single child means nothing, compared with the future of all life' (511). The care Tom fails to extend to his daughter is thus necessarily conflated with an ethic of care that must encompass the entire human race. Tom's intimate moment of connection with his daughter is the narrative stimulus for environmental change, centring on an alternative vision of a greener world based around the prototype of 'a new city, a floating city...[that] doesn't claw up the ground...doesn't eat other cities...doesn't even use up much fuel' (508–9). His empathetic vision, predicated on the deep-seated hope that the human actant – even in its degraded posthuman incarnation – is still capable of affecting change, awakens the human voice within the Stalker Fang in a series of fluctuating pronouns: "When I, when Anna first saw you together she, I knew you were meant for each other! ...I have... She has... We have..." (508; 512). Instructing the superweapon ODIN to self-destruct with the final 'We', the Stalker Fang/Anna pairing implies that it is a combination of human empathy (Anna) and environmental forethought (the Stalker Fang) that will in fact provide the key to a greener future. In merging care for the planet and care for human beings, this hybrid figure mediates human advancement with an ethic of care, as a necessary step towards a more hopeful response to environmental crisis.

Conclusion: oppression made political

Ecofeminism has much to offer, contends MacGregor (2004: 61), 'in its rethinking of hegemonic understandings of ethico-politics and its injection of hitherto "private" concerns into the political domain'. In advocating an ethic of care to counter the formal concerns of a globalised economy, these novels critique the material imbalances under capitalism that see oppression disproportionately borne by certain women, children and landscapes. The 'private concerns' of female embodiment, gendered experience, domestic responsibility and practices of care are here made political and brought to bear on the formal sphere. The political implications of female oppression are couched in the language of betrayal by Candleriggs in *Exodus*, whose own ineffectual resistance has seen her fail to negotiate her subordinate subject positioning (208):

'Well, all I can say is what I know', says Candleriggs. 'It's this – you can betray someone with a word or an action. You can betray them with silence or inaction too. And in betraying that one person you can betray a whole world. ... And I know this too: the future will not depend upon the human mind; it *belongs* to the human heart.'

A refusal to remain silent in the face of oppression characterises the protagonists' ethical interaction with the institutions that regulate them. Such a refusal gestures outwards to encompass those who are forced to remain institutionally silent, including nonhumans and the environment. In her adherence to the dualistic Enlightenment humanist position that the 'mind' is a property of the male rational individual and the 'heart' the emotional centre of the (irrational) female, Candleriggs unintentionally perpetuates a damaging hierarchy of values that historically positions the feminine as subordinate to the masculine. Her emphatic adherence to matters of the heart, however, resonates with ecofeminist assertions that the emotions are serious conduits for ethical engagement, and invites interrogation of the ways in which emotional connections between individuals are 'sites of power' (Lawson 2007: 4–5).

'The current period', argues Linda McDowell (2004: 146), is one of crisis and change in which gendered social relations are being recast into forms that are not yet clear'. In young adult fiction, the porous boundaries between masculine and feminine, public and private, formal and informal, particularly in relation to care-giving and the maintenance of affective relationships, are used to interrogate these new and recast social relations. The posthuman figure, in its 'contemporary' guise, is particularly apt for such re-envisaging since its ontological hybridity lends itself to a relational analysis with a focus on interdependency. *The Folk Keeper* is also successful in investing power in the concrete, relational capacity of language to negotiate an agential female identity within the constraints of a patriarchal superstructure. The transformative power of language, in its intimacy and its particularity, can be harnessed to counter female erasure by allowing women to write themselves new and counter-hegemonic narratives. These narratives challenge the ethical frameworks upheld by neoliberal individualism by extending care both to the self and to the earth. Corinna's success at re-appropriating language to give full expression to both her human and nonhuman identities signals the sense of hope young adult fiction invests in such alternative, earth-based feminine discourses.

The question posed by Victoria Lawson (2007: 6) – 'can care ethics move beyond the personal, the near and the familiar, to care for distant others?' – gains strength when reformulated to encompass nonhuman others as well as unfamiliar humans. The novels of this chapter suggest that environmental apocalypse – tempered by an environmental care stance – can function to offer possibilities for the negotiation of alternative, more sustainable, world orders by opening up what Amsler (2010: 142) terms 'a space of reflexive self-critique'. Such a space translates global crises into lived experience and answers Roman Krznaric's (2010: 155) call for 'a revolution of the empathetic imagination'. If taken as catalyst for the reconstitution of public and private practices and the interrogation of discourses of gendered responsibility, apocalypse can become less about ends and limits and more about renewal, change and transformation. In associating ecological crisis with care-based activities and heightened opportunities for empathetic engagement with human and nonhuman others, these novels come closer to designating apocalypse humanity's 'culmination or fulfilment' – as stimulus for collective empowerment and earth belonging – rather than its projected end or terminus (Manley Scott 2010: 265).

4
Situated Knowledges: Competing Epistemological Frameworks

The various mythic superstructures imposed onto the environment throughout history and across cultures constitute competing attempts to 'know' the world and to map epistemic thought patterns onto the landscape. A reading of nature as a discursive construct predicated on human value systems and language structures is in danger of obscuring the embodied and embedded reality of human–earth interaction and the materiality of the earth itself. In a shift that follows the move from second to third wave feminist theorising from abstract, universal understandings of female experience to acknowledgement of the differing experiences of particular women mediated through race, class, sexuality and so on, the understanding of environmental knowledge as predicated on abstract, universal and objective facts has moved towards an understanding of knowledge as emergent, subjective, and ecologically embedded. Competing epistemological standpoints – often considered to produce gendered understandings of environmental meaning – are not delineated along the lines of 'men typically construct theories, women typically tell stories' as J. Baird Callicott (1993: 336) once mistakenly claimed, but instead denote an awareness that contemporary communications technologies have rendered knowledge global whilst at the same time enabling localised – non-normative – knowledges to enter the world stage.[1] Narrative, as an appropriate conduit for ethical theorising, is found to delimit masculinist abstraction and engender localised, situated and plural understandings of the world. My analysis of varying modes of epistemic engagement in the novels interrogates the textual positioning of the environment in relation to the young reader as well as the knowledge processes that render this environment meaningful.

The 'peculiar vocabulary' common to early ecofeminist narratives, placing emphasis on restorative discourses of birth, growth and renewal, has been perceived to refute the 'sterile' vocabulary of traditional epistemic discourse (Sargisson 2001: 58). The introduction of excluded terms to established epistemic practices is undertaken by ecofeminists in what Lucy Sargisson (2001: 58) labels 'a utopian attempt at producing a new language for politics'.[2] Cheney's (1989: 132) delineation of a language that is 'intermediate between self and world, their *intersection*, carrying knowledge of both' – as delineated in my previous chapter – endows language with the capacity to open up a mediatory space between humans and the nonhuman world. If the language structures of a dislocated neoliberal culture fall short of this mediatory benchmark, the '"[r]e-mything" undertaken by ecofeminists is designed to ensure that this new language engages more successfully with the natural world (Legler 1997: 230). I here understand myth to signify 'a set of deeply encoded metaphors' or 'stories, drawn from history, that have acquired through usage over many generations a symbolising function that is central to the cultural functioning of the society that produces them' (Slotkin 1985: 16). The symbolising function of myth rests in its capacity to represent experiences of the world that resist rational or objective interpretation. According to George Schöpflin (2007: 208), myth constitutes 'the agency by which anything real becomes an object for intellectual apprehension', making visible and accessible particular aspects of experience. In a post-apocalyptic context in which the earth has become an effective blind space, mythic discourse has the potential to re-signify humanity's interaction with the earth in new and imaginative ways.

The transition from ontology to epistemology that MacGregor (2004: 60) notes in ecofeminist ethics is generally indicative of the shift from first wave to second wave ecofeminist theorising: 'from assertions about "women's nature" to assertions about what women know and, very often, what they feel'. Situated knowledges foreground local, intimate interconnections between peoples and places in a formulation that belies abstraction or universality. They embody the potential to provide concrete, theoretical groundings for responsible ecofeminist epistemologies that locate the knowing of other peoples, lands, and the environment itself, in 'places other than the "mind"' (Legler 1997: 233). Narrative modes of expression – mythic or otherwise – can be employed in the discursive formulation of ecological identity by offering alternative epistemic frameworks based on embodied ways of knowing. Myra Seaman (2007: 269) argues that identity 'does not seem possible' without stories; her contention that stories are 'grounded in an emotional life that cannot be quantitatively measured' places story in the same conceptual category as myth, with the capacity to represent non-linear and non-rational aspects of human experience. Seaman's use of the word 'grounded' usefully foregrounds the importance of narrative in the construction of individual and collective identity as well as in the conceptualisation of humanity's embeddedness in the local ecology.

Mythic frameworks can draw meaning out of the ecological landscape in an emergent narrative that discursively gives voice to the natural world; as Karen Warren (2000: 103) argues: 'Narrative provides a way of conceiving of ethics and ethical meanings as *emerging out of* particular situations moral agents find themselves in, rather than as being *imposed* on those situations as a derivation from some predetermined, abstract rule or principle'. This validation of emergent understandings has the effect of wresting 'epistemic privilege' from dominant hegemonies and allocating it instead to 'feminised' others and marginalised spatialities (Narayan 1988: 38). The term 'epistemic privilege' arises through a feminist valuation of the knowledges, feelings and needs of subordinated others on the grounds that 'members of an oppressed group have a more immediate, subtle and critical knowledge about the nature of their oppression than people who are non-members of the oppressed group' (Narayan 1988: 35). The notion of epistemic privilege is a useful tool for addressing gendered, racialised and sexualised hierarchies within neoliberal discourses. These hierarchies belie the cultural agendas that inform the 'uneven geographies' of global politics (Nagar 2004: 32). Since mythical renditions of the historical landscape are often closely tied to particular spatialities it is important to note the ways in which space and place are implicated in the processes and productions of gender difference. The feminine epistemologies, or women's ways of knowing, advocated by ecofeminists offer ways in which to address such differences and interrogate the imbrication that Patrick Murphy (1998: 23) notes 'between the values that shape how we live and the shape that such living imposes on the land'.

In my focused novels, the contradictory mythic interpretations to which the environment is subject arise through gendered epistemologies. In what follows, I identify a tendency towards abstraction and universality in environmental representation as the catalyst for ecofeminist resistance and critique. In each of the novels, the natural world is subject to imaginative engagement, whether through the imposition of myth or the drawing out of story, and each reflects overt mythic patterns in the construction of environmental meaning.

The first pattern draws on the myth of the national frontier and colonial epistemologies of moral and cultural superiority. The second constitutes ecologically-inflected narratives of origination, rebirth and renewal, and represents more meaningful or empathetic relationships between humans and the earth. These differing epistemological frameworks are constructed dialogically so that an imposition of ecological values gives way to a more empathetic and intersubjective understanding of the natural world as unfolding story. A gendered progression can therefore be noted in the novels' construction of environmental meaning. I regard this progression as key to a reading of young adult post-disaster fiction and a vehicle for expressing and engendering a responsible relationship between humanity and the natural world.

Terra nullius: colonialist epistemologies

The 'myth of progress' that Dinerstein (2006: 572) argues is crucial to the epistemic frameworks underpinning the European and American self-concept is marked by colonial ideologies that continue to reproduce themselves over time. The myth of progress is glaringly present in discourses of globalisation which posit 'development' as a marker of cultural and economic progress in the race to attain entry into the 'developed' world. In analysing the ways in which topographical data is used to maintain uneven development, Cindi Katz (2001: 1215) points to what she terms 'the integumentary nature of topographical knowledge to the imperial practices glossed as globalisation, as well as to more down-home forms of domination and exploitation'. The knowledge that figures in spatial dominance can function to shelter or mask the colonial mentality that maps oppression onto 'feminiscd' spatialities including the native lands of indigenous peoples, lower-socio economic areas, sites of environmental pollution and nonhuman habitations. Plumwood (2006: 135) charges us '[t]o recognise that both nature and indigenous peoples have been colonised' and in recognising this 'to rethink, relocate and redefine our protective concepts for nature within a larger anti-colonial critique'. In contemporary young adult fiction colonial discourses often imbricate human and nonhuman subjects and spaces and function to map global processes onto the local landscape.

The imposition of a mythic superstructure onto non-western lands is manifested most damagingly in the notion of *terra nullius*: a legal fiction that designates the natural world, with its indigenous populations, a clean slate ready for colonial rewriting.³ The artificial outdoor arena in *The Hunger Games* – 'a vast outdoor arena that could hold anything from a burning-desert to a frozen wasteland' – figures as just such a *terra nullius*: a space in which the Gamekeepers can enact a performative staging of environmental crisis (22). This artificially inscribed arena – an ecological space metonymic of the wider post-apocalyptic planet – is a hostile space of ecological extremes: a grotesque instantiation of our anthropogenically changing climate. In the arena, 'the disasters, the droughts, the storms, the fires' that saw Panem 'r[i]se up out of the ashes' of what was North America are elaborately re-staged as entertainment for the populous (21). The brutal war for resources that characterised the early years of Capitol rule is metaphorically re-enacted on the bodies of Panem's child tributes. In this colonised space, both human tributes and natural environment are designated victim *and* aggressor rendering 'nature' a contentious site of duplicitous identification.

Katniss' experience of the arena is one of scorching heat, freezing temperatures, debilitating droughts and swarms of hornet-like 'tracker-jackers' genetically programmed to hunt their victims to the death. A more spectacular instance of anthropogenic manipulation sees Katniss flee from an artificially induced forest fire designed to herd the tributes into a designated part of the arena. The Games' instigators manipulate the environment from within the confines of the control room: a view from above, mediated by screens. This dislocated perspective – akin to the disengaged planetary consciousness explored in my first chapter – further dislocates the tributes from their environments so that their experience of the natural world becomes not one of mutual interaction but of defence against attack. By turning environmental suffering into spectacle, the Gamemakers render the earth both threatened – manipulated at will – and threat: the same position as that of the young tributes who must defend themselves by learning how to kill. Both the child tributes and the environment are thus denatured in a dual enforcement of artificially imposed behaviour, and forced to negotiate their embattled ecological positioning. Faced with a hostile environment, Katniss enacts her rage not on the natural world but on the dictatorship that has engendered such abjection, willing herself 'to do something, right here, right now, to shame them, to make them accountable, to show the Capitol that whatever they do or force us to do there is a part of every tribute they can't own' (286). Under the ecophobic framework imposed by the Gamemakers, Katniss adopts a resistant subject position and refuses to perform her ideological enslavement to the colonial epistemologies imposed on her environment.

The designation of nature as a colonised space is interrogated in *Predator's Gold*, the second novel in the *Mortal Engines* quartet, via the evocation of the American myth of the frontier. Freya, the ruler of the small ice city of Anchorage, places her faith in the Dead Continent of America as the only remaining land free from roving traction cities and the threat they pose to the survival of her town. Her faith centres on the adventures of the 'alternative historian' Professor Nimrod Pennyroyal whose published journey to America – a journey that is later discovered to be fictional – 'proves' that life still remains on a continent that was thought to constitute a post-natural landscape of '"haunted red deserts, poison swamps, atomic-bomb craters, rust and lifeless rock"' (28). Whilst the text positions readers to view Pennyroyal's comedic historical mishmash as based on ignorance rather than fact – America, for instance, was '[d]iscovered in 1924 by Christopher Columbo, the great explorer and detective' – Tom and Freya are nevertheless seduced by the myth of America as a green land of safety, freedom and a surviving ecology (28). The bestseller status of Pennyroyal's alternative histories intimates a common collective desire to abnegate responsibility for the unpleasant realities of disaster or crisis and to take comfort in conventional metanarratives of heroic exploration. Here, the past is a flexible tool for manipulation in the control of the prevailing hegemonic system; Reeve posits the imposition of an originary myth onto the natural world as correlative with the assumption of epistemic privilege by the coloniser.

Appealing to the nostalgic romanticism of a repressed cultural memory, Pennyroyal blurs the dividing line between historian and storyteller, declaring that '"true historians...know that within...legends there often lurks a seed of truth"' (30). Whilst comfortably fleeing his creditors in Tom and Hester's gondola, Pennyroyal waxes lyrical about his adventures in the Dead Continent. After discovering that the land is as barren as the previous explorers had documented he almost succumbs to exhaustion, lack of food and exposure to the elements, until... (30)

'The next thing I knew I was wrapped in furs and laid in the bottom of a canoe, and some charming young people were paddling me north.

'These were not fellow explorers from the Hunting Ground, as I at first supposed. They were natives! Yes, there is a tribe of people actually *living* in the northernmost parts of that Dead Continent! ... Savage, uncivilised descendents of a nation whose greed and selfishness once brought the world to ruin – and yet they had enough humanity to rescue a poor starving wretch like Pennyroyal!'

Rescued by noble savages, Pennyroyal survives to re-propagate the myth of an empty land ready for the taking since the not-quite-human savages nevertheless 'had enough humanity' to accept him warmly into their primitive homes. Proceeding to 'rescue[] the chief's beautiful daughter... from a ravening bear' – which causes her to fall desperately in love with him – Pennyroyal accompanies his easy wooing of America's surviving peoples with an Edenic imposition of environmental purity onto the land's ecology (31):

> 'Imagine my excitement, Tom! Going up that river was like going back to the earliest beginnings of the world. To begin with, nothing but barren rock, pierced here and there by time-ravaged stones or twisted girders which were all that remained of some great building of the Ancients. Then, one day, I spied a patch of green moss, and then another! A few more days of nothing and I began to see grass, ferns, rushes clustering on either bank. The river itself grew clearer. ... And the trees, Tom! Birches and oaks and pines covered the landscape, and the river opened into a broad lake, and there upon the shore were the rude dwellings of the tribe. What a sight for a historian! America alive again, after all those millennia!'

A land of 'ravening bears' (untamed wilderness) and clear waters (untouched paradise), America 'the Beautiful' is clearly a synthesis of entrenched western desires and longings in a post-apocalyptic landscape: a *terra nullius* complete with amenable natives. In a world governed by Municipal Darwinism, human evolution – having 'once brought the world to ruin' – has forced environmental evolution to devolve, as it were: to recede 'to the earliest beginnings of the world'. Such ecological primitivism is deemed correlative with cultural innocence ('uncivilised' peoples in 'rude' tribal dwellings). If such a formulation offers a critique of present-day cultural decadence it does little to re-envisage the western ecological attitudes that have propelled civilisation from rude innocence to post-natural decay; this ironic omission ensures that the readers interpret Pennyroyal as an unreliable narrator interpellated by colonial ideologies.

A similar reiteration of the American myth of the frontier in *Uglies* inheres in the rustic farming commune of 'the Smoke' – a small-scale earth-centred community nestled in a valley – to which Tally journeys when she leaves the city. This commune is metonymic of 'the ultimate landscape of authenticity' outlined by William Cronon (1996: 80), or 'the last bastion of rugged individualism' (76). The text's glorification of such 'freer, truer, and more natural' nature overwrites nature with the mythically contoured traits of the frontier (Cronon 1996: 77). Tally's increasing physical fitness within the green spaces of the Smoke reveals her growing emotional confidence, and her new-found ability to provide for herself is indicative of her increasing subjective agency. The physical beauty of the natural world engenders in Tally a gradual rejection of her own stigmatised body image; she notes that '[n]ature, at least, didn't need an operation to be beautiful' – it 'just was' (195). In this ancient landscape that 'just was', Tally's gradually changing attitude towards the environment is perceived through a narrative foregrounding of her heightened senses and her acknowledgement of the haecceity of the natural world. That Tally goes on to use her new 'wild' subjectivity to wage war against the circumscribed mentality of the cities suggests that the 'rugged individualism' possible only in the wilderness is essential to Tally's maturational progression and that a frontier mentality is a necessary prerequisite to collective action.

Tally's increasing individualism is problematic, however, in light of the community values she must attempt to uphold if she is to resist the alienation afforded by the city. Her involvement in the Smoke's destruction at the hands of the special ops branch 'Special Circumstances' uncomfortably positions her at the intersection between the totalising discourse of the coloniser and the earth-centred epistemologies of the natural commune. Tally's ambivalent role in resisting the controlling ideologies of the city manifests itself in her outwardly changing allegiance between the Smokies and the city dwellers. The subject of others' dialogue rather than her own, Tally is positioned as the floating signifier between 'us' and 'them' (301):

> "You did this! ... Stealing my boyfriend wasn't enough? You had to betray the whole Smoke!" ...
> "Shay!" Croy said. "Calm down. Look at her. She fought them."
> "Are you blind, Croy? Look around you! *She* did this!" ...
> "Will you *look at her*, Shay?" Croy cried. "She's tied up, like us. She resisted!"

Here, the repeated invocation to '*look at her*' puts paradoxical emphasis on appearances in a text that otherwise devalues the link between outward form and inner merit. Whilst the Smokies are not primarily indigenous peoples nor are they unequivocal models of optimum human–earth interrelations, they are invested with the knowledge structures of oppressed rural peoples at the mercy of stronger urban forces and thus can be read as the victims of environmental imperialism. Both resister and betrayer simultaneously, Tally therefore vacillates between being the vehicle for imposing the city's ideologies on the natural space and being the emergent voice of an alternative epistemology that values care of the environment above colonial control.

Anita Fellman (1996: 102) notes the self-perpetuating mythologising of the frontier mentality as an 'endless series of loops' through which 'history provided characters and situations that became the stuff of myth, and historical figures interpreted their personal experiences through the lens of the mythologised frontier'. Westerfeld's positioning of Tally as the prototypical frontier American (in attributes rather than gender) relies on the mutually constitutive nature of such mythologising. Under assurance that rumours of the Smoke will exist for generations, Tally reinterprets the Smoke as a mythic space by arranging for the words 'THE SMOKE LIVES' to be written in sparklers across the sky (369). Tally accords epistemic privilege to the historic figure of David – the values by which he lives and the actual wild spaces in which such values are grounded – to perpetuate the myth of the Smoke 'whether [he's] around or not' (363). Tally thereby instigates a rift between the space of the city and the space of the wild by according the city with the ontological status of the real and the natural world with that of myth. Tally herself becomes a mythic figure, sacrificing herself for the good of humanity by volunteering to undergo the brain damage accorded by the operation to make her pretty, as test subject for David's mother's counter-pill. Under this formulation, the Smoke itself remains uninterrogated – a *terra nullius* of ecological simplicity – and the myth of the frontier retains its status as a formative and desirable epistemic model for identity formation.

In the sequel, *Pretties* [2005], in which both Shay and Tally have undergone aesthetic standardisation, such mythologising is perpetuated by the girls' decision to dress as Smokies to earn the admiration of one of the elite social groups in New Prettytown, a group that takes its inspiration from criminals who challenge the prevailing governing system. That the girls adopt such rural personas as a playfully subversive act against the rulers of New Prettytown, explicitly linking such rurality with criminal behaviour, underscores the potential of this ecological myth to offer a counter-hegemonic challenge to systemic modes of control. However, since this act has a primarily social purpose – to integrate Tally into the group which enjoys the greatest privileges within New Prettytown's tiered society – such subversive behaviour becomes instead simply a show of support for the prevailing social and political system, a system that actively marginalises and incorporates alternative communities like the Smoke. Thus the Smoke moves from being a site of active resistance against the ruling hegemony to an agent of passive support for this same hegemony in a move that foregrounds the mutually reinforcing nature of cultural and ecological imperialism. In the Smoke's mythic co-option and the girls' interpellation by the dominant ideology, the myth of the national frontier functions – like Tally – as both resistor and aid, offering up the promise of an environmental haven even whilst it undermines such a promise by revealing its falsity: that in fact such a myth simply serves to crystallise the ecological margins against which the urban centre is defined.

Cartographic control: mapping a gendered world

To understand a map, Gunnar Olsson (2007: 57) contends, is 'to approach it as a palimpsest, a parchment written on twice, the first text erased, the second covering the traces of the old'. The novels here considered demonstrate anxiety over the hubris of designating geographic spatialities the property of a certain culture or nation and of mapping *over* the landmarks of indigenous, ecocentric, and other feminised cultures. Since – as Bradford (2007: 169) notes – the very 'politics of spatiality' are 'shaped by cultural traditions steeped in the ideologies, beliefs, and practices of imperialism', this mapping of, and mapping *over*, functions to define the non-western world as a discursively gendered space. An ecofeminist reading of the spatial implications of the colonial aesthetic interrogates this imbrication of imperialist and patriarchal agendas and rejects the definition of the earth 'as [a] resource to be mapped and appropriated in bourgeois, Marxist, or masculinist projects' (Haraway 1991: 7). By resisting a construction of the land as 'passive, visually captured, something to distance from, survey and subdue' – a construction Plumwood (2006: 123) recognises as key to a colonial metanarrative of spatial dominance – these novels unsettle normative epistemic frameworks by striving towards the *unmapping* of colonial space.

   Justin D'Ath's *Shædow Master* [2003] – a novel set in an imagined ecotopia loosely modelled on Australia, in which the colonial rulers retain economic, cultural and geographic control over the indigenous Guests and their native lands – critiques the colonial myth for its imposition of controlling ideologies onto the ecological landscape. In italicised flashbacks juxtaposed throughout the narrative proper, the reader becomes aware that the colonial prince, prior to becoming king, unwittingly killed a young indigenous boy named Skiff whilst attempting to hunt the Dalfen – a mythic creature responsible for the health and wellbeing of the lake and the land. The discursive image of two bodies – that of Skiff and the magical animal – speared with the prince's harpoon is an effective visual symbol of imperial power and its dual victims: native peoples and the natural world. The deaths of Skiff and the Dalfen at the hands of King Raoul imply that controlling ideologies are simultaneously mapped onto the endangered environment and the innocent child. Raoul's admission that '"[n]othing in nature is evil, Princess. ... It is only men who are evil"', is accompanied by a romantic trope of threatened innocence employed in service of the child and the natural world (D'Ath 2003: 21). Skiff's lost childhood, the natural landscape of Folavia's indigenous peoples and the mythic figure of the Dalfen come together in this novel to render nature the semantic equivalent of childhood itself, and equally threatened for being systemically voiceless.

Since the restless spirits of Skiff and the Dalfen demand retribution in the form of gold, King Raoul's decision to sell the Guests' sacred Cloudtouchers – ancient trees that bring the rain – implicates the natural world in Folavia's economic imperialism. Yet, the king's daughter, whose name means gold, is the intended referent of the spirits' demand; Ora functions – like Mara in *Zenith* – as currency, subject to economic coercion. Destined to become the Shædow Master (guarding and guiding the Dalfen spirit) in order to counter the drought occasioned by resource depletion, Ora is narratologically positioned to critique the uneven distribution of wealth and privilege within the postcolonial diaspora for which the land itself ultimately pays the price. That King Raoul's careworn face can become 'lit by a bright boyish smile' at the sighting of an endangered meerdragon – denoting pleasure in nature an emotional response semantically linked to childhood – renders Raoul's subsequent bioregional care for the environment a displacement for his larger failure to save Ora from her fate (19). The king's delighted cry that '"[a]ll the riches in the kingdom are unequal to what we saw just now!"' thus constitutes a prophetic warning against his on-going attempts to buy nature's forgiveness with material wealth (19). The patrilineal power chain that upholds Folavia's colonial hierarchy renders Ora, as well as Skiff, the Dalfen and the natural world, similarly subject to colonial discourses of epistemic co-option.[4]

Cartographic discourse is implemented to question both the production and distribution of colonial knowledge and its material effects on the Guests and their land. When Ora consults a map of Folavia, she notes with horror that on the bend of the river where her indigenous friend Tasman's village should be 'there was not a single red stitch' (151). This colonial failure to acknowledge indigenous existence – the lack of cartographic recording signalling the Guests' cultural invisibility – underpins the ideological foundations of colonial rule. History in this novel is envisioned as a tool in the hands of the reigning hegemony: a relic of colonialism and an instrument of dominance over the indigenous Guests. The history of the kingdom, as taught by the Folavian dynasty, is a linear progression towards wealth and prosperity that accords only a passive role to the indigenous forebears (39–40):

'History starts at the Year One and goes up to Year 247,' Ora explained. 'Which is now.'

The teacher turned to his class. 'Hear that, school? History begun when Adamo Wanderer come from Outworld forty-seven and two hundred years ago. Afore that, nothall here – no lake, no land, no person. Yes, Tasman?'

The boy lowered his hand. 'Guests here.'

'But how can that be? Cordin ta Lady Ora, ent nothall here afore Adamo Wanderer.'

Ora felt her face grow hot. 'I didn't mean that. I meant Folavia was *founded* by Adamo the Wanderer.'

'Ah!' said the teacher. 'Founded. Whoall knows what founded means?'

The girl next to Tasman put up her hand. 'Found, Master?'

'Not quite, Agella. Anyall el –'

'It means established,' Ora cut in. 'To start a new country. And I know there were skiffers here already, but they weren't running it like a country.' *Guests*, she thought too late. *Call them Guests, not skiffers.*

'So Adamo Wanderer had ta come an show us how ta do it,' said the teacher.

Ora couldn't understand his tone. Was he *criticising* the Founder?

'Adamo the Wanderer opened the trading route to the Outworld,' she said. 'He brought wealth and prosperity to Folavia.'

'Yay verily,' the teacher nodded. 'Look around ee, Lady Ora, at all the wealth and prosperity im brung us.'

Marginalised culturally, economically and linguistically, the indigenous residents are subject to colonial epistemologies that delimit their moral and ethical worth and are clearly inapplicable to their lived experience. As the teacher makes clear, Ora's assumed 'right' to cultural supremacy denotes a failure to question the benefits, and beneficiaries, of colonial rule. Ora's colonial enculturation thus delimits her interpretative capacity since such a right is predicated on an assumption that there can only be one 'history'. Like the monistic truths of normative ethical theorising, this singular history is accorded authenticity – by the Folavians alone – by a since mythologised Founder. Ora's subsequent apology 'not just to Tasman but to her mother, to Solqua-Darvid and to every other Guest in the Land', and her admission that 'there is nothing I can do to undo the wrongs of the past, but I can make things different in the future', is metonymic of her attempts to dismantle such an oppressive epistemic framework and to establish a more egalitarian relationship between ethnic groupings and the land (173; 209).[5]

A colonial myth of cartographic control in *Pretties* positions both nature and human nature as fluid and historicised according to changing epistemological frameworks. After undergoing her 'pretty' operation, Tally flees the city in a stolen hot air balloon and finds herself in the middle of a forest inhabited by a tribe of primitive peoples whose blood feud with the neighbouring tribes has instituted an unending cycle of murder and revenge. The readers' introduction to these primitive peoples plays on the historically discredited empirical prototype of a violent and animalistic native tribe (255; 257):

> There were flames moving through the trees, casting jittering shadows across the clearing, darting through the air like wild, burning insects. Shrieks rose up from every side, inhuman calls strung with meaningless words. ... The two hunters closed in on her...bearded men, their ugly faces marked with scars and sores.

Apparently lacking any form of moral code, the natives are not simply ugly, inhuman and disease-ridden but also have a 'meaningless' language lacking in structural or semantic integrity. Tally's interaction predicated on a hierarchy of natural worth, with the tribe is underpinned by the sense of superiority that Kate Soper (1995: 76) argues arose through colonial expansion: 'it is only as imperialism brings about a fuller and more direct contact with the mythologised "other" that a clearer distinction gets drawn between those who are indeed men (not marvels, monstrosities, or freaks of nature), but sub-human by comparison with civilised humanity'. The tribe's oppositional positioning sees its members interpreted by Tally as 'the natural state of the species'; such naturalness, couched in the language of biological essentialism, denotes the natural human *sub*-human and the *post*human ontologically human (280).

The tribe's disease-ridden 'ugliness' exactly mirrors the 'raw, cruel wilderness with its disease and violence and animal struggle for survival' (262). Such affinity with the natural world extends from the indigenous peoples' knowledge of the forest's layout, to their use of 'clicking sounds and birdlike chirps instead of words' to camouflage their presence within their ecological surroundings (263; 264). This affinity with nature is far from romantic: it merges both humans and non-humans in their 'naturally' crude, raw and savage states. In a chapter that puts special emphasis on bodily excretions – 'unfamiliar smells and sounds: sweat and morning breath' – the text envisages indigenous peoples as grotesquely uncivilised, and an embodied relationship with the natural world as one of unpleasant proximity (272). Such an interpretation is circumscribed by the colonial ideologies of cultural supremacy that accord Tally with epistemic privilege (292–3):

> Of course, it wasn't completely fair being upset with Andrew. Probably he couldn't understand Tally's aversion to casual murder. He'd grown up with the cycle of revenge. It was just part of his pre-Rusty life, like sleeping in piles or cutting down trees. He didn't see it as wrong any more than he could understand how utterly the latrine ditch revolted her.
>
> Tally was different from the villagers – at least that much had changed in the course of human history. Maybe there was hope after all.

Relieved to find that 'there was hope after all' in her own evolutionary supremacy, Tally thus places blame for the tribe's inferiority on its members' underdeveloped epistemic capabilities ('he couldn't understand'). Tally thus accepts her labelling as a 'god' by the tribe's leaders upon the understanding that her superiority is a product of her evolutionary capacity to *know better* (262).

The mythical contouring that defines Tally's knowledge of the tribal peoples is gleaned through the discovery of a series of electronic 'little men' hanging in the trees surrounding the village that draw 'an impassable border around the villagers' world' (298). The empirical attempts of the city guardians to analyse human nature – 'someone's pet anthropology project' – has left the tribe with a limited physical existence and an equally limited epistemic capacity couched in a language of patriarchal stewardship (298). Whilst the tribal holy man, Andrew Simpson Smith, creates his own mythic framework to explain the existence of the 'little men' – 'The stories say that the gods put these here, to mark the edge of oblivion' – Tally attributes such containment to the controlling ideologies of the city guardians: 'The world goes on for a whole lot farther…[t]his is just a trick to keep you from knowing it' (301). Colonial control thus functions as a 'trick' to facilitate practices of ideological manipulation. Tally's realisation that such control is designed to exclude alternative realities is accompanied by a cartographic allusion (298; 293):

> Tally remembered an old map on the library wall at her ugly school, the words "Here be Dragons" written in flowery letters in all the blank spots. Maybe this world's edge was nothing more than the borderline of the villager's mental map of the world – like their need for revenge, they simply couldn't see beyond it.

Having initially appropriated the epistemological superiority of the coloniser to extend power over the wild ecology and the indigenous inhabitants, Tally realises that this perceived superiority is in fact simply an indication of her own adherence to a myth of colonial supremacy: 'the barriers around Tally's pretty world weren't as obvious as the little men hanging in the trees, but they were just as hard to escape' (308–9). Tally thus reveals her own interpellation by a metanarrative of evolutionary advancement that is clearly in need of its own epistemic re-framing.

Women's 'ways of knowing': generational storytelling

In these novels, global processes are mapped onto the local landscape in a formulation that John Grim (2007: 204) terms a 'grid-like mapping for control of natural processes'. Ecofeminists, by contrast, take on 'responsibility for remapping boundaries and renegotiating connections' through the interrogation of normative epistemologies (Martin and Talpade Mohanty 1986: 193). Remapping the boundaries of epistemic frameworks involves rejecting imposed knowledge structures that preclude or delimit awareness of the earth's own agency. For Plumwood (2002: 230), an embedded relationship with the natural world can be articulated in 'the essentially narrative terms' of 'interpreting the land, of telling its story'. Narrative, Plumwood (2002: 230) contends, is not a form of dominance, as it is in cartographic discourse, but instead a form of 'dialogical interaction' between humans and the land where mapping over the contours of the earth gives way to 'telling its story'. Story, as an important vehicle for ethical engagement, is here perceived to open up a creative space for the negotiation of humanity's connection with the earth by way of emergent knowledge structures. In the novels discussed, stories function as counter-hegemonic narratives, foregrounding beliefs, ideas and understandings that challenge those of 'official' metanarratives and enabling what Holmes Rolston III (1988: 351) terms 'a storied residence' in nature. Generational storytelling here authenticates the experiences of 'feminised' peoples and spatialities marginalised through colonial circumscription by basing knowledge of the world on lived and embodied experience.

In *The Folk Keeper*, Corinna uses 'the stories of Cliffsend' – folk tales passed down through generations – to structure her expectations of Cliffsend and to underpin her dealings with the nonhuman Folk (5). A dialogic interpretative frame enables either a whimsical or critical reading of the mythic networks underpinning both Cliffsend's society and Corinna's own person; she notes that others might be 'fanciful' but assures the reader that she herself is not (8). Corinna's unreliable narration vacillates between denial of mythic truths and a critical interrogation of their meaning. Having 'always loved the stories of the Sealfolk', Corinna nevertheless questions '[w]hy…they ever shed their Sealskins to walk the land as humans' on the grounds that if their skin should be lost, they would never be able to return to the sea (29). Here, Corinna's critical interpretation of the narrative teleology of Selkie myths places Corinna in the same position as the readers whose own response to these beings of legend is thus carefully circumscribed by an already-existing epistemic framework. The text in fact assumes such epistemic pre-existence, and makes intertextual reference to mythic story shapes under the expectation that the readers will recognise their narrative teleology (106):

> 'It's the old story,' said Sir Edward. 'Your father out for a moon-light sail. Your mother dancing on the Seal Rock. He fell in love with her, stole her Sealskin, insisted she marry him, live on land. What could she do? Without her Sealskin she couldn't return to the sea. Perhaps you can guess the rest. Misery, jealousy, madness, and death.'

Here, Sir Edward accords Corinna with the responsibility to 'guess the rest'; her mother's degeneration is couched not simply in the ideologies of patriarchal conquest but also in the clipped vocabulary of empirical categorisation. Corinna's subsequent success at rewriting her own story – as delineated in my previous chapter – sees her challenge the masculine metanarrative that has defined and delimited her mother's own narrative. Corinna's success suggests that a feminine 'intertwining of selves and stories in narrative constructions' is essentially, and epistemologically, empowering (Walker 1989: 7).

Shædow Master uses generational storytelling as a similarly empowering mechanism by which to undermine Folavia's colonial rule. The Guests' legends and stories provide opposing, non-linear conceptions of the past that challenge the colonial history of the kingdom. In a country facing ecological devastation, the environmental knowledge taught in schools is juxtaposed with the Guests' explanation for natural phenomena. Colonial education has no mythic schema with which to interpret the irrational and non-scientific aspects of environmental behaviour; it claims that 'shædows were mysteries of Nature, like rainbows and flying stars; nobody knew what they were' (44). The Guests rather embrace the mystery inherent in the shædows' origins, believing them to be lake spirits controlled by the Shædow Master and integral to the health of the Land. Knowledge here gives way to belief and epistemologies of control are substituted for epistemologies of faith: 'It was totally preposterous, of course. Ora didn't believe a word of it, but part of her was drawn to the story' (45). Story provokes an emotional response in Ora, despite its logical flaws, via its capacity for empathetic engagement. The mysteriousness inherent in the Guests' mythic schema is knowingly retained rather than mapped over by the quantifiable facts of scientific empiricism.

Having never heard the story of her near-drowning in the lake, Ora deems her own personal history as mysterious as that of the kingdom itself, lending it a similarly mythic status. Ora's destiny – to become the Shædow Master – is revealed in a piecemeal acquisition of fragments of knowledge gleaned from her interaction with the indigenous population and her environmental surroundings. Ora's difficult journey to gain a sense of her past is posited as a necessary rite of passage predicated on a devaluation of the colonial myth in preference for an empathetic cross-cultural connection between indigenous peoples and the land. This connection is authenticated by the long history of the country's Guests and their ancient mythic framework, inaccessible to the colonial 'squatters' – the Folavians – with their imposed hegemonic values. Such a framework centres on the Guests' sacred trees which are 'unbelievably, impossibly huge'; these trees with their 'invisible branches' from which the indigenous population must avert their gaze are a quasi-mystical product of the Guests' mythologising and exist in impossible relation to the colonisers' totalising discourse (23).

Ora's growing faith in the values embodied in the Guests' mythic framework denotes lived experience and felt sensibilities, as opposed to verifiable truths and historical fact, as central to epistemic engagement. Her realisation that the establishment of a more egalitarian society combining indigenous and non-indigenous residents in mutual respect for the land is a task that only she, as Crown Princess, can achieve is tellingly acknowledged as a consequence of shared epistemologies: 'Captain Julio's words had become imprinted on Ora's brain. *You are our Crown Princess*, she kept hearing. *That knowledge belongs to everyone in the kingdom*' (167, italics in the original). Proprietary practices of knowledge acquisition are here evoked in service of a wider earth-based 'belonging'; the shared epistemologies of *'everyone in the kingdom'* are used to envisage a land shared equally between all peoples. Ora's use of such knowledge to offer equal epistemic privilege to both Folavians and Guests reanimates the Guests' ancient mythic framework. Ora thus appropriates knowledge not to perpetuate a damaging myth of colonial superiority but to construct an ethically responsible relationship between peoples and the earth that unites both cultural groupings in reverence for the Land.

Generational storytelling is similarly evoked in *The Forest of Hands & Teeth* to critique the mythic superstructures of the prevailing hegemony. Mary's mother's stories from before the Return compete with those propagated as official history by the matriarchal religious institution, the Sisterhood. Stories 'handed down by the women of our family' provide a vital connection between generations of women in a world in which knowledge of the world before the Return is made purposefully inaccessible (8). The religious mentality superimposed by the Sisterhood onto the villagers' older collective identity follows a formulation designed to sustain the collectivity. In a biblical allusion to Adam and Eve, Sister Tabitha interprets Mary's inquisitiveness – her willingness to critique the Sisterhood's imposed religious framework – as a manifestation of the same desire for knowledge that has led to the Return. Mary's inquisitiveness signals her belief in alternative, non-prescribed ways of knowing and her desire to access the world through embodied communion, rather than through the limited epistemic frameworks available under the Sisterhood's matriarchal rule.

Religion as enforced by the Sisterhood enacts an unnatural segregation between body and spirit, freedom and desire. Narrative, on the other hand, is integral to Mary's holistic sense of identity: stories are 'a part of me that I cannot lose' (21). Stories are able to access the 'essence' of life in a way that the Sisterhood's institutional religion, with its circumscription of knowledge, cannot (8). Mary's mother's stories, moreover, have the potential to counter religion's segregation of body and soul by positing the ocean – a nostalgic space from a time before the Return – as an embodied hope for mankind.

The ocean is a mythic space that – in Mary's dreams – physically cocoons her living body and instantiates a form of death and subsequent rebirth to counter that of the Sisterhood's failed Christian alternative: 'Every night I drown and every morning I wake up struggling to breathe' (146). The ocean to which her subconscious draws her signals Mary's ability to construct a new world according to a mythic framework of spiritual renewal. The ocean becomes Mary's religion, and storytelling becomes a form of prayer: '"Pray for me, Mary,"' says Travis, '"Tell me the one about the ocean"' (54). Story-prayer enables an engagement with the world predicated on 'the things I know to be true only because of faith'; story is Mary's salvation, the crux of her desire, with her steadily increasing faith in the ocean far surpassing her belief in God (42). The passing down of stories from generation to generation mirrors the passing on of infection from body to body, yet this time re-envisioning and enabling life rather than cutting it short. Storytelling in fact enables a form of immortality that is infinitely preferable to the unending half-lives of the Unconsecrated (207):

> 'Who are we if not the stories we pass down? What happens when there's no one left to tell those stories? To hear them? Who will ever know that I existed? What if we are the only ones left – who will know our stories then? And what will happen to everyone else's stories? Who will remember those?'

Mary's fear that there will be 'no one left to tell those stories' renders narrative a transformative medium capable of giving shape to memory, agency and identity. Human identity is discursively and intersubjectively constituted ('[w]ho are we if not the stories we pass down?') such that the death of narrative enacts the death of the agential human subject. Story is located at the cognitive intersection between 'telling', 'hearing' and 'remembering'; these interlocking discourses actively produce knowledge: to 'know our stories' is to 'know that I existed'. Underlying the communication sequence is perhaps the best known utterance of Jacques Derrida: 'there is nothing outside the text' (*il n'ya pas de hors-texte*). If, in the most widely accepted understanding of this utterance, context and text are inseparable, then the disappearance of context may entail the disappearance of the text (in this case, the subject) itself; or, under an alternative formulation, if reality can only be experienced through language, then the loss of language entails the disappearance of the self. The progression in Mary's questioning from 'we' to 'I' to 'everyone else' – a move from community, to specific subject, to all humanity – affirms the centrality of story to human identity. In other words, a culture cannot exist without the narratives produced by the dialogue of social and individual discourses: the very contexts of being.

At the end of the novel, when Mary finally reaches the ocean, she enacts a 'fall', a death followed by rebirth. In the mythic space of the ocean, this fall promises redemption rather than downfall: 'I allow the water to cradle me…[to] push and pull me, lift me, hold me as I fall' (306). *The Forest of Hands & Teeth* thus poses two challenges to the Christian teleology of death and rebirth in heaven. The first resides in the Unconsecrated, whose diseased resurrection is experienced not as fulfilment but as a constant unrelenting hunger. The second inheres in a more transformative challenge to the Christian teleology: story. Stories *can* be cathartic and *can* have a resolution, one that promises not simply an end, but also a new beginning. Just as Mary's namesake gave birth to Jesus, a new hope for mankind, Mary uses the ocean as her 'cradle', carrying hope for a new life, and a new story, arisen – phoenix-like – out of 'the ashes of the Return' (64).

Alternative knowledges: creating a new myth of origin

Myths of rebirth, dream narratives, oral histories and ritual cycles are often employed by ecofeminists to envisage the ecological 're-mything' of space following a trajectory – often deemed pagan or indigenous – of ecological growth or emergence (Legler 1997: 230). Much critical attention has been paid to the portrayal of indigenous peoples and their knowledge structures in political rhetoric, the arts and the media, and critiques of essentialist notions of indigeneity have much in common with those directed towards early ecofeminist portrayals of the undifferentiated experiences of a universal 'women'. It is difficult, if not impossible, not to fall into the trap of displacing a western system of values onto the indigenous other or imagining native peoples to have a voice that is not constrained, and contained, by the dominant ideology. The overwriting of the 'the actual complexity of difference' in the 'authentic' voice of the aboriginal is something Gareth Griffiths labels 'an act of "liberal" discursive violence' (Griffiths [1994] quoted in Ashcroft *et al*. 2006: 165; 166). The importance of recognising that essentialist discourses fail to account for the vast diversity within indigenous beliefs, practices and human-nonhuman relationships experienced throughout history and today should result in qualified engagement with notions of indigeneity and preference for localised understandings of indigenous knowledge structures. Despite the dangers of essentialist readings, indigenous peoples are held up by ecofeminists as useful models for ecological embeddedness through their perceived capacity to promote embodied and storied connections to the land and, as such, helpfully enhance ecofeminist calls for sustainable engagement with place.

In young adult novels, indigenous knowledge structures are frequently adopted as counter-hegemonic alternatives capable of denaturalising colonial epistemologies or totalising discourses. *Zenith*, for instance, invokes the indigenous cultural values found within native creation myths to authenticate Mara's quest to find a new home in Greenland. My understanding of indigenous cultural values follows the working definition proposed by David Groenfeldt (2003: 919) as 'the guiding principles of a social group' that serve to 'shape the substance of thoughts and feelings, not deterministically, but through mediating between collective institutions and individual behaviour'. Such collective mythmaking offers Mara an opportunity to reject the totalising colonial discourses exploited by the New World and to instantiate an alternative epistemic framework predicated on the ecoconscious belief systems of the marginalised Treenesters. Her decision to direct the refugees northward towards the quasi-mythic space of Greenland is itself a consequence of narrative engagement. In *Exodus*, Mara gleans knowledge of Greenland's existence from the unfinished lines of a narrative fragment (154):

> *The Athapaskans*, she reads, *are a mobile people who inhabit the huge, mountainous boreal forests of the Arctic Circle, one of the emptiest, most forgotten places on Earth. They have not devastated the natural world around them as so-called civilised societies have, but have co-existed in fine balance with the land and its animals for thousands of…*

Mara's attempt to replicate the success of Athapaskan society by similarly constructing a society that can co-exist 'in fine balance with the land and its animals' is predicated on a dual set of beliefs: that narrative is capable of laying the foundation for action, and that the past is capable of laying the epistemological groundwork for future well-being.

The mythic framework that underpins Mara's journey northwards interrogates the notion of *terra nullius* whilst re-envisaging the traditional earth mother framework that is evoked in much pagan mythmaking. Bradford *et al.* (2008: 60–1) have critiqued Bertagna's portrayal of Greenland as an empty space in its recapitulation of 'the narrative directions of the many colonial texts in which the ancestral territory of indigenous people is assumed to be there for the taking'. Such critique is borne out in the representation of Greenland's native population in a double act of erasure that sees the Kalaallit Inuits not simply gone from the land but replaced by violent scavenging peoples. Bertagna's portrayal of Greenland as an *ecological* space, however, can be read productively as the focus for a semi-mythic settlement story unfolded though the 'contouring' of natural space with new meaning. An increasingly mythic and folkloric discourse is used to invest Greenland's natural spaces with the potential for belonging. Greenland in fact *is* a *terra nullius*, but one on which to let counter-hegemonic beliefs and practices emerge in place of the neoliberal values imposed on the New World sky cities. In its association with the sanctity of mythic authenticity, Greenland becomes the antidote to the first world's globalised economy with its capitalist ethos of disposable consumerism and its perpetuation of a continuous present; mythic discourse, interplayed with Christian and pagan narratives, evokes a new ecologically-inflected new world order and instils Mara's settlement with the authority of tradition.

All 'founding myths', contends Dinerstein (2006: 578), 'partake in religious concepts: they posit a story of origin, explain a people's right to a given geography, and grant a transcendent reason for that existence'. In order to create an epistemic framework for belief, the Treenester, Gorbals, mythologises the past in imitation of indigenous creation stories (258–9):

'Once upon a time, before the world's drowning, people lived in cities that covered the lands of the Earth. ... At night, the lights of the buildings and cars and buses and trains and planes sparkled like stars. But the sky grew dull with the dust and dirt from the city. Soon, it grew jealous of the city's sparkling lights. So the sky cried out to its mother sun and brother wind and sister ocean and asked them to brew up a storm of weather to punish the people of the world who had stolen its glory. And so they did'.

This mythical rendition of humanity's destruction of the natural environment posits 'mother sun', 'brother wind' and 'sister ocean' as subjective agents, responsible for punitive retribution against humanity. Gorbals' adoption of an ecophobic rhetoric, despite its failure to establish a mutually-agential relationship between humans and the earth, serves to foreground the moral urgency of environmental re-appraisal. The tale constitutes a positive rejoinder to Plumwood's (2006: 120–1) critique of the continuously retold 'land creation story' which 'follows the standard western pattern of human agency acting on a passive land'. Contemplating the story in awed silence, the refugees interpret such an existential framing story as 'a message from the past' (259). As Mara realises, it provides a powerful story to inspire change, despite its factual inaccuracies; in a world with no past in which epistemic communities have failed to learn from the lessons of history, this story will 'have to do for now' (259).

Mara's decree that the refugees remember Gorbals' story as they journey on to found a new settlement, renders the fight of the natural world against human pollutants a myth of origin upon which to base a new social order. Jonas Wellendorf (2010: 3) argues that:

> A traditional myth of origin will tell us how a particular group wishes to conceptualise its own genesis, and in this sense the interpretation of the past that is presented forms an important part of the present identity of that group. It might seek its content from the past, but the message and the values transmitted are those of the present.

The values inherent in Mara's myth of origin are overtly ecological ones, and function as 'signifiers', or 'tangible embodiments of shared values and ideas' (Layton 1994: 11). In a world with a drowned past, Greenland functions as a space onto which Mara must impress the history of the earth's destruction if its lessons are to remain tangible. As Garrison suggests, 'the past is what all people build their present and future on; without this they sit in a void waiting to reclaim their history, suspended in a bottomless pit' (quoted in Layton 1994: 21). This metaphoric void or pit recalls the abyss over which Nietzsche claims man forms the rope – a quotation with which Bertagna prefaces Mara's journey northwards. A void, pit or abyss: Greenland is discursively constructed as an epistemic blind space. Mara's use of Gorbals' story to impress a sense of the past onto this formless space functions as *mise-en-abyme* and throws meaning, like Nietzsche's rope, into the abyss in order to provide an alternative epistemic framing story for human existence.[6]

The intertextual allusions that inform a reading of Mara's journey to Greenland are numerous and serve to frame Mara's quest as a quasi-mystical myth of settlement.[7] These allusions invest Mara's journey with inherited cultural values, placing particular emphasis on oral storytelling and the importance of the collective memory in the formulation of intersubjective relations between humans and the natural world. Such a mythic register reacts against the historical specifics of globalisation, capitalism and climate change – so sharply in focus in *Exodus* – to place value instead on the universal endeavour of communities throughout history to negotiate their connection to the earth through story. Gorbals' expectations for the new land are couched in the language of an indigenous dream narrative (97):

> 'The sun was low and orange over the sea. The wind had a voice full of secrets. We had lived in this land more than ten thousand days. … It was a good place to live and it had a good name. We called our land Mara.'

Although the dream can be read as reproducing colonialist discourse, particularly in the use of 'Mara' for the new land's name, it is more helpful to read it as a myth of settlement that invests the natural world with subjective agency (the wind with its 'voice full of secrets'). Whilst Mara's greatest critic – a refugee whose name, Ruby, ties her to the New World of hedonistic consumerism – dismisses the dream as far-fetched, her voice is quickly silenced by the elderly Merlen who declares 'there's often hidden treasure tucked away in the corners of a fairy tale' (97). An oral tradition of storytelling is validated as a means of negotiating the past and imagining the future. The 'secrets' that the wind keeps are, under this formulation, indicative of the earth-based knowledge the refugees will need to acquire if they are to create an ecoconscious community.

Upon the refugees' eventual arrival on Greenland's shores, Greenland is found to be a cruel overseer of unrelenting hardship, subjecting the refugees to endless darkness, freezing temperatures and biting winds. This cold, icy and frigid entity resembles the 'cold mother figure' identified by Naomi Wood (2004: 199) in 'the discourse of the North', as a trope first inspired by Hans Christian Andersen's seductive Snow Queen (202). Huddling within a cave deep in the earth to avoid the raging winter storms, Mara imagines that an ice splinter lodges in her heart, a line that echoes Kay's fate in the *Snow Queen* at the moment when the wicked sprite's distorting mirror falls to earth and shatters in a million pieces. If the Snow Queen's distorting mirror signals an entirely self-absorbed apprehension of self and world, Bertagna's allusion to this mirror serves to posit the apocalyptic state of the planet as a grotesquely distorted mirror image of our current world. Greenland's portrayal as a disciplinary parent, demanding humility, self-denial, sacrifice and obedience from its tempestuous children – the humans responsible for the planet's destruction – serves to demand planetary reconciliation as a necessary first step towards environmental redemption. This spiritually-inflected ecological trajectory locates redemption at the intersection between two competing feminine discourses: that of the icy mother and nurturing Mother Earth. These dialogic feminine images inhere in a gendered renegotiation of spatial parameters; finding a new home is equivalent to discovering the earth's story.

Redemption, tellingly, reaffirms story as a value-laden act of giving and receiving, carving out a space for negotiation between humans and the natural world. Mara tells one of the refugees that in the netherworld she 'learned to read what was left of the world'; interpreting the signs left behind by the last vestiges of a natural ecology, Mara weaves a dialogue between the needs of the human refugees and the demands of the harsh northern clime (81). Through pagan myths of regeneration and renewal, the land of the north is gradually configured as a space of growth and rebirth, holding forth the promise of spiritual redemption and embody-ing the potential for shelter, safety, community and belonging. Mara and the refugees undergo a metaphorical re-birth in the natural space of the Greenland interior after a winter spent 'entombed' in caves deep within the earth (213). The quasi-mystical legend of the 'stone-telling' that has foreseen Mara's role in the rescue of the Treenesters has prefig-ured the need for this metaphorical resurrection since Mara had been prophesied to lead the Treenesters out of a 'deathly underworld' to find their true home (Bertagna 2003: 116).[8] If the world's cataclysmic floods have meant the death of the old world, Mara's period entombed in the earth has a similar cleansing and purifying function: a hibernation period that enables the subsequent establishment of a new social order that enacts positive intersubjective relations between humans and their environment.

With the coming of spring, the nurturing figure of Mother Nature thus replaces that of the icy mother. Mara herself becomes an embodiment of this fertile earth mother since, having conceived a baby in her time spent with Fox in the sky city of New Mungo, her gradually swelling belly prefigures the longed-for signs of the coming spring. In spontaneous adherence to oft-cited indigenous values, Mara and the refugees 'root themselves to the Earth' in a small forest beside a lake (323). Mara's baby is described as a 'tiny miracle...amid the bones and the primeval dark of the Earth': a phoenix rising from the ashes of the old world, or a seed finally planted in soil and ready to grow (233–4). Thus the initially empty land of Greenland – the epistemic blind space at the top of the world – becomes contoured with biblical narratives of exodus and quest, metanarratives of submission to parental discipline and classical and pagan myths of death and rebirth. These story shapes are not imposed on the land but rather emerge as an interlinking web of mythic values that resembles the 'interconnected web of life' of a healthy ecosystem (Orenstein 1993: 172). Such a web heralds Mara and the refugees' founding of their new settlement, a settlement with equally mythic narrative implications based on positive acknowledgement of the needs of the natural world. If the surviving climate change refugees, clinging to life in a flooded world, are to take Gorbals' story of the world's drowning as a myth of origin for a new social order, Bertagna encourages the young adult readers of her novels to take Mara's story as indicative of the same.

Conclusion: ecofeminist epistemologies and 'responsible truths'

Cultural mythologies, Jim Cheney (1989: 129) contends, can function to 'locate us in a moral space'. If myths are predicated on 'responsible truths', they can paint portraits of the world that 'ring[] true for everybody's well-being' (Cheney 2005: 112).[9] Unlike the verifiable truths of scientific fact, these responsible truths couch knowledge 'in terms of the empowerment that comes with understanding' (Cheney 2005: 112). Since scientific discourses claim universality and impartiality, amounting to what Cheney (1989: 132) refutes as 'the wrong kind of myth', we would do better, he suggests, to understand knowledge as a notion that in fact 'does not require truth' (2005: 115). Within these novels, truths that arise from a 'storied residence' in nature are heralded as epistemologically responsible (Rolston III 1988: 351). Such a storied residence can be further clarified through Margaret Walker's (1989: 16) understanding of 'the location of human beings' feelings, psychological states, needs, and understandings as nodes of a story (or of the intersection of stories) that has already begun, and will continue beyond a given juncture of moral urgency'. Walker's evocation of 'moral urgency' calls attention to the importance of epistemological reappraisal in light of environmental crisis, and the ways in which such storied thinking can negotiate a more responsible engagement with the earth.

Cheney's delineation of responsible truths requires some further delineation in relation to post-disaster fiction for young adults, and can be better understood with respect to Lorraine Code's (1987) theory of 'epistemic responsibility'. Code's (1987: 150–1) responsibilist epistemology directs attention towards knowers rather than knowledge per se, since knowers always know contextually – their knowledge is shaped by the situation, time and place of its knowing – with the result that there can be no isolated epistemologies since all knowers originate and/or function within larger communities.[10] In line with the notion of knowledge as unfolding story, contextual knowledge is best communicated through narrative, particularly when the knower lacks access to the language and theory of dominating parties. The emotions are central to epistemic theory and practice and integral to narrative engagement with the world. Understanding is a key goal of epistemological engagement and is a complex systemic process leading towards a holistic apprehension of the subject. The significance of Code's theory of epistemic responsibility to a feminist environmental ethic is foregrounded by Douglas Buege (1992: 73) who notes its capacity to highlight 'both the importance of human responsibility to the natural and the nature of particular human beings as knowers'. Responsible truths, then, are those that envision epistemic engagement in narrative terms and story as a communicative act of community engagement empowered by the collective. They are not an automatic prerequisite of epistemic engagement but inhere in the contextual positioning of myth in relation to the ethical actant. Like indigenous ways of knowing passed down through generations, responsible truths can advocate an ethically responsible life on earth.

When environmental meaning in young adult fiction is predicated on this notion of epistemically responsible truths, it can counter human–earth dislocation by foregrounding the protagonists' capacity to resist global abstraction and to become grounded in embodied understandings of the local landscape. In *Zenith*, the responsible truths gleaned from mythic interaction with the natural space instil in the young Wing and Lily the desire to 'sneak off into the mountains to track the voice of the Earth' (339). A counter-hegemonic act against authority ('sneak off'), this desire to *know* the voice of the earth renders the earth capable of telling its own story. A space is therefore opened up for the earth's own voice at the intersection between the various indigenous, pagan and literary discourses used to contour Greenland's mythic interior. The discursive scope of the blind space of the post-apocalyptic earth inheres in this potential to engender narratives of human belonging that are epistemologically responsible. 'Just as "responsible" holds within it a sense of one's response as something deeply felt, unconscious, and gratuitous', argues John Grim (2007: 203), 'so also it suggests a more conscious ability to act'. The situated knowledges communicated through myth ensure that readers are well placed to take responsibility for their interaction with the land. In the transference of epistemic privilege to those occupying the position of the 'feminine', the readers are called upon to draw meaning from the blind space and therein answer Buege's (1992: 75) call to become 'environmentally epistemologically responsible'.

5
A Poetics of Earth: Ecofeminist Spiritualities

Ecofeminist spiritualities seek to provide restorative responses to disembodiment and dislocation in human–earth relationships. They engage the alternative ethical and epistemological frameworks delineated in previous chapters to foreground both the values of care and reciprocity traditionally underplayed within neoliberal ideologies and global corporate practices, and the women's 'ways of knowing' traditionally marginalised in normative epistemic engagement. The alternative visions of ecofeminist theologies and spiritualities inhere in practices that seek to transform humanity's emotional and spiritual engagement with place. The novels discussed engage these alternative spiritualities in negotiating their protagonists' interaction with the world within – and in opposition to – the socio-political systems that secularise human–nonhuman relations. The novels seek to create an ecopoetics of embodiment and embeddedness within nature by evoking various competing spiritual paradigms. Like the epistemic frameworks analysed in my previous chapter, these formulations are more, or less, likely to engender ecoconsciousness in their young readers. Those less likely employ discourses of spiritual transcendence in place of ecological immanence, or base interaction with the earth on the instrumental use-value of the land rather than on its intrinsic value. Those more likely, by contrast, envision intimate and empathetic interaction between humans and the earth, often through allusion to indigenous notions of holistic ecological sanctity.

Apocalypse is semantically embedded in discourses of religious existentialism. As defined by Mark Levine (2010: 59), 'apocalyptic' in the western imagination 'has primarily come to be associated with a catastrophic end, or near-end, of either human society or human life, through the intervention of natural or divine beings or events'. Unlike its religious antecedent in Judaeo-Christian and Gnostic philosophy, in which such an 'end' was thought to prefigure spiritual revelation and redemption through natural disaster, apocalypse in its more recent 'Hollywood' form has become associated with a 'dominant heroic-technological mode' in which an elite few are saved from mass extinction usually through the scientific prowess and technological know-how of this select group (Levine 2010: 60). The semantic implications of apocalypse have therefore undergone a substantial shift in emphasis: from the redemption of the many to the survival of the few. In the process, the religious sense of apocalypse as revelatory of a higher purpose for humanity or meaning for human existence has been replaced by an essentially meaningless secular apocalypse as cause for individual and solipsistic acts of bravery, daring or intelligence, under a formulation that Greg Garrard (2004: 93) terms a 'blank apocalypse: an eschaton without a utopia to follow'.

In this movement from redemption to survival, apocalypse as punishment for human hubris – where humanity has challenged God's supremacy – contrasts markedly with apocalypse as encouragement of human hubris: the conviction that superior technological innovation will counter crisis or disaster. This movement from faith in God's ultimate justice and wisdom to faith in 'the false prophets of the top-down, technical fix', as Levine (2010: 61) wryly puts it, accords contemporary secular apocalypse the notion that humanity is both the cause of, and the solution to, ecological crisis. Technological progress, according to Dinerstein (2006: 591), amounts to 'a quasi-religious myth' invoked by 'a desacralised industrial civilisation' as a stand against cultural stagnation. The 'fusion of progress, technology, and religion' that he contends underpins the west's conversion of faiths from the divine to the mechanical, has seen progress secularise the idea of Christian redemption 'by inventing (and instantiating) a near-sacred temporal zone – the future – to contain its man-made utopian dreams' (2006: 572). Varying responses to the natural world at a time of environmental crisis thus see the imbrication of technological and spiritual ideologies to situate scientific progress within a secular utopian space, sustained by an ethos of human advancement.

In ecocritical engagement with spirituality, romanticism has often been used to evoke the Christian tradition of spiritual transcendence within – and through – the more sublime and transcendent aspects of the natural world. An overtly spiritual mode of narrative engagement with place, romanticism has nevertheless had an uneasy association with masculinist discourses of individual natural communion, something Code (1999: 64) terms the 'hyper-masculinity' of the '"return to nature"' metanarrative in which the natural world is 'a place for male self-discovery'. It is worth noting that these criticisms have also been directed towards the 'masculinist' tendency of first wave ecocriticism in which a largely male group of literary scholars lauded the nurturance of a special connection with the natural world through use of a canon of largely male nature writers. Feminist ecocriticism has arisen partly in response to this initial masculine bias within ecocriticism. Early, or first wave, ecofeminists have been critiqued, however, for their insistence on spirituality as a medium for serious ecological engagement. Liberal feminists, amongst others, have rejected ecofeminist goddess-worship and other embodied spiritualities as a- or anti-theoretical, arguing that they are reliant on an essentialist connection between women and nature that yokes the female body to the earth in a formulation that has lead – throughout history – to the systemic exploitation and oppression of women under western patriarchy. Note that this is a criticism similarly directed towards ecofeminism *per se*. I do not enter into this debate other than to suggest that ecofeminist spiritualities – regardless of their biological or essentialist roots – are useful to ecofeminist theorising for their capacity to provide 'alternative images' to those offered by ideologies of neoliberal individualism (Diamond and Kupp.ler 1990: 160). Whilst a plethora of alternative discourses pertaining to ecofeminist spiritualities such as that of Goddess worship, Wicca and Paganism have also been evoked as a means towards feminine empowerment, particularly in the first wave of ecofeminist theorising, I here limit my focus to a textual engagement with those earth-based beliefs that invest sanctity in the land in localised ways.

If romanticism set the benchmark in the past, today globalisation is rapidly changing the terrain of spiritual engagement with place, through processes that are similarly gendered. Carla Freeman (2001: 1007–8) points to 'the implicit, but powerful, dichotomous model in which the gender of globalisation is mapped in such a way that global: masculine as local: feminine'. Acknowledgement of the gendered underpinnings of the global–local binary informs Susan Robert's (2004: 132) contention that we must remain open to the ways in which the construction and projection of gender difference – alongside that of race, class and age – 'mediates how people experience the global and their own subjectivities'. The intersectional effects of globalisation across local and global scales can be analysed from an ecofeminist perspective by addressing the material ways in which global processes play themselves out at the local level. The 'analytical contour lines' employed by Cindi Katz (2001: 1229) to analyse the uneven geographies of globalisation can in this sense helpfully produce a 'critical topography' that makes it possible to 'excavate layers of process that produce particular places and to see their intersections with material social practice at other scales of analysis' (1228). A critical topography of the landscapes of apocalypse in young adult fiction can address the ways in which the social practices pertaining to globalisation, including the marginalisation of 'feminine' spatialities and indigenous native lands under neoliberal frameworks, are written onto the local landscape.

The novels discussed reveal recognisable, albeit sometimes limited, attempts to acknowledge the sacred in the more-than-human world according to a poetics of place designed to engender awareness, empathy and respect in young adult readers on behalf of an endangered ecology. Various spiritual positions are offered by the novels in resistance to the dislocation and disembodiment perceived to result from neoliberal progress, including sublime awe, romantic intimacy, bioregional place-situatedness and holistic embeddedness. Ashcroft *et al.* (2006: 518; 517) situate this renewal of the sacred in contemporary epistemic engagement within 'a broader rethinking of postcolonial identity':

> From the Enlightenment onwards...there has been a tendency in Euro-American thought to assume that the secular has replaced the sacral as the obvious and unchallengeable mode by which the world is best interpreted. ... It is not surprising, therefore, that resistance to these forces should have taken the form of a renewed sense of the sacral as offering an alternative to European modes of thought.

To counter the secular ethos of progress and the disembodied formulation for spiritual transcendence characteristic of such traditional modes of thought, the novels reinvest value in the local and bioregional yet exhibit tension over the difficulties of formulating a bioregional identity when confronted with the pressures of an expanding global society.

My reading centres on the dialogic relationship often invoked by the novels between intimate moments of human–earth bonding and sublime renderings of earth-inspired awe. By re-inscribing romantic values into the natural landscape, the novels attempt to sanctify humanity's relationship with the land as a space in which to invest intrinsic, rather than instrumental, value. I note the often contentious juxtaposition of these romantic values with those of traditional religious practices, and trace the beginnings of an alternative movement towards a more holistic conception of environmental sanctity modelled on indigenous spiritual practices. In what follows I use ecofeminist spiritualities as a lens through which to examine current formulations of environmental meaning and take Warren's (2000: 195) claim that ecofeminist spiritualities have the potential 'to intervene in and creatively change patriarchal (and other) systems of oppression' as generally representative of the counter-hegemonic function of spiritual contemplation and practice within the novels here discussed.

Sacred spaces: the power of new naming

Towards the end of the nineteenth century, western environmentalist conceptions of the sacred began to single out designated natural spaces for reverence (heritage sites, national parks, conservation areas and so on) and to secularise all remaining space for human dwelling (Hughes and Swan 1986). This segregation of space constitutes a significant departure from the European Romantic philosophies of place that authenticated immanental experiences of dwelling within the natural world. According to Harmon (1987: 149), the 'national park idea' is the quintessential manifestation of spatial delineation: an idea that has evolved 'into a shorthand for the belief that there are certain places inherently worth being preserved, places apart from run-of-the-mill locales, places special enough to have the capacity to fix themselves on the public consciousness to the degree that they become part of an amorphous "national heritage"'. By interpreting such a 'special' nature as ideally unaffected by, and disengaged from, human activity – whether to raise it up as a sublime and sacred manifestation of all that human society lacks, or in a more practical effort to conserve and protect nonhuman ecosystems – western environmentalism has arguably failed to envisage the human subject as already ecologically embedded. Anthropocentric boundary marking under the auspices of a culturally-inscribed hierarchy of natural worth results in humanity's further dislocation from earth-embeddedness. Within western societies that define national heritage through a lens of instrumentalism and aestheticism, ecological protection – regardless of its good intentions – becomes, as Keith Garratt (1984: 66) notes, an 'entirely...human cultural concept'.

In *Savannah 2116 AD*, the aesthetic politics that underwrite Savannah's interaction with the Wilderness formulate the natural world as a space of spiritual transcendence in which the peace of nature is so tangible that it 'reache[s] out to her through the wire, calming her' (52). Having been forbidden throughout her life from forming an embedded and embodied connection with the Wilderness, Savannah raises the wildlife reserve to Edenic levels: an originary landscape of 'first majesty' that she would 'give anything' to experience (26; 56). Savannah's longing for spiritual and emotional fulfilment sees her challenge the Cons' iron-clad rule and instantiate alternative parameters for spiritual transcendence. In a system that demands the sacrifice of 'humanity' on the Altar of Green, Savannah's escape into the Wilderness with D-nineteen and P-six is an ostensibly utopian refutation of religious fundamentalism. Despite the text's instantiation of a new spiritual framework predicated on appreciation of the beauty of the natural world, an older metanarrative of religious transcendence subsumes the ecoconscious trajectory of the text. Whilst Savannah, as narrative focaliser, imbues the natural world with beauty and freedom and joy, the text problematises her will towards ecological embeddedness by enacting the trio's metaphorical distancing from nature. If spiritual transformation is meant to engender a more egalitarian social system in which humans (unsegregated by class or race) can live side by side with the African wildlife, it conversely serves to widen the divide by instantiating a discourse of propriety and estrangement. Thus, whilst the novel purportedly communicates the sanctity of the natural landscape and the importance of human-nonhuman interrelations predicated on mutual reverence and respect, a reading against the grain reveals this trajectory to be inconsistent with the novel's implicit religious framework.

The rurals' liberating bid for freedom towards the end of the novel is positioned as engendering a newly-envisaged relationship between humans and nonhumans whereby both exist in physical symbiosis. This instantiation of cohabitationary harmony sees 'wilderness and Eden...collapsed into one and the same' in a somewhat clichéd amalgamation of utopian and Judaeo-Christian paradigms (Cloete 2009: 54). Savannah's earlier contemplation of the Wilderness – a nostalgic 'lament for Eden' to borrow a phrase coined by Mike Hulme (2010: 41) – here takes on renewed significance (88):

> She sat on the grassy slope beside D-nineteen. In front of them the giant lake rippled in a light breeze. Across on the far shore, animals had come down to take their early evening drink: impala and springbok, a few kudu, even a trio of giraffes who spread their legs awkwardly and swung their long necks down to the clear water. Beyond the lake, the sun was setting in a wide, open sky. It washed the clouds in a dusky haze of purples and pinks while the same colours rippled across the lake in answer.
>
> Paradise!

With a 'light breeze', 'clear' water and a 'wide, open' sky, Wilderness/ Paradise is subject to a discourse of spiritual transcendence: an ethereal place spatially removed from day-to-day existence: 'on the far shore'. The Homosaps' entry into this space is couched in the language of a religious dream narrative or spiritual vision, interpreted by a hazy D-Nineteen as a 'pre-death experience' (140). In this brave new world, Savannah – the lone preacher of beauty and faith – is accorded the responsibility to 'show [D-nineteen] the way, just as she had shown him the way through the Wilderness' (138). This biblical allusion serves to accord Savannah the potential to rise above natural restraints through the steadfast nature of her faith. In this biblical authentication of spiritual experience, faith has the power 'to filter into [D-nineteen's] very being, deeper than any words could reach' (136).

Having climbed up the steep slopes of the Freedom Range, D-nineteen wakes to a 'morning he was never meant to see' and a future 'stretching ahead as vast and mist-shrouded as the Wilderness' (138). Awed to find that now he has an unimpeded future, D-nineteen invests this unexpected fresh start with religious significance: an environmental resurrection haloed by 'the silvery mist of first light' (138). In allowing himself 'the joy of a little faith in tomorrow', the tomorrow of which D-nineteen dreams is a heavenly one: a post-death paradise in a natural setting in which he can lie beside Savannah each night, 'her skin warm and sweet-smelling against his' (137; 138). Such a heavenly vision conflates human and nonhuman categories; Savannah's 'sweet-smelling' skin is discursively linked to the 'sweet-smelling' air of dawn (138). Having climbed the Freedom Range slopes with D-Nineteen, Savannah becomes akin to a spiritual guru as she gazes over the ant-like rurals who rush upon the mountain and tells D-nineteen that '[i]t's my people down there' (141). Ensuring P-six that these rurals will bring food, as if in sacrificial offering after the trio's own fasting, Savannah positions 'her people' as ministering angels, flocking to 'help us survive here in the Wilderness' (141). Hand in hand, Savannah and D-nineteen stand, god-like, above the rural masses, in a spiritually-inflected new world order viewed from lofty heights.

In the new dawn of Savannah's spiritual awakening, D-nineteen allocates to her the power and importance of 'naming' (141):

> "And my name, Savannah?" said D-nineteen. "I need a proper name, not one that is just a countdown to death."
>
> "Adam," she said, without hesitation. "Adam – the first man in a wonderful new world." D-nineteen nodded, holding her close.

"Me too!" demanded P-six. "I want a new name too. I want to be called Thunderstorm. Or maybe Terminator, like in that video. Or maybe Earthquake. That's a good name, Earthquake…"

Savannah laughed. "You can have any name you want. Any name at all."

If the text here attempts to communicate Savannah's empowerment through a discourse of female naming, it does so more successfully through Savannah's disinclination to name P-six than through her *re*-naming of D-nineteen. Since naming, is – as Alaimo (1998: 131) argues – 'a proprietary act that both distances and circumscribes that which is named', it is problematic that the name Savannah chooses for D-nineteen is Adam, the man who first 'named' the earth and its creatures. Savannah's unhesitating likening of D-nineteen to Adam from her grandmother's bible configures D-nineteen as capable of imposing a name and shape on the Edenic landscape. In a nostalgic re-inscription of a time when 'everything was still right with the world', Savannah alludes to Adam standing 'with the newly created creatures crouched about him and the deep green of Eden behind him…with his face lifted to the Eden sunrise and his dark hand resting on a lion's mane' (22; 21; 57). D-nineteen/Adam is here positioned as the transcendent overlord of all creation, in the foreground of the image and physically displaced from the natural world over which he has a God-given right of dominion. In the space of the Wilderness in which old hierarchies are to be overthrown, this regressive biblical image serves to envision the future as problematically predicated on human sovereignty over feminised peoples and spatialities, including Savannah, whose name ties her to the earth. In a society in which mothers are labelled 'fat breeding machines', Mother Earth – one might assume – will similarly become subject to such interlocking discourses of ecophobic control and transcendence (48).

The potentially dystopian consequences of the Homosaps' reclaiming of the Wilderness are acknowledged when the Rurals – far from being the ministering angels of spiritual revelation – ascend the slopes of the Freedom Range brandishing spades and hoes and leaving 'an orgy of destruction' behind them (140). Savannah's earlier musings – 'to keep the chill silence and emptiness at bay' – are surely designed to be read as prophetic (137):

'They used to talk about this in the Rurals, about breaking through the fence and heading for the Freedom Range and hiding up in the caves. Thaba and his friends had such plans: they would slaughter all the game for meat and skins; they would chop down trees to build houses and make fires; they would burn the bush down to its root to make way for planting. But my aunt's friend, Mrs Vosloo, used to warn them. "That's how it all started last time round!" That's what she used to say.'

Mrs Vosloo's lone voice – we imagine – will go unheard in the 'silence and emptiness' of a newly envisaged human–earth dynamic rendering the Wilderness a human dwelling place. If Savannah's appreciation for the beauty of the Wilderness constitutes a limited attempt to sanctify the natural world, the matter of whether or not the earth will again become 'crusted over with concrete' in a desacralisation of natural worth is quietly bypassed (15). Just as D-nineteen's kiss can make Savannah's voice fade into silence, a transcendent religious framework seems likely to undermine an alternative inscription of human embodiment and embeddedness within nature.

Bioregional narratives and 'eco-cosmopolitanism'

From an ecofeminist perspective, the form of western ecological sanctification that is spatially restricted diverts attention away from humanity's need for place-situated communion with the natural world. An integrated formulation of bioregional identity can alternatively engender localised, intersubjective relations between humans and the environment. In an effort to counter global dislocation, Gaard (2010: 655) advocates 'recuperating the history of feminist and ecofeminist perspectives on place, home and bioregion', following Adamson and Slovic's (2009: 17) contention that 'even in the face of the large-scale effects of globalisation, human relationships to specific places and to other-than-human beings can and should be maintained'. Bioregionalism – as an 'alternative conception of human identity' – can offer a responsible way of living structured around a tripartite commitment to particularised place as well as to its human and nonhuman residents (Plumwood 1993: 186). Such a commitment can resacralise a secular nature – the space in which life is lived rather than the space beyond human dwelling – as a space of empathetic human (and nonhuman) belonging. Ecofeminists thus advocate place-based geographic community, or 'sustaining ecological community', in place of the segregated notions of natural worth that have traditionally structured industrialised western societies (Keough 2008: 71). If a focus on the local and bioregional can counter the diffusion and entropy often noted in globalised societies, it does so at the expense of the wider representational frameworks that structure contemporary engagement with place. Bioregionalism, in fact, must confront what Plumwood (1993: 186) terms the 'loss in modern urban life of much of the basis of [bioregional] identity, and the loss of the particular practices of care through which commitment to particular places is expressed and fostered'. Ursula Heise (2008) uses the term 'eco-cosmopolitanism' to describe the effects of processes of globalisation on humanity's evolving relationship with place. As Gaard (2010: 655) points out, however, an eco-cosmopolitan perspective can mask the radically uneven distributions of power and privilege that produce difference according to race, gender, class and species. In the post-natural landscapes of my focused novels, this masking takes on added relevance. How can a bioregional identity be constructed within the degraded, dislocated and post-natural landscapes of a post-apocalyptic planet? In societies in which global networks have failed and totalitarian systems arisen in their place, the tension between a lost globalism and an enforced localism often sees bioregional spaces become contentious sites of atavistic symbolism. The reduced parameters for action arising from an embattled local identity often lead to a reliance on regressive or anti-modern modes of environmental interaction rather than on alternative and transformative resistant positions.

In Nina Bawden's *Off the Road* [1998] – a novel set in the year 2040 in a highly technological urban suburbs, known as the Urbs, fenced off from the pre-industrial 'Wild' – a family-based pastoral lifestyle is celebrated as the desired antithesis of urban individualism yet fails to reconceptualise a non-oppressive relationship between human community and the local setting. The farming community that Tom meets in the Wild, interpellated by a series of nostalgic and gendered ideologies, envisions a relationship with the land as one of physical domination. Nature is not an agential entity deserving of reverence but a passive pastoral idyll predicated on patriarchal modes of representation and coincident with the idealisation John Cooley (1994: 3) identifies in pastoralism:

> At the heart of classical pastoralism, as a literary mode, is an idealisation of an earlier time and paradisiacal condition that are no longer achievable except in the imagination. ... [P]astorals are frequently tinged with nostalgia for or regret over the loss of an idyllic condition: childhood, a perfect love, an idealised farm, a promised land, the innocence of Eden.

The nostalgic reminiscences of Tom's grandfather Gandy about his childhood sweetheart, childhood home, childhood dreams and childhood longings, all centre on the premise that a pastoral idyll functions as memory keeper: a space in which dreams of innocence are simply waiting to be rekindled. These nostalgic dreams hinder a coterminous bioregional identity for Tom and his family by ensuring that the natural world is constructed as an oppositional space with only limited scope for embedded engagement.

In the picturesque pastoral environs of Great-uncle Jack's farmstead, value is placed on family and community, as a counterpoint to the Inside with its policy of one-child couples, policed through its ideological shaming of family- related vocabulary: the *'disgusting'* words 'brother' and 'sister' (Bawden 2000: 21). The novel denotes the large families of the Wild as ideologically superior, yet bypasses the implications of reproductive freedom by leaving uninterrogated the unstated reason behind such a policy – that of human overpopulation and its threat to the future of the planet. The Wild's counter notion that family thrives amongst nature hearkens back to the romantic ethos of natural purity. Amongst his many aunts and uncles and cousins, Tom quickly delights in the romantic joys of out-door living: playing with babies, hunting for chicken eggs and eating home-cooked meals, finding that he feels 'not only happy but *safe*' amongst the 'good smells; grassy smells, sweet, evening air smells' of the outdoors (64). The Wild's emphasis on family posits human community as the highest goal and achievement of the natural space, resonant of Dobrin and Kidd's (2004: 6) contention that the pastoral 'often has a decidedly social agenda'. Tom's move beyond the liminal space of the 'alive and malevolent' forest sees one type of anthropocentric discourse replaced by another, even if this latter discourse is grounded in a more situated portrayal of the natural world (7).

In the Wild, agrarian toil replaces urban consumerism and the land is shaped and moulded to suit the needs of the humans who work it. Nature is judged in terms of its use-value, governed and ordered by anthropocentric rules and ideologies. The foal that is newly-born is destined for a 'rope halter'; chickens provide the Jacobs family with eggs yet are eaten when they can no longer lay (92). The agrarian society's treatment of animals tellingly replicates the urban society's treatment of humans, who, at the age of sixty-five, become 'uneconomic' and are transported to the Memory Theme Park to be 'gently and permanently cared for' (74; 16). This latter policy of enforced euthanasia is positioned as a by-product of capitalism. If the text overtly interrogates the ethical implications of such a policy, the ethical framework underpinning society's treatment of animals goes unquestioned.[1] In light of the discourses of ecological domination structuring the community's relationship with nature, Tom interprets his interaction with the natural world as a physical struggle for supremacy. When working the fields, '[t]he sweat ran down his forehead and into his eyes. His back ached, his arms ached, his legs ached. His neck ached. The straw cut his hands, the stubble jabbed at his ankles. But he went on working' (92). Upset by his grandfather's doubts as to whether he is 'up to it', and proud at being labelled 'a Trojan' by Great-uncle Jack, Tom positions the natural world as a physical and maturational testing ground (34; 94). Tom's increasingly svelte physique after a few days in the Wild is the outward sign of this changing relationship with the natural world, a relationship that revolves around the hard-won domination of nature by man.

Despite being self-labelled a 'post-industrial society', the Outside retains a regressive form of social patriarchy that relies on traditional gender role allocations: whilst the men work the fields, the women stay at home and cook, clean and take care of the children (89). Tom's cousin Lizzie's refusal to look after the babies provides a counter-discourse that critiques such androcentrism, yet under the strict policy that children must be deferential to adults at all times – a power balance that replicates that of the reader's societies (it is assumed) yet tellingly inverts that of the Inside – her resistant voice goes largely unheard. Lizzie, in fact, who – as both a child and a girl – is doubly disadvantaged in a system that allocates freedom and agency to adult men, is, like nature, lacking a voice in response to patriarchal circumscription. Such rigid gendering is accompanied by a visible class hierarchy: the homesteaders versus the 'Dropouts'. These latter 'trolly-lolly boys', 'lazybones', 'sick' people and 'criminals' are envisaged as non-productive members of the community who, having been purposefully expelled from the Inside when the Wall went up, function as the waste products of a consumer society (102). With their homes in the wilder areas of the natural space, the Dropouts are associated with nature in its most primitive state, unmanaged by human systems of control.

If Tom manages to relegate the wilderness discourse with which he has been enculturated to the status of 'an old tale someone told me' and to replace it with a discourse of pastoral pre-industrialisation, the same cannot be said for the 'Wild Men' schema that colours his thinking of the Outside (42; 18–19):

> The Wild Men – the outlaws, the barbarians – were the biggest danger of all. They roamed the wilderness looking for foolish children

who had slipped off the road, away from their parents, thinking it might be an adventure to see what lay on the other side of the Wall.

The Dropouts are the quintessential 'Wild Men': outlaws and bandits who at the crux of the novel steal the baby Joshua away from Great-uncle Jack's homestead with a view to ransoming him for food and warm clothing. Wild nature – associated with a solipsistic lack of economically viable behaviour – is thus deemed an essentially non-productive space. If the Outside, then, provides a social alternative to the Inside, it is not presented as an alternative that is un-problematically superior. It dramatises, in fact, the 'limitations of localism', as argued by Gaard (2010: 657), 'which can devolve into provincialism, prejudice, and institutionalised oppression'. With rigid age, gender and class hierarchies, the Outside is a space in which an anthropocentric and secular bias thus undercuts its counter-hegemonic potential. The regressive return to a patriarchal and *pre*-disaster world order in which critical ecological issues such as human overpopulation are quietly bypassed in favour of economic productivity, make the natural space of the Outside an anti-utopian space.

As the regressive patriarchal hierarchy of Bawden's novel suggests, such a nostalgic challenge to modernisation does not necessarily engender what Eugenie Gatens-Robinson (1994: 207) terms 'genuine transformations of thought and practice in relation to the natural environment'. Westerfeld's glorification of rural community life in *Uglies*, for instance, problematically equates ecological care with ecological comfort under the implicit premise that bioregional relationships are predicated on mutual compromise rather than respect. Enculturated to believe that it is morally wrong to live in nature 'unless you want to live like an animal', Tally is initially appalled at the fact that the inhabitants of the Smoke use trees as commodities (92; 203):

The long tables had clearly been cut from the hearts of trees. They showed knots and whorls, and wavy tracks of grain ran down their entire length. They were rough and beautiful, but Tally couldn't get over the thought that the trees had been taken alive.

Having grown up in a vegetarian city, Tally is similarly horrified at David's organic and handmade clothing: 'Its patchwork appearance reminded her of Frankenstein's monster, which led to a terrible thought. What if it were made of *real* leather, like in the olden days?

Skins. She shuddered. He couldn't be wearing a bunch of dead animals. They weren't savages here' (213). Animalistic, monstrous, savage – the inhabitants of the Smoke are denoted ontologically less human than the trees, whose 'hearts' betray the ostensible heartlessness of the Smokies' ecological exploitation. The ideological ground rules for the lives of the country folk are thus clearly meant to fall short of city standards. Tally's intertextual reference to Frankenstein's monster is ironic, however, since this monstrous figure is in fact famed for being more humane than its human creator, whose appropriation of god-like powers over nature resembles that of the city guardians and their imposition of aesthetic standardisation onto Tally's 'ugly' body.

The city standards for sustainable living – 'purifying the water that we put back in the river, recycling the biomass, and using only power drawn from our own solar footprint' – are themselves problematic models for human–earth interaction (106–7). They ignore, for instance, that the manufacturing of synthetics generally has a greater negative impact on the environment than the use of organic materials, a telling indication that Tally's own biological tampering will result in similarly contentious environmental positioning. City standards – when contrasted with the bioregional lifestyles of the people of the Smoke – are equivocal models for better environmental engagement and rather serve to highlight Tally's ignorance in her ideological dealings with the environment. Tally's initial horror at the Smokies' non-ethical treatment of trees and animals is in fact, in the end, quietly bypassed. Despite claiming that she 'couldn't get over' the thought of living trees and dead animals being used as commodities, it is not long before she is content simply *not to ask* 'what was in the stew' (204). She even concedes that the animal-skin jacket 'suited David, somehow, as if growing up here in the wild allowed him to fuse with the animals that had donated their skins to his clothes' (231). This tasteless use of the word 'donated', as if the nonhuman population chooses willingly to sacrifice itself for humanity, constitutes – one assumes – an attempt to promote a more organic 'fusion' between humans and nonhumans. This 'fusion', however, simultaneously refutes animal rights by relegating animals to fashion accessories to make David appear more ruggedly attractive. As in *Off the Road*, animals are incorporated into the collective human identity in a move that defines the natural ecology in terms of its instrumental value to the humans who cultivate it. In both novels, bioregionalism thus figures as a contentious element of ecological engagement through its failure to re-envisage the economic structures and anthropocentric value systems of pre-apocalypse socio-political processes.

Rejecting the Christian paradigm: life, death and resurrection

The Platonic triune of the Christian tradition – God the Father, God the Son and God the Holy Spirit – renders spiritual fulfilment achievable through the affirmation of the immortal soul and the negation of the transient body. Ecofeminist spiritualities repudiate this now rarely instantiated model of transcendent spiritual fulfilment by alternatively embedding the human actant within the earth in embodied human-nonhuman communion. A reading of the Holy Spirit, or divine grace, as immaterial and '"airborne"', to use a phrase employed by Sharon Betcher (2007: 318), runs counter to an ecofeminist call for natural immanence since such a reading 'sacralise[s] an abhorrence of humus – of earth, our own bodies, of women, and of other earth-affiliated persons'. Betcher (332–3) terms this early Christian precedent 'think[ing] against the flesh' and foregrounds the need to resituate the notion of Spirit within the organic environment, particularly at this time of environmental crisis:

> Because Western Christianity has closed its imagination to metaphorically relating Spirit with earth, and since the collapse of the "earth" metaphor of Spirit has been coordinated with planetary decimation and with the displacement of women and children, it is crucial that we construct a pneumatology that can take into account one of the most unique, elemental particularities of our life here on earth – humus or dirt.

In the novels, the dominant hegemonies fail to metaphorically relate Spirit with earth and instead advocate spiritual transcendence through disembodiment and dislocation. The protagonists of the novels experience an alienated relationship with their own bodies and with the ecologies in which they are enmeshed, and must work to construct resistant subject positions if the abjection of the flesh, as enforced by institutionalised religion, is to be repudiated. Under this formulation the 'humus or dirt' of the natural world is at best overlooked and at worst made abject. The novels thus enact a process of abjection at the intersection of the material and the corporeal that sees the natural world and the human body similarly subject to 'airborne' discourses of spiritual transcendence.

Religious transcendence in the *The Forest of Hands & Teeth* trilogy pivots around interlocking discourses of sacrifice and choice. Whilst the cause of 'the Return' is unknown, it is blamed by the Sisterhood on social injustices of the past: on 'murder...pain and anguish...heresy and hypocrisy...[w]ars, deceit, selfishness...people allowing human beings to die of hunger outside in the cold when they had warmth and food' (Ryan 2009: 67). These social injustices within a context that we can assume reflects the neoliberal ideologies of today together amount to 'trying to cheat God. Trying to cheat death. Trying to change His will' (63). The Return is thus configured as a posthumanist Fall, a punishment for systemic asymmetries based on privilege and accompanying lack, and for man's hubristic desire for technological mastery over the limits imposed by human embodiment. Having brought about apocalypse in its original Judaeo-Christian and Gnostic form, past societies are portrayed as having waged war against God, and in so doing, challenged the natural order of things, and by implication, nature itself. In a grotesque parody of Christ's resurrection, the Unconsecrated now render the great unknown knowable; as Mary narrates: 'Now that we know what happens after death, a new question has risen to take the place of the old: why?' (16). Efforts throughout the novel and its sequels to answer this question imbricate spiritual, religious and emotional quests and centre on the successive narrators' capacity to retain a sense of embattled agency without promise of spiritual redemption.

In a world in which the word of God is not to be questioned, the Sisterhood charges the village to remember where they came from: '"Not the Garden of Eden, but the ashes of the Return"' (Ryan 2009: 64). Claiming to have '"brought heaven to this hell,"' the Sisterhood evokes a new set of existential reference points that configures the old world as a hell on earth and the new world as life after death (68). Under this new spiritual paradigm, the Sisterhood makes it their 'sworn duty' to ensure that 'questions are not asked' (68; 65). This 'duty' to shield the villagers from harm is couched in the language of sacrifice: it is a 'sacred burden' that the Sisterhood must carry 'so that we can forget what came before, can heal, become reborn without the weight of our sins before the Return' (67). To throw off the weighted shackles of previous sin is to transcend embodiment and become 'airborne'. The sacred burden that the Sisterhood carries is knowledge – that which Mary so desperately craves – without which the villagers live in perpetual, and purposefully instituted, ignorance, unable to question life outside of the village's limited coordinates: 'like fish in a glass bowl with darkness pressing in on every side' (37). In this new dichotomy of good and evil, the Sisterhood is self-configured as Christ-like in its willingness to sacrifice itself for the many. Mary realises that if she were to test the epistemological limits imposed by the Sisterhood by demanding answers to the questions that are forbidden to her, Sister Tabitha – 'so filled with the passion' – would not hesitate to 'sacrifice' her to 'the Forest' (64). Religious passion or zeal here posits the Sisterhood as Christian martyrs defending – unto death – the sanctuary they have carved out of the ashes of the old world. That Mary could become the victim of such fervour and be sacrificed 'to the Forest' suggests that the natural world in this novel is both overlord of the village's destiny – a force to be placated with human offerings – and also a space of punishment for the 'sin' of knowledge-seeking. Under this formulation, Mary – whose gaze defies containment and forever turns towards the Forest – is both Eve *and* the tempting serpent, threatened by and threatening *to* the 'Garden of Eden' that the Sisterhood has embedded within the Forest.

The history of the origins of the Cathedral are disclosed to Mary at the point at which she is forced to accept a life with the Sisterhood when no man comes to claim her for a wife. The spiritual implications of the Cathedral's construction are clear (31–2):

> "Did you know that long, long ago, centuries before the Return, this building used to belong to a plantation? Used to house a winery? ... Guardians tell us that they still encounter remnants of the vineyard, that they still find grapevines smothering the fences. ... They used to store the wine for fermentation under our Cathedral, but this is not where it was made. ... They had to stomp on the grapes, which is messy and attracts bugs, and so they had a separate well house for that. They used this tunnel to transport and store their reserves. Eventually, when the soil failed, the winery was abandoned. The old wooden well house fell apart and collapsed. But the winery itself, our Cathedral, remained standing because it was made of stone."

In this fragmented history, the Cathedral that underpins the Sisterhood's iron rule arises from the ashes of a winery. A secular site devoted to pleasure, the winery is an obvious metaphor for consumerism. The 'plantation' on which the winery stood constitutes an area of arable land marked out for human use: a monoculture brought about through crop cultivation. That the Guardians still find grapevines 'smothering' the fences alludes to the homogenising effects of this blanket importation and prefigures the 'smothering' of the living by the Unconsecrated after the Return. The winery's separation of the storage facility from the place where the wine was made – relegating the messiness, unpleasantness and disease of the natural world to a 'separate well house' – mirrors the Sisterhood's subsequent banishment of the Unconsecrated to the Forest beyond the village fences. The 'tunnel' that links the two spaces is a physical manifestation of the link that only the Sisterhood can provide between the time before the Return and the embattled present. The apocalyptic decline of the 'old wooden well house', as a metaphor for the indulgent old world, has given rise to a new world that cannot 'fail', 'fall apart' or 'collapse' since, under the will of the Sisterhood, it is 'made of stone'.

Under the new spiritual framework instantiated by the Sisterhood, the wine of pleasure has become the blood of Christ. The religious institution that has 'remained standing' after apocalypse thus 'stomp[s] on' Mary's questions just as the wine-makers trampled the grapes under foot. That Mary's dreams are also sacrificed to uphold the Sisterhood's rule becomes clear when Mary is forced to make a 'choice' to join the Sisterhood once Sister Tabitha has told her the history of the Cathedral (34). Having initially responded that she has no other choice, Mary is given the cold reply that '"[t]here is always a choice, Mary. ... It is what makes us human, what separates us from them"' (34). Sister Tabitha's instantiation of difference – between the human and nonhuman, living and dead, consecrated and Unconsecrated, duty and pleasure – is made whilst standing braced against the trapdoor leading into the forest, with 'the lower half of her body still concealed below ground' (34). Sister Tabitha's occupation of the threshold, both above and below ground, posits the 'lower half' of the body – the bodily pleasures, emotions, longings – as fit only for concealment, whilst the upper half of the body – the mental rigours, strictures, choices – are by implication deemed fit for the divine ordinance of the Sisterhood.

Choice or free will – that which separates the human population from the Unconsecrated – is thus effectively rendered redundant in a world where the Sisterhood represents both institutional law and the word of God. In a grotesque parody of the nature of choice, the only allowable exercising of free will comes in the choice of the infected to be killed by the villagers immediately after their 'turn' or to be released into the forest to roam forever amongst the undead. Mary's differing interpretation of the notion of 'choice' dissociates the Christian God from human agency: 'I do not accept the hand of God; I do not believe in divine intervention or predestination. I cannot believe that our paths are pre-chosen and that our lives have no will. That there is no such thing as choice' (174-5). Her choice to leave the sanctuary of the village to seek answers to her questions is thus positioned as an assertion of agency against the stultifying mental strictures of an imposed religious framework. Mary's entry into the Forest sees her seek spiritual fulfilment not in the stone walls of the Cathedral but in the unconsecrated ground of a banished natural world.

Spiritual fulfilment is more problematically unfolded in *The Dead-Tossed Waves* [2010] in which Mary's adopted child, Gabry, leaves the confines of her seaside town and enters the Forest where she encounters a nomadic cult that worships the Unconsecrated, in this novel termed 'Mudo'. Labelled by Gabry 'a crazy religious group', the 'Soulers' interpret the death-in-life of the Mudo as transcendent eternal life and a desired end-point of human existence (Ryan 2010: 141). Offered as a spiritual alternative to the Sisterhood's Christian paradigm, the Mudos' morbid resurrection is configured as God's salvation and draws an uneasy line between religion and ideology. Sacrifice, here, is graphically enacted on the human body; Gabry watches as a young boy cuts his skin before 'step[ping] forward into the Mudo's waiting arms' (143). Whilst such a gesture is couched in the comforting discourse of parental affection, the effects of such an embrace are violent and fierce: teeth rip into flesh in a diseased act of procreation that sees the boy himself 'turn'. The rise of the undead is circumscribed by the Soulers within a religious framework that appropriates the transcendent discourse of religious martyrdom: *'Blessed and holy is he that hath part in the first resurrection: on such the second death hath no power'* (151). Designed to render death meaningless, such resurrection is interpreted by Gabry as an empty promise couched in fundamentalist rhetoric that sees a young boy make 'an awful choice' (145). If the choice made by Mary to leave the village in search of the promised haven of a quasi-mythical ocean is one replicated by her daughter in her efforts to retrace her mother's steps, the choice left to the young Souler is one defined by waste since it lacks any redemptive spiritual framework.

The romantic and the sublime: gendered notions of natural empathy

The discourse of the 'conventional sublime', as interpreted by Christopher Hitt (1999: 611), has been critiqued for bolstering perceptions of separateness in human interactions with the earth. The sublime is a discursive formulation often mapped onto the more magnificent aspects of the natural world that affirms 'the validation of the individual through an act of transcendence in which the external world is domesticated, conquered, or erased' (Hitt 1999: 611). Hitt (1999: 605) invites us to reconsider the two most influential theorists of the sublime, Edmund Burke and Immanuel Kant, who envision the sublime as 'disorienting or overwhelming confrontations with a natural object', and notes that their invocation of nature's otherness has had a pervasive influence on the genealogy of the 'wilderness' narrative in past and present theorising. The 'asymmetrical power relations' Hitt (1999: 605) notes within the aesthetic of the sublime have instigated a set of romantic dualisms that function to 'reinforce or ratify our estrangement' from the natural world. The 'contradiction' of the sublime, however, is that 'it has tended to include *both* humbling fear *and* ennobling validation for the perceiving subject' (1999: 606).

It is in this notion of 'humility' that Hitt (1999: 607) sees the potential for a 'reconfigured version of the sublime' – an 'ecological sublime' – that would offer a 'new kind of transcendence' to resist the traditional metanarrative of humanity's supremacy over the natural world. The 'romantic project' undertaken by German and British philosophers, writers and thinkers in the early nineteenth century has laid the groundwork for this new kind of transcendence (Rigby 2004a). Kate Rigby (2004a: 12) interprets the romantics' engagement with place not as an attempt to engender an anthropocentric sense of alienation from the natural world but as an alternative attempt 'to reconstitute the grounds of hope and to announce the certainty, or at least the possibility, of a rebirth in which a renewed mankind will inhabit a renovated earth where he will find himself thoroughly at home'. Rigby (2004a: 12) terms this renewal 'the romantic turn towards the earth', arising through new understandings of nature and divinity. The spiritual relevance of these interlocking discourses rests in their capacity to 'rejuvenat[e] religious traditions in such a way as to resacralise the earth' (2004a: 12).

The romantic reconceptualisation of nature as a sacred space of human belonging prefigures much deep green thinking in contemporary philosophy and ethics, as well as the ecofeminist call for human embodiment and embeddedness within the earth. The common narrative strategy in young adult fiction of replicating or re-envisioning romantic tropes in portrayals of human–earth interaction is testament to its similar relevance for successive generations of writers. In my focused novels, an intersectional engagement with place manifests itself in a dialogic narrative structure. The aesthetic of the sublime, as delineated by Hitt, is set against the intimacy of the romantic in a progression resembling the romantic 'turn towards the earth'. In this progression, experiences of awe and wonder within the sublime natural space are replaced by earth-centred moments of embodied intimacy within nature. These latter earth-centred moments serve to cut short the protagonists' sublime communion with nature before it can lead to the spiritual transcendence that Hitt (1999: 609) deems correlative with anthropocentric supremacy. The negotiation of ecological alterity undertaken by the protagonists via the interlocking discourses of the romantic and the sublime can thus be read as symbolic of a longed for 'turn towards the earth'.

Uglies illuminates this progression from alienation to intimacy in Tally's journey from the contained cityscape to the sprawling wilderness. When Tally ventures into the forest, the changes in her perception of the environment initially place emphasis on the sublime and transcendent aspects of the natural world (151; 153):

> When Tally glanced out at the glowing horizon, her eyes opened wide. She'd never seen dawn from outside the city before. ... A band of orange and yellow ignited the sky, glorious and unexpected, as spectacular as fireworks, but changing at a stately, barely perceptible pace. ... Tally had always thought of the city as huge, a whole world in itself, but the scale of everything out here was so much grander. And so beautiful.

Glorious, spectacular, stately, grand – Tally immediately recognises that the landscape is sublime despite her limited aesthetic experience. A self-evidently sublime nature serves its purpose well: it opens Tally's eyes to the falsity and temporality of life in the cities, not simply in relation to a lack of lifestyle choice – the constant parties and required fun – but in the arbitrary and culturally-prescribed categories of ugliness and beauty that define the city population's aesthetic standards. Whilst her capacity to be awed by the power of nature is retained throughout her journey to the Smoke, Tally increasingly moves towards a more embedded interaction with the earth. Her mental turn-around is not instantaneous but signalled through gradual and tell-tale moments of embodied identification. She experiences, for instance, a new-found delight in food and is surprised and pleased at her body's resourcefulness when battling the elements. These locally-applied, earth-centred moments of empathy underpin Tally's increasingly romantic engagement with the natural landscape.

The sublime and the intimate similarly codetermine Katniss' attitude towards the natural world in *The Hunger Games*. Nature in this novel is invested with healing properties as counterpoint to the hunger, poverty and drudgery of urban life in the Seam. Having grown up in conditions of extreme poverty, Katniss is forced to venture out into the woods beyond the fence surrounding District 12 to hunt and forage for food for her family. This illegal transgression of city boundaries posits the woods as a forbidden space with counter-hegemonic potential. The woods are psychologically connected with Katniss' father, as well as with her male best friend Gale; they offer a test of strength, stamina and skill, forcing Katniss to adopt traditionally masculine character traits in order to survive. As in *Uglies*, emphasis is placed on the journey between the city and the wild and the transformation undergone in Katniss' subjectivity as she moves across nature's threshold and feels 'the muscles in my face relaxing, my pace quickening' (7). Whilst the city crushes its inhabitants under the burden of simply staying alive – its coal miners with their stooped shoulders, broken nails and sunken faces – the natural world is clean, light and rejuvenating, and emphasis is constantly placed on its surprising haecceity. A similar propensity to that exhibited by Tally for valuing nature in its more sublime manifestations sees Katniss describe the view of the valley in heightened terms (10):

> From this place, we are invisible, but have a clear view of the valley, which is teeming with summer life, greens to gather, roots to dig, fish iridescent in the sunlight. The day is glorious, with a blue sky and soft breeze.

Glorious, wonderful, iridescent – a sublime nature offers Katniss the opportunity to rediscover her true nature in a society in which she is forced to 'hold [her] tongue and turn [her] features into an indifferent mask' (7). Where the city offers scarcity, nature offers abundance ('teeming with summer life'); where the city demands closed shutters and carefully concealed thoughts, nature allows 'a clear view'. Nature here is not in need of reassessment or re-evaluation, as it is in *Uglies*, provoking reflection upon the city responsible for its marginalisation. Instead nature is positioned as counterpoint to the constrained city life of a dystopian society in a dichotomous relationship that constitutes a rather obvious attempt to foreground the flaws of the former.

Meg Rosoff's *How I Live Now* [2004] – a near-future dystopia envisaging the psychological consequences for Daisy and her four cousins of the enemy occupation of rural Britain – similarly traces city-girl Daisy's imaginative engagement with the natural world and identifies this engagement as a gradual process of increasing embeddedness. Through an ironic and comedic use of non-representative imagery, Daisy reveals her initial dislocation from the natural world as a result of growing up in the 'Concrete Jungle' of New York (even if – she qualifies – 'the Upper West Side is fairly leafy, as concrete jungles go') (Rosoff 2005: 57). In an effort to formulate a poetics of place for the unfamiliar British country-side, Daisy invokes and subsequently discards a series of archetypal nature tropes. Watching the sun rise over the fields from her bedroom window, she 'stared and stared expecting to see a deer or maybe a uni-corn trotting home after a hard night' yet 'didn't see anything except some birds' (13–14). Confronted with an abundance of wildlife, she quips that the 'squirrels and hedgehogs and deer wandering around with the ducks and dogs and chickens and goats and sheep' are 'like Walt Disney on E' (58). Daisy's mishmash of pop culture references positions nature as ecstatically removed from 'real life' and closer to a cartoon sketch by Disney. Her initial inability to think outside of city-inspired expressions manifests itself linguistically in her consistent use of hyperbole: she notes 'a hundred thousand white roses' in the garden and vegetables 'growing about six inches a day' (58). Playing in the stream with her cousins, Daisy lacks the conceptual schemata for contemplation of such a natural haven and instead relies on sensory perception: 'The feeling of the cold water and the hot sun and having the river just flow over your skin like a dolphin wasn't something I had enough words to describe but was the kind of feeling you never forget' (69). Here, the text employs the topos of the inexpressible to foreground the 'unbridgeable gap between inadequate human speech and its object of praise' (Richards 2010: 10). Daisy's inadequate speech is here evoked to dramatise the moments at which discursivity falls short and the materiality of the natural world takes precedence.

Daisy's growing willingness, as the weeks go by, to discard the non-representative words and phrases that her city acculturation has assigned to the natural world sees her engage such sensory perception in nurturing a more intersubjective relationship with her environ-ment. In a syntactical aggregation through repeated copulas, Daisy demonstrates embedding herself in the natural world as a process of 'nesting' (21):

[A]lthough the day wasn't very warm, I made a nest for myself by trampling down a little patch in the tall grass and put the blanket down and lay very still and as the sun rose up in the sky I warmed up even more and all I could hear was the sound of Edmond talking in a steady low stream of conversation to the fish, and Piper singing her odd song, and the occasional splash of the river or a bird rising into the air near us and singing its heart out.

In a repeated linguistic amalgamation of human and natural actors, Daisy merges the 'steady low stream' of Edmond's conversation with the stream of water by her side; Piper's singing similarly gives way to a bird 'singing its heart out'. 'Warming up' to nature, Daisy invests increasing emotional resonance in an embodied and embedded relationship within nature's 'heart'. For a girl who is suffering from anorexia, this willingness to embrace an embodied connection with the natural world – one even predicated on excess and abundance – is a clear sign of ecological rehabilitation. Daisy's growing emotional and sexual longing for Edmond is in fact described in the same visceral terms that render Daisy's interaction with nature meaningful. Both her appreciation for 'life' and her longing for Edmond are associated with her increasing sense of being at home in the (natural) world: 'The only thing I knew for certain was that all around me was more life than I'd ever experienced in all the years I'd been on earth and as long as no one shut me in the barn away from Edmond at night I was safe' (61). Such an apprehension of safety within nature – particularly in the context of a globalised terrorist threat – envisions the natural world as a place in which to nurture intersubjective relationships with human and non-human others under a romantic framework of spiritual and emotional wellbeing.

Ecofeminist cosmologies: holistic ecological sanctity

Ecofeminist spiritualities frequently draw on indigenous conceptions of the sacred as models for new and alternative modes of ecological engagement; as Chris Cuomo (2002: 10) suggests, 'some indigenous cultures provide specifically useful models of ecologically sustainable cultures, and systems of values and metaphysics that promote ecological flourishing, rather than degradation'. Rejecting a construction of identity based on governance over an othered ecology, ecofeminists position the earth and human life as holistically enmeshed. The ecological relevance of this form of spiritual engagement comes in a felt and lived experience of reverence and respect in human attitudes towards the environment. Moments of heightened spiritual and existential fulfilment are seen to aid a growing understanding of spiritual kinship with nature, and are correlative with an increased sense of subjective agency within nature. The popular webbed image of human place-situatedness within the wider ecology gestures towards an understanding of human identity as pluralistic, situated and collective, and not simply confined to intra-species relations.

Reeve's *A Darkling Plain* offers an intersubjective rendering of human embeddedness within nature in its portrayal of the community found to have settled at the foot of the hill on which Shrike spends several centuries guarding the dead bodies of Tom and Hester. Having become an embodied part of the landscape after centuries of stasis, Shrike's entry into this community is described as a gradual organic awakening or rebirth within nature: 'With a deep effort he began to rouse himself. ... He moved. He stood up. Gravel and owl-pellets cascaded off him; he shook himself free of cobwebs and birds' nests and moss' (530; 531). Such an organic rebirth is celebrated with an offering of flowers in a paganesque ritual that reflects the quasi-animistic beliefs of generations of villagers: 'They had hung flowers about his neck for luck each summer when they had brought their goats up to the high pastures. They had been doing it since their mothers' mothers' time' (531–2). This passing on of ritualistic belief and practice from mother to daughter in a formulation that resembles the generational transference of indigenous knowledge renders the god-like Shrike an embodied, and present, manifestation of communal beliefs.

'[C]upped' protectively in a wooded vale, the town to which Shrike is taken by his child guides with its 'meeting place' nestled in the 'city's heart' is resonant of nurturing community values based upon sound ecological principles (532). The 'airborne ships of wood and glass' that rise into the air 'like dragonflies' demonstrate a melding of human and natural systems metonymic of a successful bioregional identity (532). Whilst the simplicity of the villagers' lifestyles suggests societal primitiveness, the town has in fact accomplished the integration of old technologies with modern attitudes towards sustainability in service of a newly conceived relationship with nature. A young community with a 'redder' sun, 'clearer' air and 'kinder' climate, the town's roots nevertheless extend back to the era of the traction cities whose tracks and wheels have been perpetually grounded and made harmless in their new guise as walls and watchtowers (532). The repeated use of the word 'ancient' to describe Shrike's perception of the village ('an ancient oak wood', 'ancient metal walls', 'ancient sunlight') suggests continuity and cultural heritage: a new community sprung from the ruins of the old world like the spring nests built in the crook of Shrike's ancient arm (531; 532; 533). Shrike's self-styled designation as a 'remembering machine' posits these ancient objects as memory-keepers: telling indicators of the natural world's capacity for long-term survival (533). Whilst the 'dark, blustery day in spring' with which Shrike begins his story of the lost past is metonymic of the dark days of the traction empire, the '[g]reen light' of a 'summer morning' that greets Shrike upon his awakening suggests a new, greener future for humanity predicated on embodied and embedded community values.

Shædow Master similarly adheres to an ecofeminist spiritual framework that devalues shallow, or instrumental, re-inscriptions of the sacred, and instead employs an indigenous framework as a model for holistic ecological sanctity. The values that underpin Ora's engagement with the natural world are initially predicated on an aesthetic appreciation for the natural world, and particularly the towering Cloudtouchers: 'she was…struck dumb by their size and grandeur, by their sheer *beauty*; they simply left no room in her consciousness to take in anything else' (171). Ora's appreciation is tellingly undercut by her Guest friend Tasman's ecocentric obligation to redirect his gaze, raising the trees to a spiritual, rather than aesthetic, plane (173):

> 'You're not allowed to *look* at the Cloudtouchers?'
> His gaze returned to the ground. 'Thim's too holy.'
> Sudden tears welled in Ora's eyes. Her mother, a Guest, had spent half her life in a castle built from the wood of these same trees. And Tasman's father was there right now.

Having secularised the land that the Guests deem holy, the colonising Folavians have appropriated the Guests' sacred symbols to bolster their own imperial aspirations ('a castle built from the wood of these same trees'). Ora's growing understanding of the intrinsic, rather than instrumental, value of the earth takes shape through her parallel understanding of the earth as an agential ethical agent. According to the environmentally responsible ethical framework employed by the text, individual agency and intrinsic value are intimately associated, the former being viewed as essential to the achievement of the latter, and vice versa; if the earth is to be regarded as an entity with intrinsic value it must be acknowledged to have its own individual agency and to be capable – at some level – of influencing the course of events.

In the Guests' ecocentric worldview, stewardship is considered the defining dynamic of human-nonhuman interrelations; the ethic of care to which the Guests adhere posits the environment as a sentient and responsive entity whose voicelessness – in human terms – predicates a framework for action based on faith, trust and sacred reverence. When the king asks whether the tame 'muskotter' that disturbs his horse belongs to Tasman, the boy's answer '"[i]m belongs ta imself, Highness. I jus look after im"' refutes the proprietary practices of colonial control in favour of biosocial stewardship (91). The Guests' name, in fact, signals their status as guests only, with an ecocentric obligation to look after the Land so that the Land will let them stay. The war between the indigenous peoples and the invading Outworlder army in which women and children might get killed is therefore justi-fied on the basis that '[t]rees got killed'; women, children and trees are imbricated as comparable sites of colonial oppression, each subject to the instrumental discourses of a secular society (170). The historical failure of the country's previous residents, the Lakelanders, to abide by such ecocentric standards is taken as a moral exemplum on which to model a more intersubjective relationship with the Land. Having failed to acknowledge that 'every part of the countryside was holy: every creature, every plant, every blade of grass had its part to play in the overall health of the Land', the Lakelanders 'ma[d]e right what they done wrong' by drowning themselves in the lake to become shædows to look after the Land (243). This punishment, couched in sacrificial language, accords stewardship an essential role in the maintenance of a healthy ecosystem. In the Guests' existential belief system – a system that sees all life on earth as a manifestation of the sacred whole – a human being is to be accorded no higher value than a 'blade of grass'. With current generations facing a renewed ecological crisis, the Guests' decision to drown themselves in the lake to let the Land heal is based on this same ethical standpoint that renders humanity subject to the needs of the holistic environment.

Ecological sanctity in this novel is accompanied by a discourse of spiritual awakening. Such a discourse borrows heavily from animis-tic, or shamanistic, discourses frequently employed in young adult literature 'to enable the silenced world of nature to rediscover a voice while erasing human presence' (Bradford *et al.* 2008: 99). Shamanistic language recognises spirit in nonhuman and inanimate entities, and adheres to a belief that shamanic practices can lead to fuller acknowl-edgement of the workings of the natural world. With her half-Guest heritage, Ora's ability to speak for the ecocentric indigenous peoples becomes apparent through a shamanistic experience of earth-based identification (207):

A cloud moved across the sun. Ora looked up and the sky was gone. She was kneeling in a forest of enormous trees, their upper branches lost in a heavy belly of grey clouds. Rain fell on her upturned face. She reached up into the rain, into the trees, and felt a tingling in her fingertips, then she heard a rushing sound like a great wind and suddenly her fingers, her hands, her arms, then her whole body was filled with white light.

An experience that leaves her feeling 'almost holy', such shamanistic identification with the natural world is envisioned as a confirmation of ecological agency: 'It was the Land that claimed her attention. Starting at her knees and working all the way up to her raised fingertips, it filled her with a sense of wellbeing such as she had not experienced in all her fifteen years' (212). This image of earthly power resembles the 'totemic' ontology that Tim Ingold (2000: 112) notes in Aboriginal conceptions of the sacred; this ontology envisages 'the land' as 'harbour[ing] the vital forces which animate the plants, animals, and people it engenders'. The message is clear that a healthy earth – capable of ensuring human 'wellbeing' – is homologous with a healthy, agential human life on earth. If, as David Abram (1996: 9) contends, the 'deeply mysterious powers and entities with which the shaman enters into rapport' constitute for the modern man 'just so much scenery, the backdrop of our more pressing human concerns', the Land's ability to claim Ora's attention refutes the colonial aspirations of its human occupants and reclaims its own discursive agency.

Ora's prophetic role as Shædow Master accords her the ability to speak not simply for the Guests but also for the Land itself. Having been initially 'struck dumb' by the Cloudtouchers, Ora's re-voicing signals her increasingly spiritual, as opposed to aesthetic, engagement with the earth. Moments in which Ora's voice is defamiliarised signal the Land's reclamation of discursive agency: '[T]he voice that passed her lips was barely recognisable as her own'; 'It was as if the words had come from someone else' (212; 256). The 'voiceless' narrative often used in refugee discourse that depicts those in the developed world as having a more expert knowledge of the needs of the developing world than its own silenced people, is here dismantled in service of a natural world also traditionally deemed silent and helpless. 'The point', contends Patrick Murphy (1995: 152), 'is not to speak for nature but to work to render the signification presented us by nature into a verbal depiction by means of speaking subjects'. Ora becomes such a speaking subject, her re-voicing functioning to depict nature's self-disclosure through ecopoiesis. I here use the term ecopoiesis in the sense coined by Jonathan Bate (2000: 75), as a discursive practice designed to give 'voice' to nature in 'an attempt to transform into language an experience of dwelling upon the earth' (199). This discursive technique gives the natural world a voice that a reader would recognise not as a voice interpellated by anthropocentric notions of natural worth but as a voice representative of nature itself. Ora's subsequent decision to abolish the monarchy, rename the country Lakeland and demand equal status for all Lakeland's inhabitants accords both the Guests and the Land the potential for self-determination: 'No one shall rule over this land but the Land itself' (264). A discourse of indigenous holistic sanctity thus underwrites the novel's affirmation of a voiced and agential natural world.

Conclusion: ecological immanence

These novels engage with spirituality in their attempts to engender increasing ecological awareness in their young adult readers, particularly in relation to the young adult's capacity for emotional and empathic engagement with the natural world. An ecofeminist poetics of place refutes the 'fusion of progress, technology and religion' noted by Dinerstein (2006: 572) in contemporary western cultures as a structure upon which to base a responsible environmental ethic. Institutional religion, in particular a disembodied tradition of spiritual transcendence, is similarly rejected in favour of more embodied and embedded forms of spiritual engagement. In my focused novels, western environmentalism, normative religion and indigeneity are all used as frameworks to critique or promote such differing conceptions of the sacred. The various alternative responses to human–earth dislocation offered under these spiritual paradigms are representative of the 'spiritual phase transition', delineated in my first chapter, that Kearns and Keller (2007: xi) deem necessary for a 'green shift' in human engagement with place: 'The green shift seems to require a root change of human outlook, a mutation of collective philosophy, a spiritual phase transition'. They signal the transformations of mind necessary for ecological rehabilitation in a dislocated global society.

In *Feed*, Violet's nostalgia for a lost ecological purity is indicative of this 'spiritual phase transition' in ecological perception. Faced with the prospect of her own death, Violet seeks solace in an ancient Mayan spell to preserve dying cultures (187):

> *'Spirit of the sky, spirit of the earth, grant us descendents for as long as the sun moves, for as long as there is dawn. Grant us green roads; grant us many green paths. May the people be peaceful, very peaceful, and let them not fall; let them not be wounded. Let there be no disgrace, no captivity. O thou Shrouded Glory, Lightening Lord, Lord Jaguar, Mount of Fire, Womb of Heaven, Womb of Earth'.*

This invocation to the spirit of the sky and spirit of the earth represents a human plea for peace, health, integrity and freedom in 'the dawn' of spiritual awakening. If dawn is to be associated with spiritual transcendence – as it is in *Savannah 2116 AD* – this transcendence is not 'airborne' but deeply embedded within the 'green paths' of the natural world. A plea to the spirits of the natural world, the 'spell' locates the ancient Mayans in between the sky and the earth – in the 'Womb' of both – and intimately embedded in the earth's ecology. This prayer resonates with the ecofeminist spiritualities delineated in this chapter, which envision spiritual engagement with the natural world as key to the preservation of our own threatened cultures. Just as Violet is comforted by the holistic vision of natural cohabitation evoked by the Mayan spell, ecofeminist spiritualities are designed to create similarly restorative precedents for ecocentric engagement.

In a globalised world in which bioregional identification with the environment is impeded by transnational ideologies, Violet's turn to the spiritual beliefs of an ecoconscious culture is indicative of a common recourse within ecofeminist spiritualities to 'turn towards the earth'. The very act of '"getting grounded"', Betcher (2007: 317) argues, 'is actually a very ancient and widespread wisdom for "centring" and restoring spirit, for fitting a body back into its elemental and social niche'. The novels that offer more successful models for environmental engagement 'ground' their protagonists in embedded communion with the earth in service of such a restoration of spirit, or cosmological re-centring of the human actant within its ecological context. Novels such as *Shædow Master* counter the dislocation and disembodiment of our current cultural context by situating their sanctification of the natural environment within indigenous discourses of holistic sanctity. These ancient discourses – passed down from generation to generation as they are in *A Darkling Plain* – promote subservience to the earth, conceived as a holistic entity, to engender an intersubjective and agential relationship between humanity and the natural world.

If the place-based epistemic frameworks delineated in my previous chapter transform the blind space of apocalypse into a receptacle for responsible truths, the ecofeminist spiritualities here discussed extend such responsibility to spiritual reappraisal. Warren (1993: 120) argues that 'ecofeminist spiritualities have played a vital grass-roots role in the emergence of ecofeminism as a political movement'; 'Failure to acknowledge the potential roles care-based ecofeminist spiritualities do or could play in changing patriarchal systems', she contends, 'perpetuates the mistaken view that spirituality is not or cannot be a legitimate feminist political concern' (2000: 212). The critique to which first wave ecofeminists have been subject for attempting to legitimate ecofeminist spiritualities is testament to the contentious positioning of spirituality in current political, philosophical and ethical thinking. The novels themselves exemplify ambivalence as to whether spiritual reappraisal is an effective stimulus for change; whilst Daisy in *How I Live Now* experiences emotional renewal through her spiritual engagement with place and Ora in *Shædow Master* is politically empowered through her embeddedness in the natural world, Tom in *Off the Road* conversely fails to negotiate an intersubjective relationship with the earth just as Savannah in *Savannah 2116 AD* fails to dismantle the transcendent hierarchies on which earth-oppression is based. The impetus to look to alternative forms of knowledge, contemplation and practice is, however, political in scope, if not always in practice. As a response to the pejorative neoliberal model that fails to invest value in local community, this impetus opens up a space of resistance *within* systems of gendered power in which to negotiate, reassess and reshape current modes of environmental interaction. It is unhelpful, therefore, to dismiss ecofeminist spiritualities as inapplicable to social or political engagement; instead they should be valued for opening young readers' eyes to alternative ways of being in the world via a poetics of place grounded in immanence rather than transcendence.

6
Deep Ecology or Ecofeminism: The Embodied, Embedded Hybrid

The human subject and how he or she fits into the wider web of ecological relationships has been a contentious subject of debate for ecofeminists since the inception of the ecocritical movement. Identity – defined here as a textual construct – is determined through the construction, negotiation and redefinition of the boundaries of the self. When identity is formulated in specific relation to the natural world or the nonhuman other, these boundaries are rendered flexible enough to take the other – at some level – into the self. This dialogic relationship sees the self variously lose itself in the other, expand itself to encompass the other or develop a mutually agential relationship *with* the other. In each of these reformulations, human consciousness necessarily defines the medium of representation; as Rigby (2004b: 427) argues, 'An acknowledgement of the centrality of the human actant, however contingent, contextualised, and decentred she might be in herself, is also a necessary condition for there to be such a thing as literature'. The deep ecology and ecofeminist movements place differing emphases on human centrality, particularly in relation to the positioning of the ecological other. Deep ecologists advocate an expanded sense of self to encompass the needs of the nonhuman other, whilst ecofeminists advocate a plurality of perspectives to extend solidarity to the nonhuman other. The novels under consideration negotiate the identity formation of their protagonists within the parameters of their natural environments in ways that reflect these differing theoretical frameworks. The novels demonstrate a preoccupation with wholeness – the integration of human and nonhuman identities – in a formulation that merges insights from both deep ecology and ecofeminism. I analyse these instantiations of human-nonhuman melding by employing a discourse of ecological hybridity.

Since the deep ecology movement has had a pervasive, and often controversial, influence on popular thinking about the environment over the past few decades, I shall briefly explore its foundational concept of identification between humans and nature in light of its representational influence on contemporary young adult fiction. Recognised as a cornerstone of deep ecological thinking, identification constitutes an awareness that humans are inextricably enmeshed in broader biosocial relations. According to the founder of the deep ecology movement, Arne Naess (2002: 114), such an awareness counters the anthropocentric bias currently structuring western thought and allows humanity to 'recognise something of ourselves in the other creature, and something of the other creature in ourselves'. Human identification with the natural world is predicated on a 'cosmology of unbroken wholeness': an expansion of self that denies any bifurcation in reality between human self (or Self) and non-human other (Naess 1973: 96). Identification with the natural world, in other words, serves to allow humanity to perceive no boundaries between the human and nonhuman worlds, and thus to treat defence of the environment as self-defence; as Naess (Seed *et al.* 1988: 29) puts it, 'The requisite care flows naturally if the self is widened and deepened so that protection of free nature is felt and conceived of as protection of our very selves'.

In designating the anthropocentric separation of humans from nature a foundational problem in ecological thinking, deep ecology situates a positivist response to environmental crisis in the merging of self and other and the concomitant melding of human and nonhuman identities. Such a melding, or self-realisation, would appear to answer the ecofeminist call for an alternative ethic centring on care and mutuality in human-nonhuman interrelations. However, as Robert Session (1996: 143; 142) makes clear, identification in deep ecology is put forwards as a means of ending human domination of nature through a 'reversal' of the culture-nature dualism that has seen humanity 'split ourselves from the world'. Such a reversal, according to deep ecologists, would prevent an anthropocentric bias from defining human-nonhuman relations by placing the needs of the earth, particularly at this critical juncture in history, above (or at least on par with) our own. Such a reversal of dualisms has been seriously critiqued by ecofeminists as an unproductive alternative to ecological relations since a simple inversion of the poles serves to perpetuate, rather than dismantle, the dualistic dynamic that produces difference. Whilst deep ecology's focus on holistic attitudes towards the environment and identification between humans and the wider world is clearly a focus to which ecofeminism adheres, the two philosophies differ in the corrective responses to environmental crisis each puts forward as an alternative to dualism.

An element of critique, for ecofeminists, in deep ecology's attempt to 'reverse' the bifurcation of culture and nature, is the gendered language, theory and praxis used to interrogate current ecological thinking. Ecofeminism proposes that androcentrism, rather than anthropocentrism per se, must be critiqued in order to address the root cause of environmental oppression. Ecofeminist analysis extends this critique of androcentric discourse to the intimate, logical and historical circumstances that lead to environmental oppression. Such historicising runs counter to the abstract equality promoted by deep ecology as a solution to environmental crisis. From an ecofeminist perspective, deep ecology's abstract universalism – promoting an ethereal merging of human and nonhuman selves – ignores the complexity and diversity of human-nonhuman interrelations over time and across distance, and the logical and historical connections between environmental domination and other comparable forms of oppression. As Roger J.H. King (1996: 86) suggests, deep ecology 'remains simply the abstract negation of the original patriarchal dualism: a move from abstractly demarcated difference to abstract identity'; ecofeminism contextualises such identification within actual experience, and situates its analysis of 'the whole' within localised explorations of the particular.

In seeking unity or wholeness with nature, deep ecologists can further be accused of advocating a form of dependency in ecological relations whereby nonhuman nature is defined and circumscribed through human notions of selfhood. If the abstract expanded Self of deep ecology is to encompass nonhuman others, it lacks the capacity to distinguish the specific and particular needs of the environment it represents over the more general needs of the human who defines the medium of representation. Plumwood (1993: 180) labels this problematic tradition 'transferring the structures of egoism' and suggests that it is symptomatic of 'a general set of boundary problems encountered by forms of deep ecology which dissolve or expand the self in this way' (178). Lisa Kretz (2009: 128) similarly argues that deep ecological monistic identification with the natural world is an 'oversimplified recommendation' and instead highlights the need for ecofeminists to acknowledge multiple forms of ecological identifications. Since identification, self-realisation, self-merger and unity are all aspects of 'incorporating' the other within the self, and therefore undermine the subjectivity and agency of the other, ecofeminists prefer a reading of the ecological self as one that does not require 'any sort of identity merger, or loss of boundaries between the self and other' (Plumwood 1993: 160). The term 'solidarity' is often chosen in preference to identification in order to retain the difference and distinctness of the other but allow for an active confluence of interests and mutual understanding within (and against) an oppressive system (Mallory 2009). By taking into ethical account nature's incommensurability and alterity, ecofeminists politicise the deep ecological formulation of human selfhood.

An alternative, then, to the monism of deep ecology would be a contextualised discourse of plurality and multiplicity. Warren (1997: 30) defines such a discourse as the product of a 'contextualist ethic' that 'sees ethical discourse and practice as emerging from the voices of people located in different historical circumstances'; such an ethic, she suggests, 'is properly viewed as a *collage* or *mosaic*, a *tapestry* of voices that emerges out of felt experience'. The collage motif is important to ecofeminist theorising; Cheney (2005: 115) borrows the word to describe the multiple experiences that can come together to create 'responsible understanding[s] of the world', and proposes that – 'if plausible in relationship to [one's own] experience' – such a collage 'opens up the possibility of communication with, and invites reciprocity with, human and more-than-human worlds'. The 'quilted' nature of ecofeminist engagement with philosophy and ethics, as defined by Warren (2000: 66), denotes that ecofeminist theory will be 'made up of different "patches," constructed by quilters in particular social, historical, and materialist contexts'. As collage, mosaic, tapestry or quilt, ecofeminist theory is anti-monistic and highly contextualist; the ecofeminist contextual self seeks to include nature in its definition in order to expand the challenge to both self and status quo through the diversity of perspectives this expansion would entail.

Through its advocacy of a pluralist epistemological strategy in place of reductionist ethical reasoning, ecofeminism thus seeks to encompass a diversity of human voices, as well as those voices pertaining to the natural world. The novels discussed can be seen to participate in this dialogue by exploring the problematic notion of human identification with the natural world through the comparative lenses of deep ecology and ecofeminism: the dissolution and expansion of selfhood within nature that marks the former and the plurality of human and nonhuman voices advocated by the latter. A notable preoccupation with wholeness, or the coming together of separate parts, entities and identities underpins the ecological agenda of these novels. Whilst this preoccupation with wholeness would appear to adhere to the deep ecological call for a holistic apprehension of the natural world, I would suggest that it in fact signals less a reversal or inversion of oppressive systemic relations with nature and more an advocacy of multiplicity in identity formation as supported by ecofeminism.

I suggest the applicability of the term 'hybrid' to account for both deep ecology's notion of identification between humans and the natural world and ecofeminism's call for plurality of voice and ethical actant. I borrow the term hybridity to encompass the notion of meshing or 'coming together' in a manner helpful to an analysis of ecological representation in fiction for young adults (Roos and Hunt 2010: 8). I choose this term in reference to the importance of hybridity to inter-sectional third wave feminist discourses and in light of Cudworth's (2005: 15) contention that '[p]opular conceptions of hybridity are key to understanding contemporary developments in material relations between humans and "nature"'. This richly theorised term with its roots in postcolonial criticism (to which I can here give no more than a cursory nod) is inherently counter-hegemonic, and borrows from the critical insights embedded in other feminist hybrid figures such as Gloria Anzaldua's (1987) border-crossing 'new mestiza'. It is a term that encompasses the ontological multiplicity and plurality of voice advocated by an ecofeminist engagement with subjectivity, arising out of a discourse of challenge to normative monistic thought-patterns. In ecological terms, a human-nonhuman hybrid occupies a resistant position, posing a challenge to systemic regimes of difference that traditionally identify certain humans (adult, white, male) as outside and above nature and marginalise 'feminised' others. If hybridity chal-lenges existing borders in the identity formation of the young adult protagonists, the question to be asked is which borders, exactly, are being challenged?

In what follows I explore the hybrid form as a manifestation of ecofeminist insights gleaned from a plurality of subject positions. I find a useful forerunner to my analysis in Neil Leach's (2006: 240) theory of 'camouflage', which he understands as a 'mechanism for inscribing an individual within a given cultural setting'. Although Leach's (2006: 240) analysis is situated within cultural discourses of aes-thetic production and design, his premise that camouflage entails 'the relating of the self to the world' and thereby 'offers a medium through which to relate to the other' is applicable to a wider examination of human identity within the larger biosocial context.[1] My focus on female identity as a product of parallel human–nonhuman relationships, in a formulation that John Stephens (2010: 209) has termed the 'econarrative of dual cathexis', extends the notion of hybridity to encompass the coming together of more than one subject position. I here set the hybrid identities of my focused novels in opposition to those I explored in my second chapter, which envisioned the ecological posthuman as an eroded and disembodied man-machine hybrid arising out of crisis or disaster. The hybrid forms considered in this chapter, alternatively, are predicated on a human-nonhuman integration experienced precisely *through* the embodied nature of the subjective agent.

The dissolution and expansion of self: 'open continuity'

Ecocentric experiences of identification with the nature world have been described by Charlene Spretnak (1997: 430) as moments when 'the apparently fixed boundary between inner and outer seems to become permeable and gives way, at times, to a palpable sense of being at one with the surroundings'. In my second chapter I noted the erosion of bodily boundaries in the female protagonists as a manifestation of hegemonic interpellation. In the novels here discussed, conversely, such dissolution of boundaries or expansion of selfhood is not debilitating but desired, and reconfigured as a process of negotiation between the individual and the outside world that facilitates movement from an anthropocentric state of self-absorption to a more mutually agential interrelationship with the natural world. Metaphors of dissolution are often used in this context to dramatise a process of letting go of a previous sense of self. Metaphors of opening out or expanding, by contrast, are used to envisage a process of becoming or emerging into a new and more agential identity. These processes – dissolution and expansion – are simultaneously occurring and serve to facilitate a sense of being at one with the natural world in a formulation that sees the body inscribed as 'a threshold where nature and culture dissolve' (Alaimo 1998: 137).

Kretz's (2009) theory of 'open continuity' is useful to an analysis of identity dissolution and expansion in the novels discussed. Building on Plumwood's recommendation to alter self-concept to better reflect human-nature interrelations, Kretz (2009: 121–2) argues that:

> Ecology indicates and supports a spectrum of "open continuities," mapping a diversity of ecologically relevant boundaries. Insofar as these ecological boundaries challenge concepts of the human self as

clearly distinct from other ecological entities, the human self must be re-imagined in new and more open ways.

Kretz's (2009: 130) contention that to situate humanity within wider ecological networks, at the level of species rather than the individual, is to provide humanity with new parameters for ecological boundary marking, reflects a fluid engagement with the world that enables the rethinking of the self 'such that one has a far more intimate relationship with what is otherwise construed as other' (123). Drawing on the work of Suzuki and McConnell to claim that it is not enough merely to say we 'depend' on air, when in fact air literally 'constitutes' the human self, Kretz (2009: 126) argues that it 'follows ethically' that 'identifying in openly continuous ways can offer a strong moral imperative to care for and protect what constitutes the self'.[2] A thesis that resembles that of deep ecological thinking, Kretz's theory of open continuity differs in its engagement with the boundaries of the human body which it sees as fluid and contextual rather than static and dichotomous. Kretz's theory is useful to an analysis of identity formation in the novels under consideration since it interprets the moments of dissolution and expansion experienced by the young protagonists as exemplifying an openly continuous relationship with the natural world.

The dissolution of the body in death in *A Darkling Plain* is constituted not as an indication of trauma but as a lyrical celebration of the melding of the human and the natural. Upon the deaths of Hester and Tom, Shrike lays their bodies next to each other on the ground and watches them decompose as the days, weeks, months, years and finally centuries pass by (529–30):

> In the fitful sunlight Tom and Hester began to swell and darken beneath their shroud of flies. Worms and beetles fed on them, and birds flew down to take their eyes and tongues. Soon their smell attracted small mammals, who had been going hungry in that cheerless summer.
>
> Shrike did not move. He shut down his systems one by one until only his eyes and his mind was awake. He watched the graceful architecture of Tom and Hester's skeletons emerge, their bare skulls leaning together like two eggs in a nest of wet hair. Winter heaped snow over them; the rains of spring washed them clean. Next summer's grass grew thick and green beneath them, and an oak sapling sprouted in the white basket of Hester's ribs.

Shrike watched it all while the years fell past him, green and white, green and white. The small bones of their hands and feet scattered into the grass like dice; larger ones were tumbled and gnawed by foxes; they turned grey and crumbly and it became hard to tell whose had been whose.

Here, images that would normally be deemed grotesque and morbid – bodies swelling and darkening, animals feeding on dead flesh – are treated with a tenderness that envisions the rotting bodies not as waste but as catalyst for new life. The seasonal emphasis on death and rebirth which sees the 'two eggs in a nest' washed clean – made pure – in the spring highlights the naturalness of the body's existential cycle and the *rightness* of such a dignified human death within nature: 'If Stalkers could cry, he would have cried then, for he knew all at once that this was the right end for her, and that she would not want him to take her from this quiet valley, or from the once-born she had loved' (528–9). Bodily dissolution within nature is not associated with a loss of subjectivity but with a converse strengthening of purpose and identity since Hester 'had clutched Tom's hand as she died, and she was still clinging tightly to it' (528). Just as the jumbled bones that make it 'hard to tell whose had been whose' strengthen this indication of Hester and Tom's love, the small bones 'scattered into the grass' suggest a similar integration of purpose and identity between humans and the natural world. Through bodily dissolution, the human actant enacts less a dissolution of self and more an expansion of self in its conceptual outwards movement to encompass the natural systems it nourishes and engenders.

A dissolution of bodily boundaries in *How I Live Now*, whilst initially problematic, is reconfigured as the novel continues to become a powerful means of self-fulfilment. Dissolution is associated not with death but with a converse *denial* of death and centres on the multiply-coded female body. Daisy is aware of the threat posed to her embodied existence, even prior to the war, through her ability to manipulate the amount of food that enters her body. Daisy's refusal to eat constitutes a fear of letting the outside world penetrate her interiority; such a refusal has seen her pain over her father's re-marriage and her stepmother's pregnancy become physically written onto her emaciated body. The irony that characterises her relationship with her ecological surroundings is metonymic of an underlying fear of porous boundaries. Such a fear extends to the permeability of other mental and physical borders: the cellular membranes through which the smallpox epidemic is rumoured to strike, the locked doors of her cousins' farmhouse, the part of her psyche that stops her mind from internalising trauma. Penetration is envisaged as a threat not only to Daisy's body but also to her fragile psychological state. Daisy and her cousins, in their attempts to cope with the brutality of war, constantly struggle against the psychological dissolution of the fragile border between emotional sanity and trauma, a struggle that all but Edmond manage to eventually overcome.

The natural world exists in counterpoint to the enclosed space of Daisy's body. Whilst hunger is therefore problematic since it signals the dissolution of the fragile borders of the self, a more positive and lasting re-envisioning of the fear of bodily permeability can be found in the unexpected romance that blossoms between Daisy and Edmond. Edmond's love becomes a positive substitution for the food Daisy lacks, allowing her to relinquish the control associated with both her refusal to eat and her interaction with the outside world: 'my brain and my body and every single inch of me that was alive was flooded with the feeling that I was starving, starving, starving for Edmond. And what a coincidence, that was the feeling I loved best in the world' (50). Not only does Edmond satisfy Daisy's hunger, but also encourages her to view love and sex as an empowering, rather than disempowering, dissolution of borders: '[s]ometimes I felt like I was being consumed from within like a person with one of those freak diseases where you digest your own stomach' and '[i]t was simply a way of being in love' (58; 57). Love involves consuming and being consumed, in a positive re-envisioning of Daisy's anorexic phobia of letting the natural world penetrate her interiority.

It is because of this gradual affirmation of bodily dissolution as positive and life-enabling that Daisy and Piper's journey away from the farmhouse and into the countryside in an attempt to escape the more bloody consequences of the war – a journey in which they are forced to exist on meagre rations and forage for food – enables Daisy's changing relationship with her own body. Her evolving attitude towards hunger as means of self-control and with it her new appreciation for the natural world as enabling of subjective agency tellingly takes place after sharing with Piper their first hot meal in days after successfully foraging for mushrooms (145):

And as I started to eat the pieces of mushroom I suddenly thought All this time I've been starving, and without noticing I said it out loud, so that Piper said So have I, without even looking up and I thought No you haven't, not in the same way and I hope you never are.

That these mushrooms subsequently cause the girls to have violent hallucinations in which they hear people 'crying and screaming' suggests that the romantic ideal of self-sufficiency amongst nature is as unrealistic in the changed socio-political circumstances of globalised terror as a complete reversal of Daisy's eating habits after years battling anorexia (147). However, as a metaphor for physical and psychological healing, Daisy and Piper's journey through the British countryside is all the more powerful for its capacity to re-inscribe bodily dissolution not as the penetration of the fragile perimeters of the self but as the formulation of an embedded identity within the natural world.

Daisy's earlier empathetic connection with the natural word – before the war dissolves the close-knit family ties – is in this sense prophetic (69):

> I just closed my eyes and watched the blossom petals fall and listened to the heavy low buzz of fat pollen-drunk bees and tried to imagine melting into the earth so I could spend eternity under this tree.

'Melting' into the earth, Daisy here invokes dissolution as a blissful integration with her ecological surroundings. Her contradictory motion of closing her eyes to watch the petals fall foregrounds the imbrication of sensory perception and place-situatedness in Daisy's increasingly embodied connection to the earth. In a nod to magical realism, the text also dissolves the border between the interiority of the body and the exteriority of human interaction by instantiating a form of telepathy between Daisy and Edmond when the war forces them apart. Like that occasioned by the natural world, Edmond's ethereal 'presence' instigates a further dissolution, 'silenc[ing]' Daisy's anxiety and making her feel 'melted and soft' (97). Daisy's telepathic connection with Edmond is described as a heightening of sensory perception: she 'could smell his smell of tobacco and earth and something radiant and spicy like amber; could feel the smooth glide of his skin' (96). These embodied sensations embed an experience that is otherwise otherwordly in the earthiness of phenomenal interaction. These telepathic moments of connection empower Daisy to keep both Piper and herself safe. The dissolution of emotional and psychological barriers, then, is metonymic of the melting of the human self into the local landscape in a process of embodiment and embeddedness that engenders safe containment.

Camouflage: 'a process of "becoming other"'

The theory of camouflage propagated by Leach (2006) offers a useful lens through which to interpret the melding of human and nonhuman forms, attitudes and identities seen in much recent young adult fiction. Camouflage is taken as a term 'to encapsulate various visual strategies that have been developed in recent years in response to an image-driven culture', facilitating 'the relating of the self to the world through the medium of representation' (Leach 2006: 240). A mechanism for inscribing an individual within his or her cultural setting, camouflage is used to delineate a person's relationship with a given space. To camouflage oneself within an image-driven culture is not to disguise oneself, but rather to formulate one's identity in specific relation to that setting. Camouflage constitutes 'a mode of symbolisation' operating 'through a process of assimilation based on representation' that sees individuals interact with their environments without becoming absorbed by them (2006: 240; 243). The logic of performance underpinning such a theory posits camouflage as a 'process-based interaction with the world' used in service of self-empowerment and self-expression (2006: 245). Camouflage does not simply involve inscribing oneself within one's setting but is also 'a process of "becoming other" and seeing the self in the other' in order to relate oneself most effectively to one's given cultural setting (2006: 244). Whilst Leach's comments are made in specific relation to the man-made representational environment, his theory of camouflage is illuminating in relation to the ways in which the protagonists of the novels inscribe themselves within their wider, ecological, environments.

Katniss and Peeta's attempts to interact with the hostile environment of the arena in *The Hunger Games* constitute just such a process of inscription, a task that is not simply a recommended response to an unknown landscape but a physical necessity if they are to survive the Games. The post-disaster society of Panem, risen up out of the ashes of present-day America, is a dystopic projection of our current western social obsession with image-based media and reality television. In the Hunger Games, the tributes are under constant surveillance, their images projected into each of the Districts so that each viewer has tailored, voyeuristic, moment-by-moment access to the young peoples' movements within their ecological prison. The viewers are not simply passive spectators but have the power to affect the survival chances of chosen tributes through their ability to deliver gifts and change the trajectory of events in the arena. Camouflage within this milieu must adhere to the 'more comprehensive understanding of the term', as delineated by Leach (2006: 244), which involves 'both revealing and concealing' the self: if Katniss and Peeta are to survive their ordeal they must undertake an intimate balancing act between concealing themselves from the other tributes who pose a constant threat to their safety, and revealing themselves to the viewing public in the hope of benevolent returns.

Katniss and Peeta's televised introduction to the viewing audience reflects the role of camouflage in determining the way in which the two young tributes are subsequently to be perceived, treated and judged in the arena. Entering on stage with flaming capes and headdresses, the two tributes are instantly breathtaking. Realising that Cinna has given her an advantage by making her so unforgettable, Katniss internalises the performative logic of Leach's theory of camouflage in her subsequent interactions with the Hunger Games arena by interspersing moments of purposeful performance within her more general efforts to conceal herself from the remaining tributes (198; 198–9):

> While I've been concealed by darkness and the sleeping bag and the willow branches, it has probably been difficult for the cameras to get a good shot of me. I know they must be tracking me now, though. The minute I hit the ground, I'm guaranteed a close-up. ... So as I slide out of the foliage and into the dawn light, I pause a second, giving the cameras time to lock on me. Then I cock my head slightly to the side and give a knowing smile. There! Let them figure out what that means!

Here, Katniss very deliberately manipulates her interaction with the natural environment. The proficiency and precision with which she manages her movements involves deliberate spatial negotiation from a space of concealment to a space of visibility: she 'slide[s] out of the foliage and into the dawn light'. Here the 'dawn light' operates as the stage lights of a performance stage, investing the surrounding ecology with a theatrical role. In this merging of the ecological and the performative, Katniss must act out a pre-determined self-image. She employs mime ('I ... give a knowing smile') as she actively constitutes her identity and thereby denotes her body a discursive site in need to being read and 'figure[d] out' by the viewing public.

In the artificial arena in which the seal of the Capitol that appears to float in the sky is actually another enormous screen, Katniss' ability to acknowledge the palimpsestic nature of her contemporary image-driven society allows her to internalise the performative logic of camouflage and relate herself more effectively to the natural environment. This process of identification is also extended to her fellow tribute Peeta. Unable to decide whether Peeta is an ally or an enemy, and whether the love he has professed for her is real or an act, Katniss exhibits a confused emotional response to Peeta that is reflected in the two young people's uneasy identification with their wooded setting. Katniss' discovery of Peeta, wounded and immobile, after both tributes have spent several days alone, signals to Katniss (who here literally stumbles across him) that Peeta is invisible in more ways than one (305; 306):

> My eyes peruse the bank, but there's nothing. Just mud, the plants, the base of the rocks. ...
> "Well, don't step on me."
> I jump back. His voice was right under my feet. Still there's nothing. Then his eyes open, unmistakably blue in the brown mud and green leaves. I gasp and am rewarded with a hint of white teeth as he laughs.

Here, the odd linguistic emphasis of sight in the phrase '[m]y eyes peruse the bank' (rather than '*I* peruse the bank') sets '[m]y eyes' in opposition to '[h]is voice', 'his eyes'. These fragmented body parts are metonymic of Peeta's state of camouflage in which what Katniss 'judge[s] to be his body' could very well be simply 'mud and plants' (305). This merged landscape of mud, plants, rocks and body parts is described as a patch-work of colours: 'blue' eyes, 'brown' mud, 'green' leaves, 'white' teeth. Katniss' nihilistic denial of Peeta's subjectivity – 'there's nothing ... [s]till there's nothing' – works against this vivid image of human and nonhuman melding. Peeta's subsequent emergence from his camouflaged state signals his concomitant emergence into Katniss' consciousness. This emergence does not signify a growing intersubjective or empathetic relationship between Peeta and Katniss, or a confused one at best, but rather Katniss' realisation that she must give the audience something to root for in the form of star-crossed lovers. With a '[o]ne kiss equals one pot of broth' mentality shaping her subsequent interactions with Peeta, Katniss manipulates her use of camouflage – and her behaviour towards Peeta – to increase her chances of surviving the Games (316).

Since camouflage is 'a defensive strategy, a survival mechanism', in both an ideological and existential sense, based on the logic that an individual must 'lose the self – temporarily – in order to preserve a sense of individuality', the camouflage undertaken by Katniss and Peeta during the Games is indicative of their drive not simply to keep themselves alive but to keep themselves *themselves* in the face of such an onslaught (Leach 2006: 246). Peeta's desire to show the Capitol that he is 'more than just a piece in their Games' signals his fear of just such a loss of self in response to the physical traumas of the arena (172). Peeta and Katniss' counter-hegemonic efforts to retain their self-hood are tellingly undertaken through a deliberate use of image-based camouflage. The inscribing of their identities into the arena's landscape becomes itself a form of resistance to hegemonic control. Katniss' efforts to manipulate her surroundings constitutes as a subversive response to the Gamekeepers' own manipulation of the natural environment; this is most noticeably so in Katniss' final act of defiance against the Hunger Games' rulers that sees her threaten to poison herself and Peeta if only one of them is allowed to survive. Katniss' acts of subversion do not go unpunished: her fiery introduction to the viewing public is met with a wall of fire descending on her in the Games, just as her refusal to accept the Gamekeepers final ruling is the catalyst for the vengeful events of the next two volumes of the series.

In designating camouflage a mechanism for counter-hegemonic resistance, Katniss thus posits the natural world as a discursive space in which to constitute her identity and relate herself to the viewing public. Following the death of her fellow tribute, Rue, Katniss' stand against the Capitol is undertaken by using nature *against* those who have designated it a mode of punishment, decorating Rue's dead body with flowers: 'Covering the ugly wound. Wreathing her face. Weaving her hair with bright colours' (286–7). Katniss' decision to cover over the 'ugly wound' written onto Rue's young body with flowers that are 'bright' and 'beautiful' signifies her attempt to re-inscribe nature not as punishment but as rebellion: the means through which humanity's dissent against human rights abuses can be communicated. For a girl whose very name means a small yellow flower, and who reminds Katniss of a bird ready to take wing, such a natural tribute returns Rue to the earth in an empathetic gesture of human-nonhuman integration. 'Wreathing' and '[w]eaving' Rue into her natural surroundings, Katniss camouflages Rue's body by inscribing it into the landscape. Katniss' actions are ritualistic; they engender a sense of becoming one with the world through a peaceful process of natural dissolution. The beauty of the flowers nevertheless jars with the violence of Rue's 'ugly wound' and signifies Rue's body as a discursive site of protest against Panem's rulers. Camouflage is a mechanism for inscribing Rue's identity within the Hunger Games arena both as a symbol of hope for a relationship between humanity and the natural world predicated on peace rather than violence and as a symbol of resistance against systemic oppression.

The ancient lullaby that Katniss sings to Rue on her flowery deathbed is a mountain air used to rock children to sleep. This invocation of an older collective memory to soothe Rue as she lies dying, inscribes Rue into an older time and gentler space with a promise that 'tomorrow will be more hopeful than this awful piece of time we call today' (284). The words of the mountain air communicate an embedded identity within the natural world (284):

> *Deep in the meadow, hidden far away*
> *A cloak of leaves, a moonbeam ray*
> *Forget your woes and let your troubles lay*
> *And when again it's morning, they'll wash away.*

Safety, within the natural space invoked by the lullaby, is engendered through nature's capacity to camouflage the song's listener: to hide her deep within the natural space and cover her with a cloak of leaves. A space of safety, warmth, love and dreams, the setting of the lullaby exists in counterpoint to the 'natural' space of the arena in which the tributes' own deadly 'woes' and 'troubles' cannot be so easily forgotten. The mockingjays that take up Katniss' song, spreading its melody throughout the Hunger Games arena, serve to further re-inscribe Rue's identity into the arena, this time aurally rather than visually. These hybrid birds, able to mimic a range of human vocal sounds, are themselves symbols of counter-hegemonic resistance, joining human and nonhuman voices together in a demonstration of mutual agency. Aware of the symbolic resonance of the mockingjay, Katniss in fact adopts the name of this bird in the final novel of the trilogy – *Mockingjay* [2010] – when she becomes the face of the people's revolution. If camouflage, then, is 'a process of "becoming other" and seeing the self in the other', Katniss' successful inscription of her identity within the artificial arena sees her 'become other' to the girl whom the system forces her to be. By refusing to perform as a girl who is vulnerable, wounded, dying, murderous and who must kill in order not to be killed, Katniss refutes her designation as 'a piece in their Games' (Leach 2006: 244). Camouflage, here, is a powerful metaphor both for resistance and empowerment in the formulation of Katniss' counter-hegemonic identity.

When humans become trees: solidarity through cathexis

In the novels so far discussed, identity formation is influenced both by the protagonists' ecological embeddedness – their growing identification with the natural 'world – and by their evolving relationships with human others, usually (although not always) in the form of romantic attachments. Stephens (2010: 207) notes this paralleling of 'ecoconsciousness and cathectic relationships' in recent environmental novels for young people and suggests that the 'interpenetration of individual consciousness and natural environment' pivots around a contradiction between the impartiality of ethical engagement with the environment and the partiality of emotional attachment to other human beings. The novels on which I focus here highlight this contradiction by turning the protagonists' impartial engagement with the natural world into an emotional attachment to a particular local landscape. The loving relationship the protagonists develop with this particular environment unfolds alongside the loving relationship they develop with their fellow human beings. Yet the emotional attachment that the principle characters develop to both the ecological locales *and* human lovers is problematic since their ethical commitment to the environment precludes a complete surrendering of their emotional selves to their lovers. For the lovers, then, the environment becomes a locus of struggle, a space in which they must compete to gain the protagonists' love. Their perceived inability to displace the natural world in the protagonists' affections sees them conversely attempt to incorporate themselves within the ecological space and identify themselves with the nonhuman environment. That the principle characters are unable to let go of their emotional attachment to the natural world, suggests that the natural world constitutes their identity and determines their subjectivity more completely than does their dependency on human attachments.

The ocean in *The Forest of Hands & Teeth* is both a mythic construct and an actual space, and functions as the locus of Mary's desire; it is a discursive space in which, and against which, Travis must compete for Mary's love. His will to protect Mary from the truth of the danger that the ocean poses to her safety sees Travis attempt to contain her – both physically and emotionally – in the empty house they find in the Forest; this house enacts Travis' attempt to incorporate himself within the natural world as a substitute for the ocean Mary lacks; he declares that the days they spent together are his 'world', his 'truth' and his 'ocean' (268). In hoping that he will be 'enough' for Mary, Travis attempts – and fails – to circumscribe Mary's desire for the unknown natural space within his own human sense of self (256–7):

> 'Once I thought I could protect you. Could take care of you. ... I think that even then I knew I wouldn't be enough for you, Mary. It's no longer about the ocean. It's about you and what you want and need. ... I can't be your second-choice dream.'

The ocean becomes a discursive site of emotional contestation: a space in which Mary is forced to choose between her own identification with the natural world and her cathectic relationship with Travis. Even though '[i]t was never supposed to be about having to choose one or the other', Mary's inability to let go of the ocean signifies that her subjectivity is integrally allied with this natural space (257). In revealing the ocean to be her first choice, Mary not only demonstrates her embodied and emotional attachment to the natural world but also shows that human love cannot 'keep all other dreams at bay' (258). Upon Travis' death, Mary's desperate attempts to hold on to him – '"I choose you over the ocean"' – are thus read against her *true* choice (275). A metaphor, then, for the necessity of a human life within the natural world, the ocean, in this novel, is positioned to foreground humanity's inability to formulate an identity divorced from its ecological context.

Trees, in *Zenith*, are the locus of Mara's desire, capable of rooting her to the earth and to her own sense of self. The Treenesters identify trees as integral to their subjectivity, believing that a tree root 'entombed' in stone is a stone-telling, or prophesy, of an embedded relationship within the natural world (297). Mara's own emotional attachment to the trees is couched in the language of a dream: she 'feels in her bones' that 'trees are the key to the future' (298). Here Mara's bones 'feel' her attachment: an instinctual and embodied pull towards the natural world. Rowan's love for Mara sees him attempt – like Travis – to incorporate himself within the natural space of the Greenland interior by becoming a substitute for the trees Mara lacks; when Mara expresses her belief that trees provide the answer, Rowan reminds her of the etymological root of his own name. This interaction prefigures Mara's realisation of a change in her relationship with Rowan, one tellingly predicated on her remembrance of their shared 'roots': 'Mara remembers how she and Rowan grew up as close as two saplings in this forest of young trees. They sprang from the same patch of Earth; their roots are entwined' (325).

Invoking the meaning of his name – protector against harm – to express his love for Mara, Rowan similarly attempts to circumscribe Mara's emotional existence within his own more rooted one in order to protect her from harm. Unlike Travis, Rowan successfully aligns his love for Mara with that of her love for the trees, allowing Mara to 'root' her identity both in the natural world and in her intersubjective relationship with him. Whilst the patch of trees where the Treenesters eventually settle makes Mara feel as if she has finally found a home, Rowan's tree-like presence serves to remind her of her previous home on the island of her birth. Tellingly this remembrance centres on the image of Rowan's steady hands 'working the wood' as he builds her baby a cradle (324). Watching him work, Mara likens Rowan to the male members of her family who were able to transform driftwood into something productive or beautiful: 'Mara thinks of old Tain and his driftwood carvings that were famed all over Wing. She pictures her father mending his fishing boat with scraps of driftwood alongside the other island men on the shore' (324). In this image of generational continuity rooted in the men's ability to 'mend' old hopes or 'carve' new possibilities out of wood, Mara sees in Rowan the potential to carve out a future, questioning whether she and Rowan might 'salvage a future, together, out of the wreckage of their past' (325). This future is predicated on an intersectional engagement between Mara (human), Rowan (human-tree) and the natural world (trees), and the mutually caring relationships Rowan's mediation engenders.

The locus of Edmond's desire in *How I Live Now* is the garden of the English farmhouse: the space in which, and against which, Daisy (this time the protagonist) must compete for his love in an attempt to formulate a similarly mutually caring relationship. Having witnessed a massacre at Gateshead Farm and retreated into self-abusive silence, Edmond internalises the violence he has seen enacted by self-harming, his one apparently therapeutic outlet being the act of gardening. The 'significant literary tradition' of 'girls in gardens' that Gwyneth Evans (1994: 20) notes in children's fiction – with its roots in Frances Hodgson Burnett's *The Secret Garden* (1911) – is here re-gendered so that a male actor becomes the recipient of horticultural healing; *How I Live Now* nevertheless resonates with the 'feminine pastoral' in offering 'an intensely private and enclosed world, the image of the girl who tends it' (20). The tradition of feminine pastoral extends from children's literature to adult fiction in which, as Shelley Boyd (2006: 190) argues, 'the home, the garden, and related paradigms of femininity have contained and defined women's social roles and identities'. With the garden thus functioning as 'an infamous enclosure for submissive feminine subjects', its use here is highly symbolic (Boyd 2006: 194). 'Feminising' Edmond through containment and enclosure, the garden becomes the locus of Edmond's emotional fragility. Daisy's entry into this space is perceived as a violent act of penetration; her attempts to heal Edmond with her love, care and compassion enact a process of emasculation that sees Edmond resignify his garden as a discursive site in which to enact the increasing violence of his suppressed emotions.

Daisy's inability to reach Edmond – leaving her 'terrified and furious and guilty' – sees her project her fear and anger onto the garden, as the space in which Edmond has enacted a metaphorical death: both of his own self and of their previous relationship (197): 'I thought of the ghost of that long-dead child, watching us, its desiccated bones sunk deep into the ground below. ... And still he sat there, as still and as cold as the statue of the dead child' (195; 197). Adopting an eco-phobic discourse, Daisy subverts the regenerative schema that usually accompanies the act of gardening to use it instead to lash out against Edmond's trauma (196):

> Against another wall were white apple blossoms on branches cut into sharp crucifixes and forced to lie flat against the stone. Below, the huge frilled lips of giant tulips in shades of white and cream nodded in their beds. They were almost finished now, spread open too far, splayed, exposing obscene black centres. I'd never had my own garden but I suddenly recognised something in the tangle of this one that wasn't beauty. Passion, maybe. And something else. Rage.

Since the training of fruit trees to grow flat against a wall along horizontal and vertical lines is a standard espalier technique, and tulips, when 'almost finished', are naturally splayed, Daisy as focaliser purposefully eroticises Edmond's gardening by focusing on the flowers' 'lips', their 'bed' and their 'obscene black centres': intimate and transgressive parts that turn their viewer into a voyeur. Cut off from Edmond both emotionally and sexually, Daisy betrays her own longings by positioning the garden as an alternative discourse, a narrative expression of Edmond's subconscious. In being 'open *too* far' (my italics), the tulips are indecent, whilst the apple blossoms are 'forced' to lie flat in an unnaturally violent and abusive act of artificial control. Daisy's attribution of forced sexuality onto the garden, as well as her misinterpretation of horticultural technique, obligates a reading of the flowers as indicative of Edmond as an 'obscene' sacrifice at the altar of a dehumanised military at the behest of a global network of corporations, punished – like Christ on his 'crucifix' – for crimes he did not commit.

The circumscribed contours of the garden, symbolic of the restrained, enclosed and private feminine self, are interpreted by Daisy as prison-like: 'suffocating' and 'claustrophobic' (196; 197). Edmond's blank sterility and silence is set in relation to the fecund excesses of his private garden: 'the dense thorny branches of a Blood Rose ... wild and heavy with dark red blooms' (207). Watching 'a honeybee lurch from one fat flower to the next, drunk, and staggering under the weight of all that botanical density', Daisy signifies the garden as a grotesque substitute for the emotions Edmond lacks (207). This image of inebriation, lack of control and bodily excess, projected onto the 'fat' flowers by a girl who has suffered much of her life from anorexia, reveals Daisy's helpless-ness at her lack of control when confronted by Edmond's introversion. For Daisy, the 'Blood Rose' signifies 'unequivocally' that 'Edmond had witnessed the massacre' at Gateshead Farm (207). Reading the flowers as discursive markers of Edmond's subjectivity, Daisy conflates the horticultural landscape with Edmond's own mental landscape: 'I recognised him in the plants' (196). With Edmond's death-like silence juxtaposed with the spring garden, '[w]arm and full of life', Daisy's inability to 'reconcile' the two opposing impulses sees her retreat from her 'fear' by retreating from the garden (197; 196–7):

> After that day, I could barely enter the garden without a huge effort of will. The air was suffocating, charged, the hungry plants sucking at the earth with their ferocious appetites. You could almost watch them grow, pressing their fat green tongues up through the black earth. They emerged selfish and starving, gasping for air.

The mythic schema for emotional renewal that I have delineated in previous chapters, manifested in ecological growth and emergence, is here subverted to denote the plants as 'hungry', 'ferocious', 'selfish' and 'starving': monopolising Edmond's love. The 'crumbling earth' of Edmond's garden is thus metonymic of Daisy's self-concept: crumbling under the perceived indifference of Edmond's gaze (209).

Like Travis and Rowan, Daisy attempts to incorporate herself within the garden, becoming 'a gardener, of sorts' to provide Edmond with the reciprocal love he lacks in the flowers: 'It was the only way to talk to him, not with words, but with hard work and the feel of old tools, and with fat bulbs buried and waiting deep in the rich soil' (209). Here, the continuity of 'old tools', reaching back to older and happier times, signals the eventual emergence of a regenerative ecopoetic narrative. Whilst working together in the garden, 'fat' bulbs are no longer representative of self-absorption and excess but of the 'rich' possibilities engendered by Edmond and Daisy's growing relationship. The bulbs 'buried' in the ground are not symbolic of the desiccated corpse of the long-dead child angel but of a hopeful 'waiting' for Edmond's gradual recovery. In this new schema for ecological revival and reciprocated cathexis, the 'crumbling earth' of Edmond's fragmented and tortured subjectivity becomes the bed in which 'tiny seeds' of hope can flower (209). The 'unspeakable voices' of the people whom Edmond watched die – voices that he internalised in angry and self-abusive silence – are now quietened and silence becomes a way of rooting the two lovers in a past 'togetherness': 'Sometimes we sit together the way we did a thousand years ago and we don't say a word but just listen to the thrushes and the skylarks. He even smiles occasionally, remembering' (209–10). The textual restoration of the regenerative schema that conventionally accompanies the act of gardening thus unfolds alongside the 'unfurl[ing]' of Daisy's 'tightly clenched core of fear and fury' as she begins to open to Edmond once more (199). To care for nature, in this novel, is to care for another human being; the garden is integral to the formation of Daisy's identity as she negotiates a responsible mode of being in the world, in a formulation that Stephanie Li (2009: 20) lyrically calls 'gardening the earth with new narratives'.

In each of these novels, the negotiation of the lovers' relationships with the protagonists (I refer here to Edmond as a protagonist in this latter sequence) centres on their interaction with the natural world. Their failure to displace the natural world in the protagonists' affections sees them variously attempt – with greater or lesser levels of success – to identify with, or incorporate themselves into, the ecological space. In the end, however, it becomes clear that emotional involvement and interaction of such a kind can only engender a contentious and competitive mode of emotional engagement predicated on the 'difference' – as Plumwood (2002: 202) defines it – 'between positioning oneself *with* the other and positioning oneself *as* the other'. Plumwood's (2002: 202) conception of 'solidarity' therefore seems more applicable to the teleology of the young peoples' relationships: 'An appropriate ethic of environmental activism is not that of identity or unity (or its reversal in difference) but that of *solidarity* – standing with the other in a supportive relationship in the political sense'. This account of solidarity – through which one 'stands with' the ecological other rather than subsumes it beneath a totalising human identity – poses a challenge to the deep ecological advocacy of an assimilated or incorporated self. Travis' death as a consequence of his failed attempt to become Mary's 'ocean' is metonymic of the dangers of trying to protect, encompass or circumscribe the other within the self. Solidarity – as an ecofeminist alternative – instead allows 'the other to exist in its otherness' and still permits or, as Chaone Mallory (2009: 15) contends, even 'requires ... action on its/their behalf that does not strip the other of her/his/their agency, intentionality, and capacity to resist'. The narrative trajectory that results in an extension of solidarity by both Rowan and Daisy towards the human loved one *and* the natural world thus exemplifies this notion of 'standing with' the other in order to engender a loving and caring interrelationship.

Ecological hybridity: the melding of human and nonhuman forms

In opposition to the deep ecological tendency towards abstraction and in service of a pluralistic ecofeminist ethic, Plumwood (1993: 183) contends that 'no abstract morality can be well founded that is not grounded in sound particularistic relations to others in personal life, the area which brings together in concrete form the intellectual with the emotional, the sensuous and the bodily'. Designating 'personal life' the space in which various systemic asymmetries are brought together 'in concrete form', Plumwood prefigures the personal moments of transformation – the bringing together of self and other – in contemporary young adult fiction that see actual physical metamorphosis result from culture-nature melding. These embodied transformations, when a hybrid form becomes an expression of human-nonhuman integration, adhere to Plumwood's (1993: 186) blueprint for 'ecological selfhood': 'an attempt to obtain a new human and a new social identity in relation to nature which challenges [the] dominant instrumental conception, and its associated social relations'. These 'new' humans differ from the posthuman figures of my second chapter who are hybrid insofar as they enact the melding of man and machine but who do not necessarily signal a permanently re-envisaged earth-based interaction between humans and the natural world. Ecological hybrids, alternatively, are physiological embodiments of multiplicity; they manifest dual or plural subject positions, identities and perspectives. They actively refute the deep ecological tendency towards incorporation or assimilation of the other into the human self by articulating the distinctness of both self and other.

In *Shædow Master*, Ora's mythic transformation into the Dalfen – a magical creature capable of bringing health and prosperity to the lake and the land – is a manifestation of hybridity that has been prefigured by acknowledgement of Ora's mixed-race heritage. Her 'awful honey-blonde hair and wide, green-blue eyes' that are a physical marker of her mixed-race parentage have been viewed for much of her life as a symbol of shame (even though she is initially unaware of their significance) (8). Upon the realisation that she has a Guest mother and a Folavian father, Ora is forced to question whether her 'half and half' status makes her 'both' Folavian and Guest, or 'neither' (174). Her failure to identify herself with either the colonisers or the indigenous peoples, whilst initially hindering her accession to the Folvian throne, is in fact finally the key to her successful attempt to unify the country. Paradoxically, Ora's ability to relate to both Folavians and Guests is valued less highly, in the importance assigned to it with regards to the health and prosperity of the Land, than her ability to relate to neither since it is Ora's unique birthright – her destiny to become the Shædow Master – that prefigures her integral role in the country's ecological revival.

Physical metamorphosis is the outward sign of Ora's growing capacity to perform such an ecological rejuvenation, giving her the emotional strength to embody the needs of the Folavians and the Guests, the lake and the land. The ribbon of light that explodes 'in the very centre of Ora's being' as she resists the invading Outworlders leaves her hair and eyes a brilliant shade of gold (214; 215):

> Ora gasped when she caught her reflection in the polished steel. The eyes that looked back at her were those of a stranger. Her eyes were turquoise, these were gold. And they glared back at her with such intensity that Ora could barely meet their glowing yellow gaze.

The 'intensity' that signals Ora's strength of purpose in renouncing her throne and sacrificing her human self to guide the Dalfen's spirit is uneasily associated with the splitting of her subjectivity so that she is simultaneously both herself and 'a stranger', unable to integrate her two identities and meet her own gaze. Such unease, causing Ora to question not *who* she is but '*what*' she is, signals the necessity of her eventual total metamorphosis into the mythic Shædow Master in a move that is configured as a melding of body and spirit – her own *and* that of the Dalfen (228). With an epistemological framework structured around the uncertainty of whether this legendary creature in fact exists guiding her subsequent interactions with the natural space, Ora interprets the

Dalfen's ecological call-to-arms through a dream narrative that sees the Dalfen undergo its own necessary transformation, from 'terrifying' to 'beautiful' (189):

> [T]his time the dream continued, magical in its transformation. It stopped being a nightmare and became, instead, a kind of fairytale.
> The monster spoke to her! And the moment it spoke, it ceased being a huge, terrifying creature and became beautiful. From dull grey it turned golden. ... All she wanted to do was embrace the sleek golden form that hung suspended in the waterless space next to her.

The 'kind of fairytale' that offers such dream-logic in place of the rationalist discourse of the Folavian dynasty pre-empts Ora's final transformation into her own mythic symbol of culture-nature integration. This transformation occurs, although it is never made overt to the reader, through Ora's move to 'embrace' the golden figure in her dreams, since at this point in the narrative (when Ora has not yet reached her ageday), the Dalfen's response is: 'It is not our time. ... We are not ready' (189). Such a sensuous and embodied yielding to the Dalfen's spirit – an embrace that sees Ora's body and this ethereal entity unite in a hybrid form – is configured as a joyful, transformative act of gestation.

Ora's transformation into the Shædow Master is envisioned as having long-lasting, generational significance; a mythic register denotes her maturation into the 'girl who ... was going to end the seventeen-year drought and bring new prosperity to them, their children and their children's children' (248). Here, intersubjective human-nonhuman relations are engendered through a discourse of ecological hybridity and the sensory and embodied melding of human and natural identities. 'As the paths of humans and animals intersect', notes Stacy Alaimo (1998: 126), 'the body becomes a threshold, a site of elemental connections'. The connective capacity of the hybrid body is echoed metaphorically in the joined hands of the two young lovers, Ora and Tasman, 'forming a bridge between the land and the lake' (265). This metaphorical bridge, extending equal empathy to the land, the lake, the colonisers and the indigenous peoples, is also envisioned as a bridge into the future since the novel ends with an epilogue set several decades after Ora's transformation in a seemingly carefree, multicultural world in which the Dalfen delights in making 'new friends' with the human population (268).

Corinna's similar struggle in *The Folk Keeper* to give full expression to the several aspects of her nature follows a narrative trajectory of lack, becoming, and fulfilment. Whilst Ora's eventual hybrid form in *Shædow Master* was prefigured by her mixed-race heritage, Corinna's own prophetic hybridity is signalled by her mixed-gender status: for several years she has disguised herself as a boy and answered to the name of Corin. This re-gendering has clearly been undertaken to avoid the patriarchal prejudices that allocate to a girl of the lower classes a 'humiliating' existence: 'I remembered too well the endless carrying of water buckets and scrubbing of floors and humiliations of Corinna before I burned my skirts and turned into a boy, and a Folk Keeper' (5). An overt demonstration of feminist agency alluding to the 'bra-burning' of the women's liberation movements of the 1960s, Corinna's re-gendering is an act of camouflage, in Leach's conception of the term, that allows her to perform more effectively within the socially-stratified patriarchal society of Rhysbridge, and later Cliffsend. Narrative hints prefiguring Corinna's future acknowledgement of her own hybrid form, such as her delight at 'growing two shadows' when she leaves the cellar, centre on the multiple nature of her hidden identity: both girl and boy, human and Sealmaiden (68).

Whilst her enacted male status allocates to her a more empowering role in the household than that offered to women, it does not disguise the 'not entirely human' nature of Corinna's identity (10). With her translucent skin, her body that does not feel cold, her hair that grows two inches every night and her ability to tell the time without glancing at a clock, Corinna is aware that her 'powers set [her] apart from the rest' (19). With this knowledge comes an awareness that these secret powers prevent her from fully integrating herself into society, delimiting her ability to successfully negotiate the parameters of her own body within 'a landscape that looks flat, but is really tricked out with hidden depths and shallows' (13). Corinna interprets her unease within her social milieu as signifying the existence of a 'missing piece' of herself: 'as though I have eyes, but there are colours I cannot see. As though I have ears, but there's a range of notes I cannot hear' (19). The sensory nature of this 'missing piece' indicates that blame for her inability to function (hetero)normatively within her given setting lies in her failure to achieve an embodied and embedded relationship with her environmental surroundings.

Corinna's mediatory position in the cellar between the humans above ground and the Folk below ground is a further indication of her liminality – her existence on the threshold of the human and the non-human. Experienced as a pent-up force of nature ('shivering', 'stirring', 'straining at the boundaries'), the Folk are capable of wreaking havoc not simply on the crops and livestock of Cliffsend – and thus disrupting the contained behavioural patterns of the townspeople – but also on Corinna's body (44). Their anger threatens bodily dissolution and the alienation of Corinna *from herself*, as experienced by Ora in *Shædow Master*: 'It mixed me all together with myself...ripping through tissue and fibre into the heart of my bones' (47; 70). Here, a multiplicity of pronouns – 'me', 'myself' and 'my' – signals Corinna's struggle to retain her subjectivity in the face of diffusion. Bodily dissolution here does not signal the empowering melding of human and nonhuman identities but a capitulation to unmediated emotion through the absorption of Corinna's individual self into the stronger collective identity of the Folk. Corinna's interactions with the Folk are circumscribed by a history of ritual, passed down from generation to generation of Folk Keepers. Protecting herself from the Folk's power with a necklace of nails and concentric rings of salt, Corinna ritualises her interactions with the Folk just as her society adheres to a ritualised calendar shaped by Saints Days, Feast Days, Solstices and Equinoxes, a calendar which sees them collectively subdue the Folk through such ancient practices as 'May Day garlands ... scattered in a circle round the Manor' and 'a ring of burning torches' (44).

Whilst these group rituals serve to expel the nonhuman sphere from the safely demarcated boundaries of the human, Corinna's own dual nature serves instead to tie these two spheres more closely together. Acknowledgement of her hidden seal-self is tellingly first pre-empted by the May Day festival that sees '[t]he indoors and the out-of-doors ... all mixed together' with carpets on the lawns and roses inside the Manor (77). Such acknowledgement is given full expression in her interactions with the sea, experienced as the opening of 'a door into another dimension' (88; 87):

I was born in reverse, exploded from one medium into another, from air to liquid, from dawn into darkness; and all around there was the singing of the sea. ... There came a slowing of the world – no, not of the world. A slowing of Corinna. A slowing into new life, not into drowning and death.

In this backwards rebirth that appears so much like a death, Corinna becomes finally capable of negotiating her embodiment, no longer clumsy but buoyant and fluid in her movements. Emerging subsequently from the calm of the sea, Corinna experiences a split between her body and self, aware now that her 'land-body' does not define all that she is yet is capable of circumscribing her identity: 'I was re-inhabiting my land-body, or maybe it was re-inhabiting me' (89). Acknowledging that her missing piece is 'as real as an arm or an eye', Corinna identifies that her craving for a holistic sense of herself is contained within the need to recover her Sealskin, allowing her once more to 'be whole' (114). Like Ora in *Shædow Master*, Corinna undergoes a series of physical transformations to encompass her hybridity. A fairytale narrative of change and becoming gives shape to her metamorphosis: 'I was once a girl who became a boy who became a Folk Keeper. Now I am a girl again, looking for a way to become a Sealmaiden' (112). Corinna's ontological multiplicity is envisaged as the several layers of her being, allowing her to 'peel[] off Lady Corinna Merton in layers' (157). Tellingly it is only through completely removing the trappings of the patriarchal culture that has enforced her camouflage that she can experience the 'explosion of beauty' that signals her newly embodied relationship with the world: 'My senses have opened like flowers; everything is an exquisite pleasure. I taste... I feel... I see...' (121–2). Here, sensory perception becomes the gateway through which Corinna can escape the 'bounded space' that represents her human nature – trapped within the confines of a rigid class and gender system – and give expression to her suppressed plurality (123).

The melding of human and nonhuman identities that sees Corinna avoid a complete capitulation to her seal-self constitutes a modification of her previous desire to yield completely to the '[s]ilvered fur stretch[ing], swallowing skin, binding thigh to thigh' that would see her mesh forever with her Sealskin (159). Such 'swallowing' and 'binding' echoes her absorption within the strictures of the patriarchal society to which she had previously been subject. Whilst Ora in *Shædow Master* achieves her hybrid form through rejecting the human she loves in order to create an alternative bond with the Dalfen spirit, Corinna's transformation conversely takes place through acceptance of her love for Finian and the necessity of therefore integrating her seal-self into her human identity. Realising that she need not become a Sealmaiden to have a life with the sea since she 'was a part of it already', Corinna configures the integration of her identities as a process of awakening into a selfhood that in fact 'already' was (161). Corinna configures such embodied hybridity as an act of resistance and uses her multiplicity to re-write her mother's failure to negotiate her own hybrid nature under patriarchal systems of oppression (161):

> My mother went mad when her Sealskin was destroyed. She turned her back forever on the sea. She may never have known her powers,

that the sea was open to her still. But I won't go mad; I'll make the sea my second home. This is how we are different.

Corinna's identification with both the human world and the natural world is paradoxically achieved through a *denial* of both: neither a Sealmaiden or Lady Corinna. Empowerment comes through achieving an intimate balance between her 'solid' human self and her 'liquid' non-human self and thus an integration of her various subjectivities (140). Unlike the cellar, with its walls communicating her mother's alienation (*'Poor Rona: take pity on her'*), the liminal space Corinna comes to occupy – '[b]oth in and out of the water' – is able to open up new possibilities for agential belonging and communion between the human and nonhuman worlds (162). Here, ecological hybridity facilitates the generational overcoming of the oppressive strictures that have seen Corinna's mother fail to negotiate the parameters of her own self and body within her alien environment, and that see Corinna become conversely empowered through acknowledgement of her counter-hegemonic potential.

In both of these novels ecological hybridity allows for an extension of empathy towards natural entities that are not normally considered sentient: the 'Land' in *Shædow Master* and the 'sea' in *The Folk Keeper*. This extension of empathy enables these now-sentient natural spaces to develop a discursive agency of their own; as Corinna marvels: 'The beach has a language of its own, with its undulating ribbons of silt, the imponderable hieroglyphs of bird tracks. ... A new language, with a new alphabet, which I will learn to read' (20–1). Corinna's inability to understand why she craves the flesh of fish, like Ora's inability to understand the physical changes that are happening to her own body, foregrounds the intentionality of their nonhuman selves and the power of such nonhuman discursivity to actively shape the protagonists' identities. The 'deep human eyes' of the seals that guide Corinna back to shore when she becomes lost at sea prefigure this awareness of ecological intentionality (99). The seals' gaze serves to reverse the anthropocentric tendency noted by John Berger (1980: 16) to make animals 'the object of our ever-extending knowledge' and instead invests the seals with their own capacity to gaze back at us.

In these novels, then, the natural world becomes a space in which to enact 'in concrete form' the integration of human self and nonhuman other (Plumwood 1993: 183). Through the foregrounding of the nonhuman gaze and nonhuman intention, this integration does not involve incorporation or assimilation of the other within the self but mutual recognition of a shared ontological framework for identity formation. These hybrid forms are closely allied with possibilities for human and nonhuman self-fulfilment. They counter the 'centrality' of the human by offering alternative subject positions for the human actant beyond those of the 'contingent, contextualised, and decentred' subject noted by Rigby (2004b: 427). Human identity formation within the natural world therefore moves beyond political solidarity to the construction of ecologically-oriented 'cyborg' subject positions, in a modification of Haraway's (1991) seminal theory of hybridity. In their capacity to interrogate asymmetric power relations, as delineated in my second chapter, Haraway's cyborgs undertake a '"political struggle" to see from both perspectives at once' according to the premise that 'each reveals both domination and possibilities unimaginable from the other vantage point' (Haraway 1991: 154). The hybrid forms here discussed manifest far more successful attempts to offer such a 'political struggle' against productions of difference than do the man-machine hybrids explored in my second chapter since they give full body and voice to the human *and* nonhuman actant.

Conclusion: ecopoiesis and the 'traitorous' human

Transformation, contend Gaard and Murphy (1998: 3), 'may very well be the single term to which all adherents of ecofeminism would assent'. In the novels discussed, transformation of the self – through identification, incorporation or solidarity with the other – foregrounds the vital importance of intersubjectivity to the growth of a young person's ecoconsciousness. These novels enact the protagonists' autopoiesis, understood as 'self-fashioning and self-disclosure', through their integration and immersion within the natural space (Stephens 2010: 210). The 'econarrative of dual cathexis' that Stephens (2010: 210) notes in recent young adult fiction sees this autopoiesis occur in parallel with *eco*poiesis; self-disclosure discursively engenders a 'mode of writing that is to some extent mimetic of nature's self-disclosure' (Stephens 2010: 210). Through discourses of self-dissolution, camouflage, cathexis and hybridity, these novels attempt to render these parallel modes of self-inscription a product of the protagonists' embodiment and embeddedness within the natural world. The novels are relatively successful at representing those 'rare moments' that Stephens (2010: 214) suggests affirm 'a continuity and interpenetration of anthropocentric subjectivity and ecocentric awareness' (210):

> Such ecopoiesis is perhaps only evident in rare moments, as, for example, when the text represents an interpenetration of subject

(focaliser) and object (world), in which the focaliser becomes the locus for a perception of the haecceity ('thisness' or self-immanence) of the phenomenal world.

Personal transformation, in these novels, is predicated on the inter-penetration of self and world, or the 'open continuity' of the human self-concept (Kretz 2009). In novels that envisage personal transforma-tion as a physical process of metamorphosis, the binary categories of subject-object are reconstituted in a hybrid form. These openly con-tinuous hybrid bodies enact the haecceity noted by Stephens.

An ecoconscious conceptualisation of human identity that recognises the self as a product of the ecological whole thus offers an alternative to the individual self of western humanism. Kretz's (2009: 130) contention that '[t]he story of human selfhood is impoverished and incomplete if one solely construes their functional role in the world as that of an individual human being' supports a reading of human self-concept as materially embedded and embodied. If embodiment can engender holistic awareness of the needs of the earth, it follows that it can also re-envisage the culture-nature axis around which western conceptions of human culture and nonhuman nature have traditionally revolved. Whether these categories can be *dismantled* in service of an ecofemi-nist ethic of environmental embeddedness, is, however, dependent on whether, and to what extent, the novels retain previous parameters for individual selfhood. Both the deep ecological notion of identifica-tion with, and self-realisation in, nature and the ecofeminist call for multiplicity of voice and ethical agent are capable of re-envisaging conventional notions of individual autonomy and subjectivity. The novels that adhere most strongly to ecofeminist conceptions of identity find in hybridity a representation of the multiplicity necessary for the expanded parameters of ecological selfhood. If Haraway's faith in the cyborg's potential to dismantle dualisms was found to be too idealistic for the hybrid figures of my second chapter, the ecological hybrids here delineated go some way towards embodying such potential.

Plumwood's (2000: 69) notion of '[t]raitorous kinds of human identity' provides a useful tool with which to analyse this ecological hybridity:

> Traitorous kinds of human identity involve a revised conception of the self and its relation to the non-human other, opposition to oppressive practices, and the relinquishment and critique of cultural allegiances to the dominance of the human species and its bonding against non-humans.

As Mallory (2009: 9) argues in her nuanced interpretation of Plumwood's work, such 'traitorousness' rests 'in recognition that the human is ecosocially positioned as superior, and that one must "betray" one's own kind, become a "traitor" to a certain narrative of the human, in order to allow the more than human world to flourish on its own terms'. Ecoconsciousness entails a 'traitorousness' to the metanarrative of ecological otherness that has engendered a definition of human identity divorced from its ecological context. It also involves a certain 'traitorousness' to the deep ecological 'wider, or big Self' in its failure to give expression to the incommensurability and alterity of the ecological other (Fox 1990: 199). 'Traitorousness' is grounded in multiplicity – both of subject positioning and perspective – thus making the traitor perfectly poised to extend solidarity to the other. As Plumwood (2000: 69) herself suggests, the traitor is 'someone with a view from both sides, able to adopt multiple perspectives and locations that enable an understanding of how he or she is situated in the relationship with the other from the perspective of both kinds of lives'. The traitor is a 'quilted' figure – to adapt the phrase employed at the beginning of this chapter – that functions as the 'collage', 'mosaic' and 'tapestry' of ecofeminist theorising (Warren 1997: 30).

The hybrid figures of the novels discussed are quintessentially 'traitorous'. With their hybrid bodies, Ora and Corinna most fully manifest such traitorousness since they represent the melding of the multiple perspectives and plural subject positions advocated by ecofeminist practitioners. Hester and Tom's dissolving bodies in *A Darkling Plain* and Rue's camouflaged body in *The Hunger Games* are also semantically hybrid since they represent the melding of the human and the earth in a manner that rejects epistemological monism. The reciprocated cathexis of Mara and Rowan and Edmond and Daisy shows a similar impetus towards hybridity since human love is predicated on a more encompassing love for the ecological other. Under this formulation, neither human attachment nor environmental attachment is sufficient on its own to engender responsible ecological engagement. Westerfeld's *Specials* [2006] provides a metonymic example of this form of human traitorousness. Tally's decision to remain in the wild with David after the cities' guardians have been overthrown can be read as the adoption of an overtly traitorous subject position: *'from now on, David and I are here to stand in your way. … Whenever you push too far into the wild, we'll be here waiting, ready to push back'* (371). This message, left to the remaining city dwellers and, by implication, to the novel's readers, sees Tally 'betray' her own kind and become a traitor to 'the narrative of the human' that desires anthropocentric expansion and exploitation in a progress-led trajectory that has engendered environmental crisis (Mallory 2009: 9). Standing in humanity's way is here equivalent to standing *with* the ecological other in an extension of solidarity. That Tally accomplishes this act of solidarity with David, her erstwhile love interest, suggests traitorousness inheres in a rejection of normative cultural allegiances in favour of a tripartite relationship between a human self, a (specific) human other and an ecological locale. The abstract universal bonds of deep ecological thinking are here concretised in particular, localised relationships and feminine values of care, trust and love.

The advocacy of multiplicity – in a manner that is often overtly counter-hegemonic – reveals the novels' wider political motivations. Whilst the will towards personal transformation resonates with the self-fulfilment promulgated by the ecofeminist spiritualities of my previous chapter, the politicisation of personal transformation through solidarity and cathexis sees the novels delve more deeply into the socio-political dimensions of ecological selfhood. Whilst the novels of the previous chapter displayed ambivalence as to whether spiritual reappraisal could be an effective stimulus for change, the novels of this chapter are relatively consistent in foregrounding the social and political possibilities engendered by ecological selfhood. If the blind space of the post-apocalyptic earth is a space in which to instil alternative ecofeminist ethics, epistemologies and spiritualities, it is also, therefore, a space in which to formulate a more embodied and embedded ecological identity. Here we might find an answer to the question I posed at the start of this chapter: 'if hybridity challenges existing borders, which borders, exactly, are being challenged?'. Through challenging the borders of the self – not simply the body but the emotions, mind and identity – these novels extend a further challenge to the discursive borders structuring contemporary environmental representation. To imagine the environment not as setting or background but as a fully agential ecological entity is to reconceptualise the borders of human identity according to humanity's intimate enmeshment in the earth. As young adults approach that further border – the far more permeable border separating childhood from adulthood – such a reconceptualisation is not only ecologically relevant and appropriate, but also ethically, epistemologically and spiritually responsible.

Conclusion: Apocalypse as Ecopoiesis

Listing a series of worrying trends that signal worsening environmental crisis, including rising world temperatures, water shortages, soaring populations, clearcutting and global violence, Gaard (2009: 321) begins an article on the importance of responsible ecopedagogy by asking the question 'what in the world are we doing by reading environmental literature?'. We may well ask this question of young adult post-disaster fiction, at a time in which our own planetary disaster – our own environmental crisis – is not post- but imminently upon us. Gaard answers her own question, in fact, in her discursive turn of phrase: 'what in the world' we are doing is precisely being (and doing) 'in the world'. The post-apocalyptic novels that I have explored throughout this study aim to embed their young adult readers firmly in the earth. By adopting implicit, or explicit, ecofeminist frameworks, they attempt – more, or less, successfully – to negotiate embedded and embodied subject positions for their young adult readers. These subject positions are contextual, predicated on situated knowledges and lived experiences; they are plural, encompassing multiple viewpoints and collective perspectives; they are local, finding strength in place-situatedness and empathetic engagement with the local landscape; and they are resistant, posing a challenge to the neoliberal representational frameworks that delimit phenomenal belonging. By situating their young protagonists 'in the world', these novels refute human–earth dislocation and systemic – and often violently-imposed – regimes of difference. These novels imply that if the dislocation and disengagement engendered by crisis is countered by ecofeminist principles, not only will young adults be in a better position to resist hegemonic interpellation, but they will also be in a more agential and empowered position to meet the challenges of climate crisis. This discursive 'turn towards the earth', to use Rigby's

(2004a: 12) phrase, can best be described in the narrative trajectory frequently evoked in these novels from a planetary consciousness to an embedded ecoconsciousness: a poetics of planet to a poetics of earth. Code (2006: 4) contends that 'the creative possibilities of ecological thinking for interrupting and restructuring the dominant social and philosophical imaginary have yet to be adequately explored'. I have sought to answer this call by employing an ecofeminist framework to analyse the creative possibilities of ecologically-oriented fiction for young adults. The successes of these novels – their capacity to respond creatively and responsively to environmental crisis – lie in envisaging sustainable modes of earth interaction predicated on foundational ecofeminist principles rather than on the abstract, universal and monistic thought patterns of normative ecological engagement. They include ethical stances that abide by the 'feminine' values traditionally underplayed within ideologies of neoliberal individualism, such as care, love and community; epistemological frameworks that value narrative modes of ecological engagement whereby 'responsible truths' emerge through human–nonhuman interaction; and spiritual frameworks that invest intrinsic value in the earth through personal and community embeddedness. These sustainable modes of earth interaction are achieved not without struggle; they emerge – as these novels show – out of resistance towards institutions and systems whose proprietary and oppressive ideologies preclude or delimit social and environmental change. I have undertaken both a negativist and restorative critique of ecological engagement within my focused novels, foregrounding the ways in which these novels imagine new world orders to arise in the old world's stead.

A planetary interruption, or apocalyptic tipping point, lays the groundwork for these new world orders. Apocalypse here engenders an epistemic 'blind space': a space in which humanity's relationship with the earth can – and, for the novels' protagonists, must – be reassessed. The blind space is discursively constructed; it renders the earth a site of cultural production and functions as a mechanism for exploring rights abuses towards 'feminised' peoples and spatialities, including non-heteronormative men, women who refuse to abide by principles of self-advancement, ecologies that have no instrumental value, and young adults who refuse to submit to the controlling ideologies of asymmetric socio-political systems. In each of my focused texts, masculinist ideologies of consumerism, capitalism and globalism are implicated in the 'planetary consciousness' that dislocates humans from their ecological embeddedness. Alternative ecofeminist insights are employed to re-signify the earth as a space of human belonging, as argued in my first chapter. Acknowledgement of the earth as a material entity ties the earth to other 'bodies' and particularly the female body. Whilst 'bodiliness' has engendered the female characters' subordinate subject positioning via discourses of gendered power, the capacity of these female characters to re-appropriate their own bodies in order to write themselves new narratives, as argued in Chapter 2, offers a challenge to the ideologies of individualism and self-advancement that characterise institutionalised neoliberalism.

The counter-hegemonic potential of ecofeminist thought inheres in attempts to resignify traditionally feminine values as conduits for empowerment and care. Subject positions predicated on an ethics of care and mutuality – as argued in Chapter 3 – can be formulated through the re-appropriation of feminine values into a largely masculinist history of philosophical thought and via an evolving discourse of posthumanism. The epistemic frameworks underpinning such ethical re-visioning render the earth subject to competing mythic discourses, as argued in Chapter 4. These novels demonstrate that the earth becomes a *terra nullius* available for anthropocentric inscription when controlling and totalising imperial epistemologies are mapped onto the landscape. Responsible epistemic engagement, by contrast, is shown to inhere in the emergent positioning of myth in relation to the ethical agent. A 'storied residence' in nature, according to this framework, allows for a discursive readjusting of epistemic privilege so that the earth can begin to tell its own story. This earthly capacity for self-inscription arises through acknowledgement of the earth as an entity with intrinsic value, as argued in Chapter 5. A local and bioregional engagement with place – whilst rendered more difficult under the pressures of globalisation – can produce a spiritually responsible and sustainable mode of earth interaction. These novels refute the disembodied spiritual transcendence of normative religion and instead advocate ecological immanence.

The ecofeminist insights gleaned from ethical, epistemological and spiritual reappraisal come together in my final chapter to inhere in matters of identity. The hybrid bodies and/or identities of the protagonists enact the melding of human and ecological exigencies. These hybrid bodies are radical in scope; they open up a space for the negotiation of an integrated and embodied subjectivity for the young protagonists. Identification, or solidarity, with the earth is shown in these novels to arise through a reconceptualisation of human identity as not simply dependent on, but *constituted by*, the ecological context in which humans are enmeshed. The blind space of the (female) body, then, and the blind space of the earth together engender – and enact – a variety of ecoconscious ethical responses to environmental crisis. The hybrid identities of my final chapter foreground the relevance and importance of ecofeminist theorising to children's literature criticism. Bradford *et al.* (2008: 91) have noted that:

> Children's texts remain constrained by the intrinsic commitment to maturation narratives – narrative structures posited on stories of individual development of subjective agency, or of bildungsroman. This tends to ensure that any environmental literature remains anthropocentric in emphasis, rather than engaging with the biocentrism of 'deep ecology'.

This comment foregrounds the importance of individual maturation and subjectivity to children's and young adult fiction in lieu of wider ecological exigencies. If this commitment to maturation delimits the texts' potential for effective ecological engagement, an ecofeminist commitment to multiplicity of voice and ethical agent can challenge this tendency. The hybrid identities of my focused novels affect a repositioning, or decentring, of the young adult individual in relation to his or her ecological context. This decentring has the effect of wedding the material needs of the earth to those of the young adult through the engendering of ecoconsciousness. Autopoiesis is here enacted through ecopoiesis, so that the personal growth or maturation of the young adult arises through, and is occasioned by, his or her ecological embeddedness. The narrative strategies through which such embeddedness can be affected are multiple; bodily dissolution, camouflage, reciprocal cathexis and metamorphosis are all mechanisms by which the hybrid integration of human and natural identities can be constituted.

By adding 'the child' and young adult as a third category of analysis in ecofeminist theorising, I have outlined a productive new area for ecocritical engagement. This linking of the child to women and nature follows naturally from the romantic delineation of the 'natural child'. The hopeful possibilities engendered by this tripartite association inhere in their shared capacity to decentre normative standpoints. In her delineation of the child as 'a source of hope', Roni Natov (2003: 7) notes the common conception that 'no matter how devastating the world, healing can come through the use of childhood to create a poetics, an imagined but tangible state, inspired and illuminated by the child, to return to'. In light of environmental crisis, we might expand this statement to argue that no matter how devastated the world, healing can come by investing the natural world with this same capacity. An ecopoetic is a similarly 'imagined but tangible' construct. Inspired and illuminated by the natural world, it can likewise become a space for the human imaginary 'to return to'. If this tendency towards constructivism appears to run counter to an acknowledgement of the materiality of the earth, this tendency is nevertheless inherent in narrative engagement with the world. As Rigby (2004a: 8) suggests:

> If we are not to fall prey to ecopoetic hubris, we must ask of the literary work not only how it can help us to see the earth anew and to dwell caringly amidst its multifarious more-than-human denizens: we must also consider how it alerts us to the inevitable loss entailed in the translation into merely human words of an experience of the givenness of more-than-human nature.

The 'inevitable loss' of a felt and lived experience of the world is a fact of the literary text. Unlike childhood, however, nature is a space we actually *can* 'return to'. Its 'givenness' is something each of the young adult readers of these novels can experience. In imagining post-apocalyptic landscapes, contemporary authors highlight the very real ways in which this earth is under threat; our current ecological context is one that some already deem 'post-natural'. In translating the earth into literary text, these authors engender in their readers an awareness of, and emotional engagement with, the threatened natural landscape. Far from precluding a real or embodied connection between humans and the earth, these novels can actively encourage their readers to experience, and engage with, the natural world on a material and not simply textual level.

This engagement, I have argued, is particularly important for the young adult reader. Positioned on the brink of adulthood – the young adult's own ontological tipping point – an awareness of the earth and its manifest fragility can be socially and politically transformative. Mary Mellor (2000: 119) foregrounds both the necessity and the difficulty in confronting this fragility, particularly in the context of a 'dominant elite':

> [A] transcendent dominant elite mediated by sex/gender and other relations of exploitation are unlikely to be motivated to 'see' the vulnerability of human immanence. Even when this vulnerability is grasped, this does not mean that hu(man)ity can reclaim an original harmony that has been lost or a teleological harmony to come as many green thinkers imply. If anything, hu(man)ity is *essentially* in

conflict with nonhuman nature in using human consciousness and reflexivity to create a special and privileged niche.

The centrality of human consciousness – made particularly apparent in narrative modes of engagement in which such consciousness is discursively constituted – cannot do otherwise but create for humanity a 'special and privileged niche'. Whilst children's fiction, especially, retains emphasis on the autonomy of the human subject, this does not preclude possibilities for ecological engagement. Whilst the novels of my corpus do allude to an 'original harmony', often under a romantic framework, this harmony is invariably too amorphous, too tenuous and too lost in some deep, pre-apocalypse past to engender hope of reclamation; nostalgia for a lost harmony is in fact less conducive to current wellbeing than hope for a new, green harmony to come. These novels suggest most effectively, in fact, that human 'privilege', rather than obfuscating the agency or subjectivity of the human actant, should instead obligate human beings to 'see' the vulnerability of human immanence and the fragility of the earth. In other words, these novels encourage their readers to look into the blind space and make visible the oppressive conceptual frameworks that lead to earth oppression. Young adults occupying that threshold preceding integration into adult systems of social and political responsibility are in an especially privileged position to engender change.

Throughout this study I have explored theoretical insights grounded in ecofeminist literary theory, philosophy and ethics, using these standpoints to illuminate environmental representation in contemporary young adult fiction. A larger work would wish to extend this critique to include insights gleaned from related ecologically-oriented disciplines such as political and social ecology, ecopedagogy, eco-socialism, environmental politics, environmental justice ethics and glocalisation studies as well as the wider ecocriticism movement out of which ecofeminist literary criticism has sprung. A work with a larger scope would also wish to explore the ways in which ecofeminism is currently being used creatively and productively to translate theory into practice and provide empowering responses to particular world-wide crisis situations. I would further wish to practice the hybridity I embrace in my final chapter by attempting not simply an analysis of children's literature through an ecofeminist lens but also an examination of how the theoretical work of children's literature and childhood studies can productively enhance the insights of ecofeminist theory and praxis. I hope these further areas of exploration will be tackled by theorists to come. In the meantime

I note the positive contributions ecofeminism can make to a study of young adult fiction; not only does it allow for a reappraisal of ideological frameworks that are oppressive to certain women, children and local landscapes, it also offers an empowering framework for change in both human actions and attitudes towards the environment.

Despite its necessarily limited parameters, then, this study has gone some way towards achieving the 'cross-fertilisation' of literature and ecology with 'related disciplines' that Cheryll Glotfelty (1996: xvii–xix) suggested – in her seminal introduction to the field of ecocriticism – would be so important to ecocritical theory. It has made moves towards correcting the gender imbalance in ecocritical theorising that currently 'marginalises both feminist and ecofeminist literary perspectives' (Gaard 2010: 643). It has extended the integrative boundaries of an ecocritical tradition that explores its mainstay theories primarily within adult literature to encompass young adult fiction alongside adult texts. My active conceptualisation of fiction for young adults as a relevant and appropriate genre of analysis for current ecofeminist theorising has also gone some way towards answering Bradford *et al.*'s (2008: 85) call for a widening integration of ecofeminism in children's literature criticism. Such an integration is, they suggest, 'yet to come, although we envisage that it will eventually play an oppositional, interrogative role in the field, with a potential to reshape the nature and direction of environmental advocacy in children's texts and to disclose the operation of the culture/nature duality in a text's orientation towards the material environment' (85). In attempting to answer this call, and to fill what Dobrin and Kidd (2004: 9) label a 'critical gap' in the ecocritical analysis of children's fiction, I have explored ecofeminist philosophical and ethical insights and applied them to current theorising on subjectivity, identity formation and agency within children's literature. Such a melding of critical perspectives, echoing the hybrid forms of my final chapter, can be of manifold relevance to both ecofeminist thinking and children's literature criticism alike at this propitious moment in our own, and the earth's, history.

Notes

Introduction

1. See Greta Gaard (2011) for a comprehensive account of the antifeminist backlash against North American ecofeminism over the past thirty years and her useful recuperation of ecofeminist insights.
2. This is not to say that these first wave notions preclude or delimit the social and political dimensions of ecofeminist engagement; as I shall go on to show, the personal transformations of the protagonists in these novels – whether through spiritual or emotional fulfilment – are political in scope, if not always in practice.
3. Children's literature scholars, on the other hand, have undertaken some useful and productive analyses of how feminist insights can be applied to children's texts. See for instance Beverly Lyon Clark and Margaret R. Higonnet (1999) and more recently Kerry Mallan (2009).
4. See Colleen Mack-Canty (2004) for a useful reading of the ways in which this acknowledgement of the feminist present informs youth feminism.
5. John Locke's *An Essay Concerning Human Understanding* [1690] argued that the child's mind is a blank slate, or 'tabula rasa', and that knowledge of the world is acquired through experience in a cumulative process of sensation and reflection. In *Émile, or On Education* [1762] Jean-Jacques Rousseau countered contemporary notions of original sin by arguing that children are born innocent. He formulated a view of childhood as a separate developmental stage – rather than simply a pre-adulthood – and argued for the importance of sensory perception and emotional engagement in a child's interaction with the world.
6. It should be noted that Ryan himself denies that this shift has occurred and instead advocates historical continuity.
7. See John Stephens (2010) for an exploration of the relevance of Zapf's principles to children's literature.
8. Susannah L. Hollister uses the phrase 'the Poetics of the Planet' in the title of her 2008 article 'A.R. Ammons and the Poetics of the Planet'. My use of the term 'poetics of planet' here and elsewhere thus derives from Hollister.
9. See Curry (2010) for a more detailed examination of the concept of 'blind space' and its origins in film theory.

1 A 'Poetics of Planet'

1. See for instance the 'Cuban Missile Crisis Debate' between Adlai Stevenson and V. A. Zorin in the United Nations Security Council on 23 October 1962: http://www.fordham.edu/halsall/mod/1962-cuba-un1.html.
2. In 1968 the *Apollo 8* mission produced the first widely publicised image of the globe from space. This planetary image – as Hollister (2009: 664) suggests – had been anticipated by the development of satellite technology in the 1950s

and was therefore present in the public consciousness long before these first photographs were taken.

2   Ideologies of Advancement

1. See Carol J. Adams (1990) for a thorough examination of the culturally-prescribed historical link between sex and species.

3   Regimes of Gender Difference

1. See, for example, the early theorists Mary Dietz (1985), W. Savarsy and Berta Siim (1994) and K. B. Jones (1994) for a fuller exploration of the notion of citizenship.

4   Situated Knowledges

1. Such recuperation has been aided by French feminists Luce Irigaray, Genevieve Lloyd and others, who had early success in arguing for 'difference' between masculine and feminine voices within ethics, legitimating women's right to 'speak as women'. See Luce Irigaray (1988) and Genevieve Lloyd (1984).
2. An example of the mythic language sometimes evoked by early ecofeminists to challenge patriarchal modes of representation can be found in Anne Cameron's narrative 'First Mother and the Rainbow Children' (1989): 'First there was the Great Egg and, inside it, the promise of all life. That promise of life began to stir, to swell, to grow, and the shell holding the promise began to stretch. The shell cracked and, from inside the egg, the water of life began to flow: a single river of hope and commitment' (54).
3. *Terra nullius* was a myth first adopted by European imperialists in the eighteenth century to facilitate the colonial occupation and exploitation of non-western lands by declaring these lands ownerless and thereby taking away any claim indigenous peoples had to their age-old living spaces. This legal term was first used in the context of the British take over of Aboriginal lands in modern-day Australia. It was a term used as a legal justification for land-seizure in Australia up until 1990 (Bauman 2007). Not simply a legal fiction, *terra nullius* is '[a] fiction whose power has extended well beyond the law courts. It is one of those dominant, organising fictions of a culture which can coexist with lack of explicit belief' (Lloyd 2000: 31). This 'organising fiction', interiorised and therefore uninterrogated, suggests that 'there is "no prior presence" in conquered or "discovered" territories' and that these territories can therefore 'be owned and "made useful" through colonisation' (Bauman 2007: 355). The 'ownership' of indigenous lands under European expansion allowed for the legal exploitation of the lands' natural resources; with the indigenous occupants 'doomed' to die out to make way for white settlers, such exploitation was not only justified but also lauded as advancing a metanarrative of techno-scientific progress and white expansionism (Lloyd 2000).
4. Ora's obligation to sacrifice herself to redeem her father for his depletion of Folavia's natural resources is reminiscent of our current preoccupation

that future generations will pay the price tomorrow for fossil fuel consumption today. Her father's guilt, in fact, has much in common with that upon which 'climate debt' is predicated. Friends of the Earth International defines 'climate debt' as 'a special case of environmental injustice where industrialised countries have over-exploited their "environmental space" in the past, having to borrow from developing countries in order to accumulate wealth, and accruing ecological debts as a result of this historic over-consumption'. If the novel is read in light of Australia's own colonial history, it is clear that D'Ath's critique of the colonial myth is as much a political interrogation into current attitudes towards climate change as it is a cry of protest against the country's treatment of its indigenous forbears. See 'Climate Debt: Making Historical Responsibility Part of the Solution', Dec 2005. www.foei. org/en/publications/pdfs/climatedebt.pdf. Accessed: 09.02.11.

5. Ora's apology foreshadows former Australian Prime Minister Kevin Rudd's national apology of February 2008 to the Aborigines and Torres Strait islanders – the indigenous victims of colonial oppression – and in particular to the 'stolen generations' of children who were taken away from their families at an early age to be integrated into non-indigenous society. Rudd's apology – on behalf of the government of Australia and the parliament of Australia – places blame for past wrongs firmly in the hands of the current government, not as a parallel instigator of racist policy but as a co-conspirator in historical events if knowingly leaving Australia's formative cultural heritage unacknowledged. D'Ath's novel, although preceding Rudd's official apology to Australia's indigenous population by half a decade, is infused by the values of cultural reconciliation upon which it stands. Rudd's apology echoes other public instances of national regret such as German President Johannes Rau's apology in 2000 to the Israeli parliament for the Holocaust, American President Barak Obama's signing of the Apology Resolution to Native Americans in 2009 and British Prime Minister David Cameron's apology in 2010 to the people of Northern Ireland for the Bloody Sunday killings of 1972. See the following website for the full text of Kevin Rudd's 'sorry speech' to parliament: http://www.smh. com.au/articles/2008/02/13/1202760379056.html. Accessed: 07.02.11.

6. My usage here differs from the more common interpretation of *mise-en-abîme* (or *abyme*) – as that describing a self-contained episode which reflects upon, sums up or thematises a larger framing narrative – and follows the less frequently cited sense that refers to the determination of meaning outside of a given frame. See Hawthorn (1998: 28) for a more detailed account of the differing interpretations of the term.

7. The most overt allusions to inform Mara's journey northwards are the biblical narratives of Noah's Flood (Genesis 8) and the Israelites flight from Egypt (Exodus 14). In this latter quest narrative, the Israelites, under the guidance of Moses and with Pharaoh's army in pursuit, despair at the strength of the Egyptian army and desire to turn back for fear of what lies ahead. In Mara's quest for her own promised land, the dissenting voices are many; like the Israelites, too, Mara's ship is pursued across the sea, this time by the 'gypsea' city of Pomperoy – a pirate fleet demanding vengeance for Mara's destructive passage through their floating city. The passage that describes the Israelites' willingness to betray their God and their country for fear of the Egyptians directs attention to the necessity of faith. It is interesting to note that the

word gypsy in fact originates in the name Egypt; the intertextual framework underpinning Bertagna's novel is overt.

8. An allusion to the Greek myth of Orpheus and Eurydice, Mara's challenge, like that of Orpheus, is not to look back at the life she could have led if she had stayed cocooned in New World luxury with her baby's father.

9. Cheney (2005) uses the term 'responsible truths' to develop his notion of 'ceremonial worlds', following Louise Profeit-LeBlanc's own delineation of responsible truth.

10. Code's (1987) responsibilist epistemology centres on five main concepts, summarised under the headings: knowers, emotions, understanding, normative realism and epistemic community. By 'normative realism' Code suggests that knowers have a moral responsibility to understand the world 'as it is' rather than adhere to biased viewpoints or favoured theories (Buege 1992: 74). This point is problematic, particularly since the notion of a normative ethics or normative philosophy, and hence normative realism, is critiqued by ecofeminism for often being established within ethical frameworks that are themselves inherently gendered. Code's point, however, is to highlight the dangers of a constructivist reading of the environment that interprets the natural world solely as a screen on which to impose biased viewpoints; to understand the world 'as it is' gestures towards an essentialist reading of epistemic engagement with the environment.

5   A Poetics of Earth

1. The text's rendering of human euthanasia at 65 is a dystopic exaggeration of the UK government's 2006 *Employment Equality (Age) Regulations* and their introduction of a Default Retirement Age, whereby employers are able to terminate or deny employment to people over 65 without a reason.

6   Deep Ecology or Ecofeminism

1. My thanks go to Tanya Kiermaier for introducing me to the work of Neil Leach at the *International Research Society for Children's Literature* biennial congress in July 2011.

2. Suzuki and McConnell (1997: 32) suggest that 'when we look carefully at the interaction at every level between our bodies and the elements that surround us, we see how completely we are embedded in air, all of us caught together in the same matrix. Air is a physical substance; it embraces us so intimately that it is hard to say where we leave off and air begins'.

Bibliography

Anderson, Matthew Tobin. *Feed* (Cambridge, MA: Candlewick Press, 2004).

Bawden, Nina. *Off the Road* (London: Puffin Books, 2000).

Bertagna, Julie. *Exodus* (London: Young Picador, 2003).

—— *Zenith* (London: Young Picador, 2007).

—— *Aurora* (New York: Macmillan, 2011).

Billingsley, Franny. *The Folk Keeper* (New York: Aladdin Paperbacks, 2001).

Collins, Suzanne. *The Hunger Games* (London: Scholastic, 2009).

—— *Catching Fire* (London: Scholastic, 2009).

—— *Mockingjay* (Australia: Scholastic, 2010).

D'Ath, Justin. *Shædow Master* (Sydney: Allen and Unwin, 2003).

Reeve, Philip. *Mortal Engines* (London: Scholastic, 2002).

—— *Predator's Gold* (London: Scholastic, 2004).

—— *Infernal Devices* (London: Scholastic, 2009a).

—— *A Darkling Plain* (London: Scholastic, 2009b).

Robson, Jenny. *Savannah 2116 AD* (Cape Town: Tafelberg, 2004).

Rosoff, Meg. *How I Live Now* (London: Penguin Group, 2005).

Ryan, Carrie. *The Forest of Hands & Teeth* (London: Gollancz, 2009).

—— *The Dead-Tossed Waves* (London: Gollancz, 2010).

—— *The Dark and Hollow Places* (New York: Ember, 2011).

Westerfeld, Scott. *Uglies* (New York: Simon Pulse, 2005a).

—— *Pretties* (New York: Simon Pulse, 2005b).

—— *Specials* (New York: Simon Pulse, 2006).

Works Cited

Abbruzzese, Teresa V. and Gerda R. Wekerle. 'Gendered Spaces of Activism in Exurbia: Politicizing an Ethic of Care from the Household to the Region' *Frontiers: A Journal of Women Studies* 32.2 (2011): 140–69.

Abram, David. *The Spell of the Sensuous: Perception and Language in a More-Than-Human World* (New York: Pantheon, 1996).

Adams, Carol. 'Why Feminist-Vegan Now?' *Feminism & Psychology* 20.3 (2010): 302–17.

—— (ed.) *Ecofeminism and the Sacred* (New York: Continuum, 1993).

—— *The Sexual Politics of Meat: A Feminist/Vegetarian Critical Theory* (New York: Continuum, 1990).

Adamson, Joni and Scott Slovic. 'The Shoulders We Stand On: An Introduction to Ethnicity and Ecocriticism' *MELUS* 34.2 (2009): 5–24.

Alaimo, Stacy. '"Skin Dreaming": The Bodily Transgressions of Fielding Burke, Octavia Butler, and Linda Hogan' in G. Gaard and P. D. Murphy (eds) *Ecofeminist Literary Criticism: Theory, Interpretation, Pedagogy* (Urbana and Chicago: University of Illinois Press, 1998), pp. 123–38.

—— 'Cyborg and Ecofeminist Interventions: Challenges for an Environmental Feminism' *Feminist Studies* 20.1 (1994): 133–52.

Alaimo, Stacy and Susan Hekman (eds) *Material Feminisms* (Bloomington and Indianapolis: Indiana University Press, 2008).

Amsler, Sarah S. 'Bringing Hope "To Crisis": Crisis Thinking, Ethical Action and Social Change' in S. Skrimshire (ed.) *Future Ethics: Climate Change and Apocalyptic Imagination* (London and New York: Continuum, 2010), pp. 129–52.

Anzaldua, Gloria E. *Borderlands/La Frontera* (San Francisco: Aunt Lute, 1987).

Ashcroft, Bill, Gareth Griffiths and Helen Tiffin (eds) *The Post-Colonial Studies Reader* 2nd edn (London and New York: Routledge, 2006).

Bakker, Karen and Gavin Bridge. 'Material worlds? Resource geography and the "matter of nature"' *Progress in Human Geography* 30.1 (2006): 5–27.

Barad, Karen. 'Posthumanist Performativity: Toward an Understanding of How Matter Comes to Matter' in S. Alaimo and S. Hekman (eds) *Material Feminisms* (Bloomington and Indianapolis: Indiana University Press, 2008), pp. 120–54.

Bate, Jonathan. *The Song of the Earth* (Cambridge, MA: Harvard University Press, 2000).

Bauman, Whitney. *Theology, Creation, and Environmental Ethics: From Creatio Ex Nihilo to Terra Nullius* (New York and Abingdon: Routledge, 2007).

Beckwith, Sarah. 'Preserving, Conserving, Deserving the Past: A Meditation on Ruin as Relic in Postwar Britain in Five Fragments' in C. A. Lees and G. R. Overing (eds) *A Place To Believe In: Locating Medieval Landscapes* (Pennsylvania: Pennsylvania University Press, 2006), pp. 191–210.

Berger, John. *About Looking* (New York: Vintage International, 1980).

Betcher, Sharon. 'Grounding the Spirit: An Ecofeminist Pneumatology' in L. Kearns and C. Keller (eds) *Ecospirit: Religions and Philosophies for the Earth* (New York: Fordham University Press, 2007), pp. 315–36.

Bowman, Andrew. 'Are We Armed Only With Peer-Reviewed Science?: the Scientisation of Politics in the Radical Environmental Movement' in S. Skrimshire (ed.) *Future Ethics: Climate Change and Apocalyptic Imagination* (London and New York: Continuum, 2010), pp. 173–96.

Boyd, Shelley. 'Domestic Gardening: Gabrielle Roy's Bower of Innocence in Enchantment and Sorrow' *ESC* 32.4 (2006): 189–211.

Bradford, Clare. *Unsettling Narratives: Postcolonial Readings of Children's Literature* (Ontario: Wilfred Laurier University Press, 2007).

—— 'The Sky is Falling: Children as Environmental Subjects in Contemporary Picture Books' in R. McGillis (ed.) *Children's Literature and the* Fin de Siecle (Westport, CT: Praeger Publishers, 2003), pp. 111–20.

Bradford, Clare, Kerry Mallan, John Stephens and Robyn McCallum. *New World Orders in Contemporary Children's Literature: Utopian Transformations* (London: Palgrave Macmillan, 2008).

Bronfen, Elizabeth and Sarah Webster Goodwin (eds) *Death and Representation* (Baltimore: The Johns Hopkins University Press, 1993).

Buege, Douglas. 'Epistemic Responsibility and the Inuit of Canada's Eastern Arctic: an Ecofeminist Appraisal' in K. J. Warren (ed.) *Ecofeminism: Women, Culture, Nature* (Bloomington and Indianapolis: Indiana University Press, 1997), pp. 99–111.

—— 'Epistemic Responsibility to the Natural: Toward a Feminist Epistemology for Environmental Ethics' *American Philosophical Association Newsletter on Feminism and Philosophy* 91 (1992): 73–8.

Buell, Lawrence. *The Future of Environmental Criticism: Environmental Crisis and Literary Imagination* (Oxford: Blackwell Publishing, 2005).

—— *Writing for an Endangered World: Literature, Culture, & Environment in the US and Beyond* (Cambridge: Belknap, 2001).

—— *The Environmental Imagination: Thoreau, Nature Writing and the Formation of American Culture* (London: Princeton University Press, 1995).

Butler, Judith. *Gender Trouble: Feminism and the Subversion of Identity* (London: Routledge, 1990).

Callicott, J. Baird. 'The Search for an Environmental Ethic' (revised version) in T. Regan (ed.) *Matters of Life and Death* 3rd edn (New York: McGraw-Hill, 1993).

Cameron, Anne. 'First Mother and the Rainbow Children' in Judith Plant (ed.) *Healing the Wounds: The Promise of Ecofeminism* (Philadelphia, PA: New Society Publishers, 1989): 54–66.

Carlassare, Elizabeth. 'Socialist and Cultural Ecofeminism: Allies in Resistance' *Ethics and the Environment* 5.1 (2000): 89–106.

Castree, Noel and Catherine Nash. 'Posthuman Geographies' *Social and Cultural Geography* 7.4 (2006): 501–4.

Cheney, Jim. 'Truth, Knowledge and the Wild World' *Ethics and the Environment* 10.2 (2005): 101–35.

—— 'Postmodern Environmental Ethics: Ethics as Bioregional Narrative' *Environmental Ethics* 11 (1989): 117–34.

Clark, Beverly Lyon. 'Fairy Godmothers or Wicked Stepmothers? The Uneasy Relationship of Feminist Theory and Children's Criticism' *Children's Literature Association Quarterly* 18.4 (1993): 171–6.

Clark, Beverly Lyon and Margaret R. Higonnet (eds) *Girls, Boys, Books, Toys: Gender in Children's Literature and Culture* (Baltimore: Johns Hopkins University Press, 1999).

Cloete, Elsie. 'Ecofutures in Africa: Jenny Robson's *Savannah 2116 AD*' *Children's Literature in Education* 40 (2009): 46–58.

Code, Lorraine. *Ecological Thinking: The Politics of Epistemic Location* (New York: Oxford University Press, 2006).

—— 'Flourishing' *Ethics and the Environment* 4.1 (1999): 63–72.

—— *Epistemic Responsibility* (Hanover, NH: University Press of New England, 1987).

Cohen, Michael P. 'Blues in the Green: Ecocriticism under Critique' *Environmental History* 9.1 (2004): 9–36.

Cooley, John. 'Introduction: American Nature Writing and the Pastoral Tradition' in J. Cooley (ed.) *Earthly Words: Essays on Contemporary American Nature and Environmental Writers* (Ann Arbor: University of Michigan Press, 1994), pp. 1–15.

—— (ed.) *Earthly Words: Essays on Contemporary American Nature and Environmental Writers* (Ann Arbor: University of Michigan Press, 1994).

Corsaro, William A. *The Sociology of Childhood* (Thousand Oaks, CA: Pine Forge Press, 1997).

Cronon, William. 'The Trouble with Wilderness; or, Getting Back to the Wrong Nature' in W. Cronon (ed.) *Uncommon Ground: Rethinking the Human Place in Nature* (London and New York: W.W. Norton & Company, 1996), pp. 69–90.

—— (ed.) *Uncommon Ground: Rethinking the Human Place in Nature* (London and New York: W.W. Norton & Company, 1996).

Cudworth, Erika. *Developing Ecofeminist Theory: The Complexity of Difference* (Basingstoke: Palgrave Macmillan, 2005).

Cuomo, Chris. 'On Ecofeminist Philosophy' *Ethics and the Environment* 7.2 (2002): 1–11.

Curry, Alice. 'The "Blind Space" that Lies Beyond the Frame: Anne Provoost's *Falling* (1997) and John Boyne's *The Boy in the Striped Pyjamas* (2006)' *International Research in Children's Literature* 3.1 (2010): 61–74.

DeFalco, Amelia. 'Moral Obligation, Disordered Care: The Ethics of Caregiving in Margaret Atwood's *Moral Disorder*' *Contemporary Literature* 52.2 (2011): 236–63.

Di Chiro, Giovanna. 'Polluted Politics? Confronting Toxic Discourse, Sex Panic, and Eco-Normativity' in C. Mortimer-Sandilands and B. Erickson (eds) *Queer Ecologies: Sex, Nature, Politics, Desire* (Indiana: Indiana University Press, 2010), pp. 199–230.

Diamond, Irene and Lisa Kuppler. 'Frontiers of the Imagination: Women, History and Nature' *Journal of Women's History* 1.3 (1990): 160–80.

Diamond, Irene and Gloria. F. Orenstein (eds) *Reweaving the World: The Emergence of Ecofeminism* (San Francisco: Sierra Club Books, 1990).

Dietz, Mary. 'Citizenship with a Feminist Face: The Problem with Maternal Thinking' *Political Theory* 13.1 (1985): 19–37.

Dinerstein, Joel. 'Technology and Its Discontents: On the Verge of the Posthuman' *American Quarterly* 58.3 (2006): 569–95.

Dobrin, Sidney I. and Kenneth B. Kidd (eds) *Wild Things: Children's Culture and Ecocriticism* (Detroit: Wayne State University Press, 2004).

Estok, Simon C. 'Theorising in a Space of Ambivalent Openness: Ecocriticism and Ecophobia' *ISLE* 16.2 (2009): 203–25.

Evans, Gwyneth. 'The Girl in the Garden: Variations on a Feminine Pastoral' *Children's Literature Association Quarterly* 19.1 (1994): 20–4.

Fellman, Anita Clair. '"Don't Expect to Depend on Anybody Else": The Frontier as Portrayed in the Little House Books' *Children's Literature* 24 (1996): 101–16.

Fincher, Ruth. 'From Dualisms to Multiplicities: Gendered Political Practices' in L.A. Staeheli, E. Kofman and L.J. Peake (eds) *Mapping Women, Making Politics: Feminist Perspectives on Political Geography* (New York: Routledge, 2004), pp. 49–69.

Foote, Bonnie. 'The Narrative Interactions of Silent Spring: Bridging Literary Criticism and Ecocriticism' *New Literary History* 38.4 (2007): 739–53.

Fox, Warren. *Toward a Transpersonal Ecology* (Boston: Shambhala, 1990).

Freeman, Carla. 'Is Local: Global as Feminine: Masculine? Rethinking the Gender of Globalization' *Signs* 26.4 (2001): 1007–37.

Friedman, Andrea. 'The Politics of Consumption: Women and Consumer Culture' *Journal of Women's History* 13.2 (2001): 159–68.

Gaard, Greta. 'Ecofeminism Revisited: Rejecting Essentialism and Re-Placing Species in a Material Feminist Environmentalism' *Feminist Formations* 23.2 (2011): 26–53.

—— 'New Directions for Ecofeminism: Toward a More Feminist Ecocriticism' *ISLE* 17.4 (2010): 643–65.

—— 'Children's Environmental Literature: From Ecocriticism to Ecopedagogy' *Neohelicon* 36 (2009): 321–34.

—— (ed.) *Women, Animals, Nature* (Philadelphia, PA: Temple University Press, 1993).

Gaard, Greta and Patrick D. Murphy. 'Introduction' in G. Gaard and P. D. Murphy (eds) *Ecofeminist Literary Criticism: Theory, Interpretation, Pedagogy* (Urbana and Chicago: University of Illinois Press, 1998), pp. 1–13.

—— (eds) *Ecofeminist Literary Criticism: Theory, Interpretation, Pedagogy* (Urbana and Chicago: University of Illinois Press, 1998).

Garb, Yaakov Gerome. 'Perspective or Escape? Ecofeminist Musings on Contemporary Earth Imagery' in I. Diamond and G. F. Orenstein (eds) *Reweaving the World* (San Francisco: Sierra Club Books, 1990), pp. 264–78.

Garratt, Keith. 'The Relationship Between Adjacent Lands and Protected Areas: Issues of Concern for the Protected Area Manager' in J. A. McNeely and K. R. Miller (eds) *National Parks, Conservation, and Development: The Role of Protected Areas in Sustaining Society, Proceedings of the World Congress on National Parks, Bali, Indonesia, 11–22 October 1982* (Washington, DC: Smithsonian Institution Press, 1984).

Garrard, Greg. *Ecocriticism* (Abingdon: Routledge, 2004).

Garry, Ann and Marilyn Pearsall (eds) *Women, Knowledge and Reality* (Boston: Unwin Hyman, 1989).

Gatens-Robinson, Eugenie. 'Finding Our Feminist Ways in Natural Philosophy and Religious Thoughts' *Hypatia* 9.4 (1994): 207–28.

Glotfelty, Cheryll and Harold Fromm (eds) *The Ecocriticism Reader: Landmarks in Literary Ecology* (Athens: University of Georgia Press, 1996).

Godfrey, Phoebe C. 'Ecofeminist Cosmology in Practice: Genesis Farm and the Embodiment of Sustainable Solutions' *Capitalism Nature Socialism* 19.2 (2008): 96–114.

Gordon, Suzanne, Patricia Benner and Nel Noddings (eds) *Caregiving: Readings in Knowledge, Practice, Ethics, and Politics* (Philadelphia: University of Pennsylvania Press, 1996).

—— 'Introduction' in S. Gordon, P. Brenner and N. Noddings (eds) *Caregiving: Readings in Knowledge, Practice, Ethics, and Politics* (Philadelphia: University of Pennsylvania Press, 1996), pp. vii–xvi.

Greenway, Betty. 'Introduction: the Greening of Children's Literature' *Children's Literature Association Quarterly* 19.4 (1994): 146–7.

Griffiths, Gareth. 'The Myth of Authenticity' in C. Tiffin and A. Lawson (eds) *De-Scribing Empire* (London: Routledge, 1994).

Grim, John. 'Indigenous Knowing and Responsible Life in the World' in L. Kearns and C. Keller (eds) *Ecospirit: Religions and Philosophies for the Earth* (New York: Fordham University Press, 2007), pp. 196–214.

Groenfeldt, David. 'The Future of Indigenous Values: Cultural Relativism in the Face of Economic Development' *Futures* 35 (2003): 917–29.

Grossberg, Lawrence, Cary Nelson and Paula A. Treichler (eds) *Cultural Studies* (London and NY: Routledge, 1992).

Groves, Jason. 'The Ecology of Invasions: Reflections from a Damaged Planet' *Global South* 3.1 (2009): 30–41.

Gruen, Lori. 'Attending to Nature: Empathetic Engagement with the More than Human World' *Ethics and the Environment* 14.2 (2009): 23–38.

Gunn Allen, Patricia. 'The Woman I Love Is a Planet; the Planet I Love Is a Tree' in I. Diamond and G. F. Orenstein (eds) *Reweaving the World* (San Francisco: Sierra Club Books, 1990), pp. 52–7.

Halberstam, Judith and Ira Livingston. *Posthuman Bodies* (Bloomington and Indianapolis: Indiana University Press, 1995).

Haraway, Donna. 'The Promises of Monsters: A Regenerative Politics for Inappropriate/d Others' in L. Grossberg, C. Nelson and P. A. Treichler (eds) *Cultural Studies* (London and New York: Routledge, 1992), pp. 295–337.

—— *Simians, Cyborgs, and Women: The Reinvention of Nature* (New York: Routledge, 1991).

Harmon, David. 'Cultural Diversity, Human Subsistence, and the National Park Ideal' *Environmental Ethics* 9.2 (1987): 147–58.

Hawthorn, Jeremy. *A Glossary of Contemporary Literary Theory* (London: Arnold, 1998).

Hayles, N. Katherine. *How We Became Posthuman: Virtual Bodies in Cybernetics, Literature, and Informatics* (Chicago: The University of Chicago Press, 1999).

Heise, Ursula. *Sense of Place and Sense of Planet: The Environmental Imagination of the Global* (New York: Oxford University Press, 2008).

Hengst, Heinz. 'Complex Interconnections: The Global and the Local in Children's Minds and Everyday Worlds' in J. Qvortrup (ed.) *Studies in Modern Childhood: Society, Agency, Culture* (Houndmills, Basingstoke: Palgrave Macmillan, 2005), pp. 21–38.

Herles, Cecilia. 'Muddying the Waters Does Not Have To Entail Erosion: Ecological Feminist Concerns with Purity' *International Journal of Sexuality and Gender Studies* 5.2 (2000): 109–123.

Hess, Scott. 'Imagining an Everyday Nature' *Interdisciplinary Studies in Literature and Environment* 17.1 (2010): 85–112.

Hickel, Jason and Arsalan Khan. 'The Culture of Capitalism and the Crisis of Critique' *Anthropological Quarterly* 85.1 (2012): 203–27.

Hillard, Tom J. '"Deep Into That Darkness Peering": An Essay on Gothic Nature' *Interdisciplinary Studies in Literature and Environment* 16.4 (2009): 685–95.

Hitt, Christopher. 'Toward an Ecological Sublime' *New Literary History* 30.3 (1999): 603–23.

Hollister, Susannah L. 'The Planet on the Screen: Scales of Belonging in A.R. Ammons's Sphere' *Contemporary Literature* 50.4 (2009): 662–94.

—— 'A. R. Ammons and the Poetics of the Planet' *ThoughtMesh: National Poetry Foundation* (2008) http://vectors.usc.edu/thoughtmesh/publish/84.php. Accessed: 15 September 2011.

Hughes, J. Donald and Jim Swan. 'How Much of the Earth Is Sacred Space?' *Environmental Review: ER* 10.4 (1986): 247–59.

Hulme, Mike. 'Four Meanings of Climate Change' in S. Skrimshire (ed.) *Future Ethics: Climate Change and Apocalyptic Imagination* (London and NY: Continuum, 2010), pp. 37–58.

Ingold, Tim. *The Perception of the Environment: Essays in Livelihood, Dwelling and Skill* (London and New York: Routledge, 2000).

Irigaray, Luce. *Speculum* (Ithaca: Cornell University Press, 1988).

Jaggar, Alison M. 'Love and Knowledge: Emotion in Feminist Epistemology' in A. Garry and M. Pearsall (eds) *Women, Knowledge and Reality* (Boston: Unwin Hyman, 1989).

—— *Feminist Politics and Human Nature* (Lanham, Maryland: Rowman and Littlefield, 1983).

James, Kathryn. *Death, Gender and Sexuality in Contemporary Adolescent Literature* (London and New York: Routledge, 2009).

Jenks, Chris. *Childhood* 2nd edn (London and New York: Routledge, 2005).

Jones, K. B. 'Identity, action and locale: Thinking about citizenship, civic action and feminism' *Social Politics* 1 (1994): 256–71.

Katz, Cindi. 'On the Grounds of Globalization: A Topography for Feminist Political Engagement' *Signs* 26.4 (2001): 1213–34.

Kearns, Laurel and Catherine Keller (eds) *Ecospirit: Religions and Philosophies for the Earth* (New York: Fordham University Press, 2007), pp. 196–214.

Keough, Noel. 'Sustaining Authentic Human Experience in Community' *Earthographies: Ecocriticism and Culture* 64 (2008): 65–77.

King, Roger J. H. 'Narrative, Imagination, and the Search for Intelligibility in Environmental Ethics' *Ethics and the Environment* 4.1 (1999): 23–38.

—— 'Caring about Nature: Feminist Ethics and the Environment' in K. J. Warren (ed.) *Ecological Feminist Philosophies* (Bloomington and Indianapolis: Indiana University Press, 1996), pp. 82–96.

King, Ynestra. 'The Ecology of Feminism and the Feminism of Ecology' in J. Plant (ed.) *Healing the Wounds: The Promise of Ecofeminism* (Philadelphia: New Society, 1989), pp. 18–28.

Knebusch, Julien. 'Planet Earth in Contemporary Electronic Artworks' *Leonardo* 37.1 (2004): 18–24.

Kretz, Lisa. 'Open Continuity' *Ethics and the Environment* 14.2 (2009): 115–37.

Kristeva, Julia. *Powers of Horror: An Essay on Abjection* (New York: Columbia University Press, 1982).

Krznaric, Roman. 'Empathy and Climate Change: Proposals for a Revolution of Human Relationships' in S. Skrimshire (ed.) *Future Ethics: Climate Change and Apocalyptic Imagination* (London and New York: Continuum, 2010), pp. 153–72.

de Lauretis, Teresa (ed.) *Feminist Studies/Cultural Studies* (Bloomington: Indiana University Press, 1986).

Lauro, Sarah Juliet and Karen Embry. 'A Zombie Manifesto: the Non-Human Condition in the Era of Advanced Capitalism' *Boundary 2* 35.1 (2008): 85–108.

Lawson, Victoria. 'Geographies of Care and Responsibility' *Annals of the Association of American Geographers* 97:1 (2007): 1–11.

Layton, Robert. *Who Needs the Past? Indigenous Values and Archaeology* 2nd edn (London and New York: Routledge, 1994).

Leach, Neil. *Camouflage* (Cambridge, MA: MIT Press, 2006).

Lees, Clare A. and Gillian R. Overing (eds) *A Place to Believe In: Locating Medieval Landscapes* (Pennsylvania: Pennsylvania University Press, 2006).

Legler, Gretchen T. 'Ecofeminist Literary Criticism' in K.J. Warren (ed.) *Ecofeminism: Women, Culture, Nature* (Bloomington and Indianapolis: Indiana University Press, 1997), pp. 227–38.

Levine, Mark. 'The Apocalyptic as Contemporary Dialectic: From Thanatos (Violence) to Eros (Transformation)' in S. Skrimshire (ed.) *Future Ethics: Climate Change and Apocalyptic Imagination* (London and New York: Continuum, 2010): 59–80.

Li, Stephanie. 'Domestic Resistance Gardening, Mothering and Storytelling in Leslie Marmon Silko's *Gardens in the Dunes*' *Studies in American Indian Literatures* 21.1 (2009): 18–37.

Lloyd, Genevieve. 'No One's Land: Australia and the Philosophical Imagination' *Hypatia* 15.2 (2000): 26–39.

—— *The Man of Reason* (London: Methuen, 1984).

Lovelock, James. *The Revenge of Gaia: Why the Earth Is Fighting Back – and How We Can Still Save Humanity* (Santa Barbara: Allen Lane, 2006).

MacGregor, Sherilyn. 'From Care to Citizenship: Calling Ecofeminism Back to Politics' *Ethics and the Environment* 9.1 (2004): 56–84.

Mack-Canty, Colleen. 'Third-Wave Feminism and the Need to Reweave the Nature/Culture Duality' *NWSA Journal* 16.3 (2004): 154–79.

MacLeish, Archibald. 'A Reflection: Riders on the Earth Together, Brothers in Eternal Cold' *New York Times* 25 December 1968.

Mallan, Kerry. *Gender Dilemmas in Children's Fiction* (Houndmills, Basingstoke: Palgrave Macmillan, 2009).

Mallory, Chaone. 'Val Plumwood and Ecofeminist Political Solidarity: Standing with the Natural Other' *Ethics and the Environment* 14.2 (2009): 3–21.

Manley Scott, Peter. 'Are We There Yet?: Coming to the End of the Line – a Postnatural Enquiry' in S. Skrimshire (ed.) *Future Ethics: Climate Change and Apocalyptic Imagination* (London and New York: Continuum, 2010), pp. 260–79.

Mann, Bonnie. 'World Alienation in Feminist Thought: The Sublime Epistemology of Emphatic Anti-Essentialism' *Ethics and the Environment* 10.2 (2005): 45–74.

Marston, Sallie, and Lynn Staeheli. 'Citizenship, Struggle, and Political and Economic Restructuring' *Environment and Planning A* 26 (2004): 840–8.

Martin, Biddy and Chandra Talpade Mohanty. 'Feminist Politics: What's Home Got To Do with It?' in T. de Lauretis (ed.) *Feminist Studies/Cultural Studies* (Bloomington: Indiana University Press, 1986), pp. 191–212.

Martin, Patricia. 'Contextualising Feminist Political Theory' in L.A. Staeheli, E. Kofman and L.J. Peake (eds) *Mapping Women, Making Politics: Feminist Perspectives on Political Geography* (New York: Routledge, 2004), pp. 15–30.

McDowell, Linda. 'Work, workfare, work/life balance and an ethic of care' *Progress in Human Geography* 28.2 (2004): 145–63.

McGillis, Roderick (ed.) *Children's Literature and the* Fin de Siecle (Westport, CT: Praeger Publishers, 2003).

McNeely, Jeffery A. and Kenton R. Miller (eds) *National Parks, Conservation, and Development: The Role of Protected Areas in Sustaining Society, Proceedings of the World Congress on National Parks, Bali, Indonesia, 11–22 October 1982* (Washington, D.C.: Smithsonian Institution Press, 1984).

Mellor, Mary. 'Feminism and Environmental Ethics: A Materialist Perspective' *Ethics and the Environment* 5.1 (2000): 107–23.

—— 'The Politics of Women and Nature: Affinity, Contingency or Material Relation?' *Journal of Political Ideologies* 1.2 (1996): 147–64.

Mies, Maria and Vandana Shiva. *Ecofeminism* (Halifax, Nova Scotia: Fernwood Publications, 1993).

Mortimer-Sandilands, Catriona and Bruce Erickson (eds) *Queer Ecologies: Sex, Nature, Politics, Desire* (Indiana: Indiana University Press, 2010).

Murphy, Patrick D. *Farther Afield in the Study of Nature-Oriented Literature* (Charlottesville and London: University Press of Virginia, 2000).

—— (ed.) *Literature of Nature: An International Sourcebook* (Chicago: Fitzroy Dearborn, 1998).

—— *Literature, Nature, and Other: Ecofeminist Critiques* (New York: State University of New York Press, 1995).

Naess, Arne. *Life's Philosophy: Reason and Feeling in a Deeper World* (Athens and London: University of Georgia Press, 2002).

—— 'The Shallow and the Deep, Long-Range Ecology Movement: A Summary' *Inquiry* 16 (1973): 95–100.

Nagar, Richa. 'Mapping Feminisms and Difference' in L.A. Staeheli, E. Kofman and L.J. Peake (eds) *Mapping Women, Making Politics: Feminist Perspectives on Political Geography* (New York: Routledge, 2004), pp. 31–48.

Nagar, Richa, Victoria Lawson, Linda McDowell and Susan Hanson. 'Locating Globalization: Feminist (Re)readings of the Subjects and Spaces of Globalization' *Economic Geography* 78.3 (2002): 257–84.

Narayan, Uma. 'Working Together Across Difference: Some Considerations on Emotions and Political Practice' *Hypatia* 3.2 (1988): 31–47.

Natov, Roni. *The Poetics of Childhood* (London and New York: Routledge, 2003).

Oelschlaeger, Max. *The Idea of Wilderness: From Prehistory to the Age of Ecology* (New Haven: Yale University Press, 1991).

Olsson, Gunnar. *Abysmal: A Critique of Cartographic Reason* (Chicago and London: the University of Chicago Press, 2007).

Orenstein, Gloria Feman. 'Toward an Ecofeminist Ethic of Shamanism and the Sacred' in C. J. Adams (ed.) *Ecofeminism and the Sacred* (New York: Continuum, 1993), pp. 172–90.

Plant, Judith (ed.) *Healing the Wounds: The Promise of Ecofeminism* (Philadelphia: New Society, 1989).

Platt, Kamala. 'Environmental Justice Children's Literature: Depicting, Defending, and Celebrating Trees and Birds, Colours and People' in S.I. Dobrin and K. Kidd (eds) *Wild Things: Children's Culture and Ecocriticism* (Detroit: Wayne State University Press, 2004), pp. 183–97.

Plumwood, Val. 'The Concept of a Cultural Landscape: Nature, Culture and Agency in the Land' *Ethics and the Environment* 11.2 (2006): 115–50.

—— *Environmental Culture: The Ecological Crisis of Reason* (New York: Routledge, 2002).

—— 'Deep Ecology, Deep Pockets, and Deep Problems: A Feminist Ecosocialist Analysis' in D. Rothenberg (ed.) *Beneath the Surface: Critical Essays in the Philosophy of Deep Ecology* (Cambridge, MA: MIT Press, 2000), pp. 59–84.

—— 'Nature, Self, and Gender: Feminism, Environmental Philosophy, and the Critique of Rationalism' in K. J. Warren (ed.) *Ecological Feminist Philosophies* (Bloomington and Indianapolis: Indiana University Press, 1996), pp. 155–80.

—— *Feminism and the Mastery of Nature* (London and New York: Routledge, 1993).

—— 'Feminism and Ecofeminism: Beyond the Dualistic Assumptions of Women, Men and Nature' *The Ecologist* 22.1 (1992): 8–13.

Prout, Alan. *The Future of Childhood: Towards the Interdisciplinary Study of Children* (London: Psychology Press, 2005).

Qvortrup, Jens (ed.) *Studies in Modern Childhood: Society, Agency, Culture* (Houndmills, Basingstoke: Palgrave Macmillan, 2005).

Raglon, Rebecca. 'The Post Natural Wilderness and Its Writers' *Journal of Ecocriticism* 1.1 (2009): 60–6.

Regan, Tom (ed.) *Matters of Life and Death* 3rd edn (New York: McGraw-Hill, 1993).

Richards, Page. 'The Topos of the Inexpressible and Self-Critique' *GRAAT* On-Line issue 8 (2010): 10–27.

Rigby, Kate. *Topographies of the Sacred: The Poetics of Place in European Romanticism* (Charlottesville and London: University of Virginia Press, 2004a).

—— 'Earth, World, Text: On the (Im)possibility of Ecopoiesis' *New Literary History* 35.3 (2004b): 427–42.

Roberts, Susan M. 'Gendered Globalisation' in L.A. Staeheli, E. Kofman and L.J. Peake (eds) *Mapping Women, Making Politics: Feminist Perspectives on Political Geography* (New York: Routledge, 2004), pp. 127–40.

Rolston III, Holmes. *Environmental Ethics: Duties to and Values in the Natural World* (Philadelphia: Temple University Press, 1988).

Roos, Bonnie and Alex Hunt (eds) *Postcolonial Green: Environmental Politics and World Narratives* (Charlottesville and London: University of Virginia Press, 2010).

—— 'Introduction: Narratives of Survival, Sustainability, and Justice' in B. Roos and A. Hunt (eds) *Postcolonial Green: Environmental Politics and World Narratives* (Charlottesville and London: University of Virginia Press, 2010), pp. 1–13.

Rothenberg, David (ed.) *Beneath the Surface: Critical Essays in the Philosophy of Deep Ecology* (Cambridge, MA: MIT Press, 2000).

Ryan, Patrick J. 'How New is the "New" Social Study of Childhood? The Myth of a Paradigm Shift' *Journal of Interdisciplinary History* 38.4 (2008): 553–76.

Salleh, Ariel. 'Moving to an Embodied Materialism' *Capitalism Nature Socialism* 16.2 (2005): 9–14.

—— *Ecofeminism as Politics: Nature, Marx and the Postmodern* (London: Zed Books, 1997).

Sargisson, Lucy. 'What's Wrong with Ecofeminism?' *Environmental Politics* 10.1 (2001): 52–64.

Savarsy, W. and Berta Siim. 'Gender, Transitions to Democracy and Citizenship' *Social Politics* 1 (1994): 249–55.

Schöpflin, George. 'The Functions of Myth and a Taxonomy of Myths' in R. A. Segal (ed.) *Myth: Critical Concepts in Literary and Cultural Studies* Vol. 1 (London and New York: Routledge, 2007), pp. 205–20.

Seaman, Myra J. 'Becoming More (than) Human: Affective Posthumanisms, Past and Future' *Journal of Narrative Theory* 37.2 (2007): 246–75.

Seed, John, Joanna Macy, Pat Fleming and Arne Naess. *Thinking Like a Mountain: Towards a Council of All Beings* (Philadelphia, Pennsylvania: New Society, 1988).

Segal, Robert A. (ed.) *Myth: Critical Concepts in Literary and Cultural Studies* Vol. 1 (London and New York: Routledge, 2007).

Session, Robert. 'Deep Ecology versus Ecofeminism: Healthy Differences or Incompatible Philosophies?' in K.J. Warren (ed.) *Ecological Feminist Philosophies* (Bloomington, Indianapolis: Indiana University Press, 1996), pp. 137–54.

Skrimshire, Stefan (ed.) *Future Ethics: Climate Change and Apocalyptic Imagination* (London and New York: Continuum, 2010).

Slotkin, Richard. *The Fatal Environment: The Myth of the Frontier in the Age of Industrialisation, 1800–1890* (New York: Atheneum, 1985).

Soper, Kate. *What Is Nature?: Culture, Politics and the Non-Human* (Oxford: Blackwell, 1995).

Spretnak, Charlene. 'Radical Nonduality in Ecofeminist Philosophy' in K. J. Warren (ed.) *Ecofeminism: Women, Culture, Nature* (Bloomington and Indianapolis: Indiana University Press, 1997), pp. 425–36.

Staeheli, Lynn A., Eleonore Kofman and Linda J. Peake (eds) *Mapping Women, Making Politics: Feminist Perspectives on Political Geography* (New York: Routledge, 2004).

Staeheli, Lynn A. and Eleonore Kofman. 'Mapping Gender, Making Politics: Toward Feminist Political Geographies' in L.A. Staeheli, E. Kofman and L.J. Peake (eds) *Mapping Women, Making Politics: Feminist Perspectives on Political Geography* (New York: Routledge, 2004), pp. 1–14.

Stephens, John. 'Impartiality and Attachment: Ethics and Ecopoeisis in Children's Narrative Texts' *International Research in Children's Literature* 3.2 (2010): 205–16.

—— 'Post-Disaster Fiction: The Problematics of a Genre' *Papers: Explorations into Children's Literature* 3.3 (1992): 126–30.

Suzuki, David and Amanda McConnell. *The Sacred Balance* (Vancouver: Greystone Books, 1997).

Tiffin, Chris and Alan Lawson (eds) *De-Scribing Empire* (London: Routledge, 1994)].

Tseëlon, Efrat. *The Masque of Femininity* (London: Sage, 1995).

Twine, Richard T. 'Ma(r)king Essence-Ecofeminism and Embodiment' *Ethics and the Environment* 6.2 (2001): 31–58.

Vakoch, Douglas A. (ed.) *Ecofeminism and Rhetoric: Critical Perspectives on Sex, Technology, and Discourse* (New York: Berghahn Books, 2011).

Vakoch, Douglas A. 'Preface' in D. Vakoch (ed.) *Ecofeminism and Rhetoric: Critical Perspectives on Sex, Technology, and Discourse* (New York: Berghahn Books, 2011), pp. xix–xxi.

Walker, Margaret. 'Moral Understandings: Alternative "Epistemology" for a Feminist Ethics' *Hypatia: A Journal of Feminist Philosophy* 4.2 (1989).

Warren, Karen J. *Ecofeminist Philosophy: A Western Perspective on What It Is and Why It Matters* (Lanham, Maryland: Rowman and Littlefield, 2000).

—— 'The Power and the Promise of Ecological Feminism' in K. J. Warren (ed.) *Ecofeminism: Women, Culture, Nature* (Bloomington and Indianapolis: Indiana University Press, 1997), pp. 19–41.

—— (ed.) *Ecofeminism: Women, Culture, Nature* (Bloomington and Indianapolis: Indiana University Press, 1997).

—— 'Ecological Feminist Philosophies: An Overview of the Issues' in K. J. Warren (ed.) *Ecological Feminist Philosophies* (Bloomington and Indianapolis: Indiana University Press, 1996), pp. ix–xxvi.

—— (ed.) *Ecological Feminist Philosophies* (Bloomington and Indianapolis: Indiana University Press, 1996).

—— (ed.) *Ecological Feminism* (London and NY: Routledge, 1994).

—— 'A Feminist Philosophical Perspective on Ecofeminist Spiritualities' in C. J. Adams (ed.) *Ecofeminism and the Sacred* (New York: Continuum, 1993), pp. 119–32.

—— 'The Power and Promise of Ecological Feminism' *Environmental Ethics* 12 (1990): 125–46.

Wekerle, Gerda R. 'Framing Feminist Claims for Urban Citizenship' in L.A. Staeheli, E. Kofman and L.J. Peake (eds) *Mapping Women, Making Politics: Feminist Perspectives on Political Geography* (New York: Routledge, 2004), pp. 245–59.

Wellendorf, Jonas. 'The Interplay of Pagan and Christian Traditions in Icelandic Settlement Myths' *Journal of English and Germanic Philology* 109.1 (2010): 1–21.

Whatmore, Sarah. 'Humanism's Excess: Some Thoughts on the "Post-human/ist" agenda' *Environment and Planning* A 36.8 (2004): 1360–3.

White, Frank. *The Overview Effect: Space Exploration and Human Evolution* 2nd edn (Reston, VA: American Institute of Aeronautics and Astronautics, 1998).

Wood, Naomi. 'Embracing Icy Mothers: Ideology, Identity, and Environment in Children's Fantasy' in S. I. Dobrin and K. B. Kidd (eds) *Wild Things: Children's Culture and Ecocriticism* (Detroit: Wayne State University Press, 2004), pp. 198–214.

Worden, Daniel. 'Neo-liberalism and the Western: HBO's Deadwood as National Allegory' *Canadian Review of American Studies* 39.2 (2009): 221–46.

Zapf, Hubert. 'Literary Ecology and the Ethics of Texts' *New Literary History* 39.4 (2008): 847–68.

Index

A Darkling Plain (Reeve), 28, 30–1,
    152–3, 158, 166–7, 190
Abbruzzese, Teresa V. and Gerda
    R. Wekerle, 75
Abjection
    environmental, 31, 105, 143
    female, 53, 66–7, 71, 81–5, 87
    and the figure of the zombie, 81–5
    of the animal/animalised body, 53,
        57, 59, 70
    posthuman, 45, 56
    religious, 143–4
Abram, David, 156
Activism
    and crisis rhetoric, 14, 20
    and ecofeminism, 2, 10, 180
Adams, Carol, 58–9, 61, 200n2.1
Adamson, Joni and Scott Slovic, 137
Aestheticism
    and nature, 133, 148–9, 154, 156
    and beautification, 47–8, 52–4, 71
    and standardisation, 38, 48–51,
        109, 142
    artificial, 36, 38, 42
Agency
    constitution of, 23, 26, 41, 50, 53,
        56, 67, 89–90, 93, 119, 144,
        146–7, 168, 197–8, 5, 10, 89, 195
    female, 64, 66, 70, 72, 77, 85, 140,
        184
    of the child, 12, 13, 34, 35, 44–5,
        116, 123, 124
    of the natural world, 115, 154, 156,
        162–3, 174, 187
Alaimo, Stacy, 52, 60, 136, 165, 183
    and Susan Hekman, 11
Alienation
    from the natural world, 15, 18, 24,
        26–8, 31–33, 41–4, 58, 108, 148–9
    from the self, 63, 78–80, 185, 187
Amsler, Sarah, 20, 41, 100
Anderson, Matthew Tobin
    see Feed

Anthropocentrism, 18, 19, 35, 40–1, 47,
    72, 133, 139–43, 148–9, 156, 161–2,
    165, 187–8, 191, 193, 194, 195
Anthropogenesis, 31–5, 37, 49, 68, 105
Anzaldua, Gloria E., 164
Apocalypse
    and fiction, 1, 13–17, 20–1, 22–6,
        40–2, 68, 71, 87, 102, 192
    and landscape, 27, 42, 90, 105, 107,
        132, 138, 196, 129–30, 143–7
    as motif, 18, 20, 22–6, 65, 100, 125,
        128, 158, 191, 193
    and religion, 129–30, 144
Ashcroft, Bill, Gareth Griffiths and
    Helen Tiffin, 121, 132

Bakker, Karen and Gavin Bridge, 3
Barad, Karen, 90
Bate, Jonathan, 156–7
Bauman, Whitney, 200n4.3
Bawden, Nina
    see Off the Road
Beckwith, Sarah, 89
Berger, John, 187
Bertagna, Julie
    see Exodus
    see Zenith
Betcher, Sharon, 143, 158
Billingsley, Franny
    see The Folk Keeper
Bioregionalism
    and agrarianism, 139
    and stewardship, 115, 154–5
    and the local, 111, 132, 137–43,
        153, 158, 194
    and the pastoral, 138–40, 177
'Blind space', 15, 17, 19–21, 25, 38,
    40–2, 44, 46, 71, 102, 124, 126,
    128, 158, 191, 193–5, 197,
    199Intro.119
Body
    animal, 56–63
    earth, 8, 21, 26, 43, 44, 64–66, 194

Body – *continued*
  emancipation from, 46–51, 119,
    143–4, 146, 158
  female (*see Female Body*)
  hybrid (*see also Hybridity*), 17,
    181–8, 190, 194
  male, 62–3
  posthuman (*see Posthumanism*)
  theories of, 43, 45, 49, 60, 75, 81
Bowman, Andrew, 74
Boyd, Shelley, 177–8
Bradford, Clare, 22, 110
  and Kerry Mallan, John Stephens
    and Robyn McCallum, 14, 15, 46,
    122, 155, 195, 198
Bronfen, Elizabeth and Sarah Webster
  Goodwin, 83
Buege, Douglas, 127, 128
Buell, Lawrence, 18, 31, 44, 46
Butler, Judith, 45

Callicott, J. Baird, 101
Cameron, Anne, 200n4.2
Care
  and gender difference, 77–81, 193,
    194
  and language, 89–94
  and motherhood, 84–8
  and sexuality, 81–5
  and politics, 98–100
  and posthumanism, 94–8
  ethic of, 1, 16, 74–7, 98–100
  of the environment, 109, 111, 138,
    141, 154, 159, 161, 177, 180, 181,
    191
Carlassare, Elizabeth, 2, 6
Cartography, 110–15, 116
Castree, Noel and Catherine Nash, 68
Catching Fire (Collins), 94–5
Cheney, Jim, 89, 93, 102, 126–7, 163,
  202n9
Child, the
  and adult-child dualism, 7–9
  and childhood studies, 7, 8–10,
    197–8, 199n5
  and ecofeminism, 1, 6–10, 13–15,
    195–6, 198, 199n3
  and innocence, 7, 111–12, 139,
    199n5

  and Romanticism, 7–8, 195–6
  see also Young Adult
Clark, Beverley Lyon, 6
  and Margaret R. Higonnet, 199n3
Class, 2, 6, 44, 47–8, 53, 59–62,
  66, 101, 131, 138, 140–1, 184,
  186
Climate change, 16, 18–21, 23, 41–2,
  124, 201n4
Cloete, Elsie, 60–1, 134
Code, Lorraine, 5, 9, 127, 130, 193,
  202n10
Cohen, Michael, 19
Collins, Suzanne
  see The Hunger Games
  see Catching Fire
  see Mockingjay
Colonialism
  and environmental imperialism, 32,
    38, 44, 109–10, 110–15, 155, 156,
    200n3, 201n4
  and indigenous peoples, 15, 64,
    104–5, 109, 110–15, 116–18, 121,
    122, 124, 132, 155, 182–3, 200n3,
    201ns4 & 5
  and *terra nullius*, 104–10
  and the national frontier,
    104–10
  see also *Cartography* and *Landscape*
Community
  and ecofeminism, 19, 21, 25, 33,
    75–7, 81, 94, 108, 120, 124, 127,
    137–43, 153–4, 159, 193, 194,
    202n10
  in opposition to neoliberalism, 16,
    43, 193
Conservationism, 44, 133
Consumerism
  and animals, 52–3, 56–63, 142
  and neoliberalism, 22, 33, 43–4, 51,
    63–7, 71, 90, 122, 124, 139, 140,
    145, 193
  and politics, 54–5, 62
  and sex, 51–6, 62–3, 81–5
Cooley, John, 138–9
Corsaro, William A., 9
Cronon, William, 108
Cudworth, Erika, 2, 164
Cuomo, Chris, 5, 72, 152

D'Ath, Justin
  see Shœdow Master
d'Eubonne, Frances, 1
Deep ecology
  and ecofeminism, 5, 166, 181,
    188–91, 195, 160–5
DeFalco, Amelia, 75
Diamond, Irene and Lisa Kuppler,
  131
Di Chiro, Giovanna, 45
Dietz, Mary, 200n3.1
Dinerstein, Joel, 47, 72–3, 104, 122,
  130, 157
Discourse
  abstract, 4, 10, 11, 16, 35, 42, 58,
    76, 101–4, 127, 162, 181, 191,
    193
  constructivist, 1, 6, 8, 11, 44, 45,
    196, 202n10
  gendered (*see Gender*)
  masculinist, 16, 25, 26, 46, 52, 63,
    74, 77, 89, 101, 110, 130–1, 193
Disembodiment, 3, 16, 17, 24, 28,
    35–40, 46, 73, 78, 129, 132, 143,
    157, 158, 165, 194
Dissolution
  of self/subjectivity, 50, 54, 64, 66,
    67–9, 83, 90, 92, 162–5, 165–169,
    172, 181–8
  of the body, 66–70, 165–9, 172,
    173
Dobrin, Sidney I. and Kenneth
  B. Kidd, 13, 139, 198
Domination
  male, 3, 46, 138, 140
  systems of, 2, 14, 87, 104, 161, 162,
    188
Dualism, 2, 5, 35, 59, 68, 72, 80, 148,
    161–2, 189
  see also Child

Earth
  and agency (*see Agency*)
  and belonging, 18, 21, 27, 30–1,
    32, 33, 41–2, 100, 118, 122, 128,
    137–8, 148, 192, 194
  and commodification, 44, 64–5
  and materiality, 18–21, 26–31, 42,
    101, 131–2, 151, 195–6

  and Mother Earth imagery (*see also
    Myth*), 26, 122, 125–6, 136
  dislocation from, 15–20, 24,
    26–31, 32, 36, 37, 41–2, 73, 127,
    129, 132, 133, 143, 151, 157–9,
    192
  versus planet (*see Planet*)
Ecoconsciousness, 18, 32, 36, 42, 121,
    124, 129, 134, 175, 188–91, 193,
    195
Ecocriticism
  and children's literature, 13–14,
    195–198
  theory of, 11–12, 19, 21, 130–1,
    160, 198
Ecofeminism
  and deep ecology (*see Deep Ecology*)
  and epistemology
    (*see Epistemology*)
  and ethics (*see Ethics*)
  and gender (*see Gender*)
  and hybridity (*see Hybridity*)
  and literature, 10–13
  and neoliberalism
    (*see Neoliberalism*)
  and philosophy (*see Philosophy*)
  and place (*see Place*)
  and spirituality (*see Spirituality*)
  and the child (*see Child*)
  theory of, 1–5, 15–17, 20–1, 25–6,
    33, 41–2, 56, 68, 72, 76, 81,
    98–9, 101, 102–3, 110, 115–16,
    120–1, 131, 137–8, 143, 148,
    152, 159, 181, 188, 189–90,
    192–5, 197–8
Economics
  and inequality, 4, 84, 104
  capitalism, 3, 4, 22, 43–6, 62, 63–7,
    71, 82, 98, 111–13, 122, 140, 146,
    193
  labour, 3, 8, 62, 63, 71, 72, 76
  see also Female body and
    Consumerism
Ecopedagogy, 13, 192, 197
Ecophobia, 40–2, 47, 48, 51–3, 54, 68,
    70, 105, 123, 136, 178
Ecopoiesis, 31, 129, 156–7, 180,
    188–91, 195–6, 188–91, 195–6
  and autopoiesis, 188–91, 195–6

Ecosystem, 11, 38, 66, 126, 133, 155
Embeddedness, 3–4, 9, 11, 17, 20,
    25, 28, 31–4, 35–6, 38, 42,
    46–7, 56, 76, 83, 89, 91, 101,
    103, 116, 121, 129, 132–4,
    137, 139, 143, 145, 148–9,
    151–2, 153–4, 155, 157–60,
    169, 174, 175–6, 184, 188–91,
    192–5
Embodiment
    crisis of, 15, 40, 44, 46–50, 54, 69,
        71, 81–2, 144, 3, 7, 11, 36, 47, 52,
        54, 56, 62, 98
    human, 37, 45, 72–3, 93
    posthuman, 125–6, 129, 137, 148,
        152, 169, 181
    within nature, 185, 188–9, 195
    see also Body, Disembodiment and
        Emotion
Emotion
    and attachment, 30, 36–7, 61, 75,
        78, 79, 90, 99, 175–81, 196
    and narrative, 103, 127
    and posthumanism, 96–7
    and the 'feminine' 4, 78, 79, 83,
        85, 87, 88, 93, 95, 99, 108,
        199Intro.n2, 202n10
    as embodied response, 69, 111, 117,
        129, 134, 144, 146, 152, 157, 159,
        169, 172, 181, 182, 185, 191,
        199Intro.n5
Empathy, 12, 16, 41, 58, 87–8, 98,
        132, 147–52, 183, 187, 194
    'storied', 12
Environment
    see Nature
Environmental crisis, 1–2, 5, 14–17,
        18–21, 21–6, 28, 31–2, 36, 40–2,
        43, 66–7, 76–7, 78, 94, 97–8,
        100, 105–6, 127, 130, 137, 143,
        155, 161–2, 165, 191, 192–3,
        195–6, 197
Epistemology
    colonialist (*see also Colonialism*),
        104–10, 110–15, 121
    Ecofeminist, 4, 6, 7, 16, 74, 79,
        101–4, 115–20, 120–6, 126–8,
        129, 132, 145, 154, 158, 163,
        182, 190, 191, 193–4,
        202n10

epistemic privilege, 24, 92, 103,
        114–15
    normative (masculinist), 18, 25, 45,
        66, 75, 92, 101–4, 116, 129
Essentialism
    biological (child), 6, 9
    biological (women), 3, 4, 63, 76, 80,
        81, 84, 131
    ecological, 11, 202n10
    indigenous, 114, 120–1
Estok, Simon, 40–41, 44, 52
Ethics
    and ecofeminism, 1, 6, 7, 10, 16,
        18, 23, 42, 65, 73, 74–7, 78, 80–1,
        99, 101, 102–3, 116, 127–8, 129,
        148, 154–5, 157, 159, 161, 162–4,
        166, 175, 180, 181, 189, 191,
        193–5, 197–8, 200n1
    and literature, 10–13
    normative, 4, 16, 40, 44–5, 100,
        113, 202n10
    of care (*see Care*)
Evans, Gwyneth, 177
Evolution
    Darwinian, 47, 49, 107, 114–15
    technological, 68–70
Exodus (Bertagna), 23, 24, 27, 33–4,
        37–40, 78–81, 98, 121, 124

Feed (Anderson), 34–5, 37, 38,
        54–6, 65–7, 72, 73, 89–92, 93,
        157–8
Fellman, Anita Clair, 109
Female body
    and anorexia, 50, 152, 169, 179
    and consumption, 51–6
    animalisation, 56–63
    as a discursive site, 16, 17, 44, 46,
        70–2, 77, 83, 85, 131, 167, 171,
        173, 194–5
    commodification, 63–7
    sexualisation, 51–6
    see also Dissolution
Feminisation
    of environment, 1, 26, 77, 103, 104,
        116, 193
    of peoples, 1, 26, 57, 76, 78, 103,
        116, 164, 193
    of space, 1, 26, 74, 96, 103, 104,
        116, 193

Feminism, 1–5, 6–7, 11, 21, 27, 43, 62, 74–6, 80, 81, 101, 103, 127, 131, 137, 159, 164, 184, 198, 199Intro.ns1, 3 & 4, 200n4.1
Femininity, 47, 50, 69, 70, 75, 77, 83–5, 97, 177
  and home/domesticity, 75, 79, 81–2, 94–5, 99, 140, 177
Fincher, Ruth, 2
Foote, Bonnie, 11, 13
Fox, Warren, 190
Freeman, Carla, 131
Friedman, Andrea, 81–2

Gaard, Greta, 13–14, 21, 42, 52, 63, 137, 138, 141, 192, 198
  and Patrick D. Murphy, 188
Garb, Yaakov Gerome, 26, 29
Garratt, Keith, 133
Garrard, Greg, 130
Gatens-Robinson, Eugenie, 21, 141
Gender
  and difference, 1, 3, 4, 6, 26, 42, 44–5, 49, 56–7, 63, 69, 73, 74–7, 77–81, 85–6, 88–9, 94, 103, 138–41, 159, 162, 194, 198, 202n10
  and ecofeminist reappraisal, 2, 7, 98–9, 100, 101, 104
  and sexuality, 81–5
  and space (*see Feminisation*)
Global warming
  see Climate Change
Globalisation
  and corporate practice, 2, 12, 56, 129
  processes of, 5, 12, 16, 21, 44, 45, 63, 64, 98, 104, 122, 131–2, 137–8, 158, 193, 194
Glotfelty, Cheryll and Harold Fromm, 198
Godfrey, Phoebe C., 4
Gordon, Suzanne, Patricia Benner and Nel Noddings, 75
Greenway, Betty, Epigraph, 18, 42
Griffiths, Gareth, 121
Grim, John, 115, 128
Groenfeldt, David, 121
Groves, Jason, 60
Gruen, Lori, 12
Gunn Allen, Patricia, 73

Halberstam, Judith and Ira Livingston, 84
Haraway, Donna, 72, 110, 188, 189
Harmon, David, 133
Hawthorn, Jeremy, 201n6
Hayles, N. Katherine, 35, 40, 67
Heise, Ursula, 138
Hengst, Heinz, 7
Herles, Cecilia, 2
Hess, Scott, 19
Hickel, Jason and Arsalan Khan, 43
Hillard, Tom J., 40
Hitt, Christopher, 147–9
Hollister, Susannah L., 199Intro.n8, 199n1.2
How I Live Now (Rosoff), 150–2, 159, 167–70, 177–81
Hughes, J. Donald and Jim Swan, 133
Hulme, Mike, 134
Hybridity
  and ecofeminism, 5, 17, 72, 98, 99, 160, 164–5, 181–8, 188–91, 194–5, 197–8
  and metamorphosis, 181–8
  and the cyborg, 30, 45, 72–3, 188–9
  see also Body

Identity
  and camouflage, 170–4, 184, 186, 188, 190, 195
  and cathexis, 165, 175–81, 188, 190, 191, 195
  and 'open continuity', 165–9, 189
  and performance, 12, 40, 45, 49, 59, 69, 70, 80, 83, 105–6, 170–2, 174, 182, 184
  and plurality, 4, 7, 75, 101, 153, 160–5, 181–8
  and solidarity, 163, 175, 180–1, 188, 190–1, 194
  and 'traitorousness' 188–1
Indigenous
  and colonialism (*see Colonialism*)
  creation myths (*see Myth*)
  cultural values, 81, 117–18, 120–1, 124, 126, 127–8
  spirituality, 16, 129, 132, 152, 153, 154–7, 158
  see also Essentialism

Inequality, 12, 62, 89, 193
Ingold, Tim, 156
Intertextuality, 48, 115, 118, 124, 125, 135, 142, 201ns7 & 8
Irigaray, Luce, 200n4.1

Jaggar, Alison M., 77–8
James, Kathryn, 83, 84
Jenks, Chris, 7
Jones, K. B., 200n3.1

Katz, Cindi, 104, 131
Kearns, Laurel and Catherine Keller, 20, 21, 41, 157
Keough, Noel, 137
King Roger J. H., 10, 162
King, Ynestra, 51
Knebusch, Julien, 20
Knowledge
    and 'responsible truths' (*see Responsibility*)
    indigenous (*see Indigenous–cultural values*)
    situated, 4, 5, 9, 11, 75, 101–4, 192
    and women's 'ways of knowing' 102, 103, 115–20, 129
    see also Epistemology
Kretz, Lisa, 162, 165–6, 189
Kristeva, Julia, 82
Krznaric, Roman, 100

Landscape
    colonised, 15, 104, 110–15, 194
    degraded/post-natural (*see also Apocalypse and Waste*), 10, 14, 15, 21, 25–31, 31–5, 42, 45–6, 68, 72, 89, 90, 106–7, 132, 138, 196
    garden (*see also Religion*), 8, 15, 151, 177–80
    local/natural, 2, 8, 9, 21, 23, 45, 99, 103, 108, 121, 127, 131–2, 134, 136, 149, 169, 175–81, 192, 196, 198
    virtual/artificial (*see also Virtual*), 38–40, 78
Language
    and ecofeminism, 81, 89–94, 99–100, 102, 157, 187, 200n4.2
    and postmodernism, 20, 120

and spirituality, 38, 52, 81, 124, 135, 144, 155, 157
    as a site of power, 47, 74, 88–94, 114, 127
    normative (masculinist), 16, 44–5, 101, 102, 162
    see also Discourse
Lauro, Sarah Juliet and Karen Embry, 81
Lawson, Victoria, 75, 94, 99–100
Layton, Robert, 123
Leach, Neil, 164, 170–4, 184, 202n6.1
Legler, Gretchen T., 102, 120
Levine, Mark, 129–30
Li, Stephanie, 180
Lloyd, Genevieve, 200ns4.1 & 4.3
Lock, John, 7, 199nIntro.n5
Lovelock, James, 25

MacGregor, Sherilyn, 75–7, 98, 102
Mack-Canty, Colleen, 2, 199Intro.n4
MacLeish, Archibald, 26
Mallan, Kerry, 199Intro.n3
Mallory, Chaone, 163, 181, 190–1
Manley Scott, Peter, 100
Mann, Bonnie, 19, 20
Marston, Sallie and Lynn Staeheli, 94
Martin, Biddy and Chandra Talpade Mohanty, 115
Martin, Patricia, 75, 88
McDowell, Linda, 78, 99
Mellor, Mary, 3, 71, 90, 196
Mies, Maria and Vandana Shiva, 65
Mise-en-abyme, 124, 201n6
Mockingjay (Collins), 95, 174
Murphy, Patrick D. and Greta Gaard, 188, 90, 103, 156
Motherhood, 81, 84–8
    and madness, 84–8
Mortal Engines (Reeve), 23, 27, 29–31, 32–3, 36–7, 94, 95–8
Mutuality, 12, 75, 77, 94, 161, 194
Myth
    and literature, 15, 32, 67, 111, 113, 175, 201n8
    colonial (*see Colonialism – national frontier; Colonialism – terra nullius*)
    symbolising function of, 37, 87, 101, 102–104, 106, 115–20, 126–8, 194, 200n4.2

pagan/ of rebirth/ of origin/ of settlement, 120–6, 179, 182–3
of 'progress', 73, 104, 130

Naess, Arne, 161
Nagar, Richa and Victoria Lawson, Linda McDowell and Susan Hanson, 45, 103
Narrative
and ecoconsciousness, 14–15, 16, 21, 26, 32, 36, 46, 77, 85, 93, 100, 115–20, 121–122, 148, 165, 180–181, 18, 184, 186, 188, 193–7, 200n4.6
and ecofeminism, 102–4, 115–20, 127, 130
master/metanarrative, 26, 27, 41, 42, 48, 67, 74, 106, 110, 115, 116, 117, 130, 134, 148, 190–1, 200n4.3
see also Discourse, Emotion, Ethics and *Myth*
Narayan, Uma, 103
Natov, Roni, 7–8, 195–6
Natural
and naturalisation, 8, 37, 39, 43, 50, 60, 62, 63, 68, 75, 85, 86, 88, 121
and unnatural, 35, 48, 54, 57, 71, 72–3, 84, 85, 97, 119, 178
and monstrous, 34, 50–1, 87, 96, 114, 142
contempt for the, 51–6
versus cultural, 4, 7, 33–35, 47, 49, 68, 69, 78, 114, 166, 167
Nature
and literature, 11–13, 13–15, 22, 46
and the child (*see Child*)
and women, 1–7, 8, 22, 76–7, 78, 80, 85, 102, 131, 164
segregation from culture, 2, 5, 12–13, 19, 24–5, 40–1, 44, 68, 133, 161–2, 181, 183, 189, 198
see also Spirituality, the *Sublime* and *Romanticism*
Neoliberalism
and ecofeminism, 43–6

ideologies of, 2, 5, 14, 16, 22, 41, 43, 45, 63, 72, 74–5, 102–3, 122, 129, 132, 144, 159, 192, 194
and individualism, 15, 16, 21, 43, 44, 74, 77–8, 81, 99, 108, 131, 138, 193–4
and self-advancement, 2, 16, 21, 43–4, 47, 74, 193–4
see also Economics
Nostalgia, 27, 34–5, 50, 97, 106, 111, 119, 134, 136, 138–9, 141, 197

Oelschlaeger, Max, 44
Off the Road (Bawden), 138–41, 142, 159
Olsson, Gunnar, 110
Orenstein, Gloria Feman, 11, 126
Otherness, 11–12, 44, 75, 78, 94, 160–4, 170, 174, 180–1, 187, 188–91

Patriarchy, 3, 4, 59, 67, 71, 79–80, 84, 87, 88, 92–4, 99, 110, 115, 117, 131, 133, 138, 140–1, 159, 162, 184–6, 200n4.2
Pedagogy
see Ecopedagogy
Philosophy
and ecofeminism, 1, 5, 10, 41, 148, 157, 159, 162, 163, 193, 197–8
and Romanticism, 133, 148
normative, 4, 10, 74, 129–30, 202n10
Place
and mapping (*see Cartography*)
bioregional (*see Bioregionalism*)
situatedness, 3–4, 12, 15, 132, 153, 169, 192
poetics of (*see Poetics*)
Planet
and decline/destruction, 15, 16, 18, 20, 22, 23, 32, 34, 41, 42, 97, 125, 143, 192, 193
and planetary consciousness, 19–21, 26–31, 32, 42, 43–4, 46, 105, 193
and 'whole earth' image, 21, 26–31
Platt, Kamala, 14–15

Plumwood, Val, 44, 58, 75, 78, 80, 104, 110, 115–16, 123, 137, 138, 162, 163, 165, 180, 181, 187, 189–90

Poetics
  of childhood, 7–8, 195–6
  of earth/ecopoetics (*see Ecopoiesis*)
  of place, 7–8, 132, 150, 157, 159, 193
  of planet, 15, 26–31, 193, 199Intro.n8

Politics
  and difference, 2, 3, 12, 19, 43, 63, 65, 103, 110, 120, 143, 193
  and ecofeminism, 2, 4, 5, 6, 10, 13, 17, 20, 44–5, 46–8, 74–7, 81, 94, 98–100, 102, 129, 159, 163, 180, 199, 191, 199Intro.n2
  and responsibility (*see Responsibility*)
  of childhood, 8–9
  of consumerism (*see Consumerism*)
  of dissent, 57, 65, 72, 95, 191

Posthumanism
  and the body, 16, 36, 46, 62, 66–7, 70, 71–3, 95, 144
  discourse of, 35, 37, 45–6, 50, 54, 56, 67–8, 72–3, 91, 96, 98–9, 114, 144, 165, 181

Predator's Gold (Reeve), 28–9, 106–7
Pretties (Westerfeld), 109–10, 113–15
Prout, Alan, 9

Race
  and difference, 6, 101, 131, 138, 182
  racism, 2, 40, 50

Raglon, Rebecca, 31

Reeve, Philip
  see Mortal Engines
  see Predator's Gold
  see Infernal Devices
  see A Darkling Plain

Religion
  and apocalypse (*see Apocalypse*)
  and Christianity, 119–20, 122, 129–30, 134, 142–7
  and doctrine, 82–5, 97, 118–119, 122, 133–137, 143–7, 157, 194
  and Garden of Eden, 32–3, 107, 134, 136, 139, 144–5

  and resurrection, 118–20, 135, 142–7
  see also Spirituality

Renewal
  and beauty, 15, 19, 26–8, 33, 35–40, 48–51, 61, 96, 108, 134–5, 137, 149, 154, 173, 178, 186
  and ecological growth, 21, 32, 34, 35, 42, 100, 102, 120, 125, 148, 159, 179
  and resilience/adaptability, 31–2, 33, 35, 42

Reproduction
  female, 3, 8, 81–2, 139
  see also Motherhood

Responsibility
  and care practices (*see also Care*), 86, 94, 99
  and ecological engagement, 20, 26, 28, 30, 41, 77, 100, 104, 106, 137, 154, 157, 180, 190, 194
  and pedagogy (*see also Ecopedagogy*), 10, 13, 192
  and truth/understanding, 17, 21, 41, 75, 115, 126–8, 158, 163, 193, 202n4.9, 202n10
  ethical, 22, 154, 191, 200n4
  epistemological, 24, 102, 118, 191, 194
  political, 7, 14–15, 19, 20, 22, 23, 41, 73, 196, 197, 200n4
  young adult (see *Young Adult*)

Richards, Page, 151
Rigby, Kate, 148, 160, 188, 192–3, 196
Roberts, Susan M., 63

Robson, Jenny
  see Savannah 2116 AD

Rolston III, Holmes, 116, 126
Romanticism, 7–9, 17, 35, 40, 106, 111, 114, 130–2, 133, 139, 147–52, 169, 195, 197
Roos, Bonnie and Alex Hunt, 164

Rosoff, Meg
  see How I Live Now

Rousseau, Jean, 7, 199Intro.n5

Ryan, Carrie
  see The Forest of Hands & Teeth
  see The Dead-Tossed Waves
  see The Dark and Hollow Places

Ryan, Patrick J., 7, 8–9

Salleh, Ariel, 8, 63
Sargisson, Lucy, 102
Savannah 2116 AD (Robson), 23,
  59–63, 133–7, 157–8, 159
Savarsy, W. and Berta Siim, 200n3.1
Schöpflin, George, 102
Seaman, Myra J., 95, 102–3
Seed, John and Joanna Macy, Pat
  Fleming and Arne Naess, 161
Session, Robert, 161
Sex
  and death, 81–5
  and power, 152, 168, 178–9
  sexism (*see also Species*), 2, 6, 40, 44,
    62, 73, 76, 85, 101, 103, 196
  see also Female Body
Shædow Master (D'Ath), 110–13,
  117–18, 154–7, 158, 159, 182–4,
  185, 186, 187
Shamanism, 155–6
Skrimshire, Stefan, 41
Slotkin, Richard, 102
Solidarity, 12, 160, 163, 175–81, 188,
  190, 191, 194
Soper, Kate, 113
Specials (Westerfeld), 190–1
Species
  'sexism/speciesism nexus' 51–6, 59,
    63, 70, 200n2.1
  speciesism, 2, 40, 59, 138, 153, 166
Spirituality
  and ecofeminism, 3, 4, 5, 129–33,
    142, 152–3, 158–9, 191,
    199Intro.n2
  and ecological immanence, 41, 73,
    79, 125, 129, 143, 148–9, 152–6,
    157–9, 189, 193, 194, 196
  and Shamanism (*see Shamanism*)
  and the sacred, 16, 32–3, 37, 111,
    118, 112, 129, 130–3, 137, 144–5,
    148, 152, 154–7, 158
  and transcendence, 17, 34, 36, 38,
    119, 133–7, 142–7, 149, 157–9, 194
  see also Religion
Spretnak, Charlene, 165
Staeheli, Lynn A., Eleanore Kofman
  and Sallie Marston, 75, 76, 94
Stephens, John, 11, 22, 46, 165, 175,
  188–9, 199Intro.n7

Subjectivity
  and child/young adult (*see Young
    Adult*)
  and interdependency, 2, 5, 9,
    11–12, 45, 75, 99
  and intersubjectivity, 12, 26, 69,
    94, 104, 119, 124–5, 137, 151–2,
    153, 155, 158–9, 172, 177, 183,
    188
  and subject positioning, 4, 11, 13,
    18, 24, 36, 71, 77–8, 80, 93, 96,
    98, 105, 143, 164, 165, 181, 188,
    190, 192, 194
  and self-erasure (*see Dissolution*)
  constitution of, 3, 5, 9, 46, 75, 82,
    150, 164, 175–6, 179–80, 188–9,
    194, 197
  see also Otherness, Agency and
    Identity
Sublime, the, 26, 40, 130, 132, 133,
  147–52
Surveillance, 21, 30, 170
Sustainability, 1, 18, 21, 22, 26, 27,
  33, 41, 42, 77, 100, 121, 142,
  152–3, 193–4
Suzuki, David and Amanda
  McConnell, 166, 202n6.2

Technology
  and progress, 17, 21, 26, 37, 41, 43,
    73, 130, 157, 200n10.3
  and hybridity, 35–6, 37–8, 46, 68
  and advancement, 16, 24–6, 30–1,
    33, 39–40, 44, 50, 130, 138
  defunct/pre-modern, 24–5, 34, 153
  masculinist/abstract, 16, 50, 73, 98,
    130, 144
The Dead-Tossed Waves (Ryan), 147–8
The Folk Keeper (Billingsley), 85, 87–9,
  91–4, 99–100, 116–17, 183–8
The Hunger Games (Collins), 22,
  47–8, 52–4, 57–9, 69–70, 70–1,
  85–6, 88, 94, 105–6, 149, 170–4,
  190
The Forest of Hands & Teeth (Ryan),
  68–70, 82–5, 86–7, 118–20,
  143–7, 175–6, 180–1
Tipping point, 15, 21–6, 41, 193,
  196

Transformation
  as metamorphosis
    (*see also Hybridity*), 69, 70, 93, 95,
    181–3, 186
  personal and social, 5, 12–13,
    16–17, 100, 134, 141, 150, 157,
    181–8, 188–91, 199Intro.n2
Tseëlon, Efrat, 55
Twine, Richard, 49, 56–7, 73

Uglies (Westerfeld), 22, 48–51, 107–9,
  141–3, 149, 150

Vakoch, Douglas A., 43
Virtual
  and the internet, 24, 37–40
  reality, 24, 27, 36, 42

Walker, Margaret, 117, 126–7
Warren, Karren, 2, 5, 103, 133, 158–9,
  163, 190
Waste
  and toxicity, 31–5, 45
  human, 34, 55, 66, 140, 167
  wasteland, 30, 31, 34, 51, 105
Wekerle, Gerda R., 76
  and Abbruzzese, Teresa V., 75
Wellendorf, Jonas, 123
Westerfeld, Scott

  see Uglies
  see Pretties
  see Specials
Whatmore, Sarah, 68
White, Frank, 19, 21
Wilderness, 15, 44, 59–60, 62, 107–8,
  114, 133–7, 140–1, 148, 149
  and Eden, 134–5
Wood, Naomi, 124
Worden, Daniel, 43

Young adult
  as borderline identity, 6, 14, 17, 23,
    191, 196–7
  constructivist discourses, 1, 5, 6,
    8–9, 193, 195
  fiction, 1, 5, 6, 8–9, 10, 13, 15–17,
    19–21, 25, 43, 45–6, 67–68, 77,
    99–100, 104, 121, 126, 127, 132,
    148, 155, 157, 161, 164, 170, 181,
    188, 192–3, 195, 198
  maturation, 5, 108, 140, 183, 195
  responsibility, 6–7, 23, 89, 101, 197
  subjectivity, 1, 5–6, 9, 10, 195, 198

Zapf, Hubert, 10–12, 199Intro.n7
Zenith (Bertagna), 24–6, 27–8, 29,
  30, 63–5, 89, 111, 121–6, 127–8,
  176–7, 181, 190